STYLE VERSUS SUBSTANCE

GEORGE V. HIGGINS

•

Macmillan Publishing Company

NEW YORK

Style

Versus

Substance

•

BOSTON, KEVIN WHITE, AND

THE POLITICS OF ILLUSION

Macmillan Publishing Company
866 Third Avenue, New York, N.Y. 10022
Collier Macmillan Canada, Inc.

Library of Congress Cataloging in Publication Data
Higgins, George V., 1939-
Style versus substance.
Includes index.
1. White, Kevin H. 2. Boston (Mass.)—Politics and government.
3. Communication in politics—Massachusetts—Boston. 4. Boston
(Mass.)—Mayors—Biography. I. Title. F73.54.W48H54 1984
974.4′61043′0924 [B]   84-15468 ISBN 0-02-551450-4

Macmillan books are available at special discounts
for bulk purchases for sales promotions, premiums, fund-raising,
or educational use. Special editions or book excerpts
can also be created to specification.
For details, contact:
Special Sales Director
Macmillan Publishing Company
866 Third Avenue
New York, New York 10022

10   9   8   7   6   5   4   3   2   1

Designed by Jack Meserole

Printed in the United States of America

If ever this free people, if this government itself is ever utterly demoralized, it will come from
the incessant wriggle and struggle for office,
which is but a way to live without work.

—Abraham Lincoln

INTRODUCTION

In August of 1975, late on a Sunday morning, Charles Street at the foot of Beacon Hill was closed to cars and trucks, and to the odd MBTA bus lumbering along ahead of its thick black screen of diesel exhaust smoke. The street was turned over to the people for their annual fair. The celebration, benefiting various Good Causes that abound on Beacon Hill, was deemed by the authorities adequate reason to suspend for one day both the official and the actual rules under which Boston traffic so thrillingly proceeds.

For those who have not visited the city, Boston's official traffic rules, like those of other old and crowded metropolitan centers, grudgingly accord to vehicular traffic certain minimal rights of passage, hedged about and stymied by thousands of traffic lights that function whimsically when they work at all and by signs arbitrarily designating connecting streets as one-way thoroughfares (Charles Street, for many years one way from south to north, was one Sunday morning in 1982 made one way north to south; that significantly increased the intellectual challenge of commuters to the Hill on Monday morning). The official rules also declare that people traveling on foot shall stay out of the streets and remain on the sidewalks, except when traversing the streets at intersections where the flow of vehicular traffic may be periodically interrupted.

The actual rules of Boston traffic commence with the consensus of both drivers and pedestrians that the official rules shall be ignored. The drivers disregard the red lights and the street signs. The people walk in the streets whenever and wherever they please. Since the streets are fairly short, and constricted by drivers who have parked illegally for brief outings as pedestrians, the drivers cannot get up much speed between right- or acute-angle intersections. Because the streets are narrow, the pedestrian of average speed afoot has a reasonably good chance of reaching safety on the opposite curb before the approaching vehicle runs over him, at least in fine weather.

There are, it is true, regular instances of bad form on both sides. Pedestrians emerging in large groups from subway stops, or gathering at busy intersections during morning, lunch, and evening hours, often form roving bands on an *ad hoc* basis and bring all the cars and trucks to a standstill by streaming across the thoroughfares without interruption. Often these aggregations follow a bumptious oldster, or a legally blind person, who by waving a white cane or holding one arm high slows the wheeled traffic just enough to let the horde step off. Drivers, too, are guilty of unsportsmanlike behavior: on the broader, straighter, longer avenues, such as Commonwealth, Atlantic, and Huntington, they accelerate when a distant jaywalker steps out, instead of maintaining steady speed, allowing him to stroll. Generally, though, conformity to the actual code is fairly dependable and results in surprisingly few deaths or serious injuries. Those are usually ignorant people recently arrived from elsewhere, unschooled in local customs.

The relatively minor carnage is attributable to the Bostonian understanding of the importance of eye contact and its significance in all human intercourse, however transient. Drivers stare straight ahead at all times, whether approaching pedestrians standing poised upon the curbs or being approached by other drivers bent upon preceding them through crossings. Pedestrians, whether following the officious elderly or lame person who has made the traffic pause or darting out on solo ventures when the streets are wet or icy, do not allow their gazes to lock with those of drivers. Boston's workaday version of the rules of modern warfare is extremely strict; it forbids not only maiming, or attempted maiming, but even the wrongful interruption of ongoing passage of another person whose gaze has met one's own. Its practice requires vigilance, alertness, great strength of character, and fortitude, and it is required for the performance of all ordinary business within the city limits.

The sawhorses blocking Charles Street on that August day therefore warranted the happy belief of the people strolling there that this was a day of festive peace and secure recreation. Vendors took up stations with carts of spicy hot foods, chilled beverages, and ice cream. Three young women hitched a garden hose up to a spigot and employed it to fill a huge galvanized tub with water, floating small boats on its surface. A young man in a top hat rode a high-wheeled unicycle. Clowns and mummers, street musicians, artists with more zeal than skill: all mingled with young parents, cheerful babies, friendly dogs, cordial matrons, beaming elders, and the occasional lost child.

Mayor Kevin H. White, earlier that day, had gone to Charlestown's new high school to confer with voters there. There was a reporter with him. There was a small group to greet him, perhaps forty people. They were white and of the age when most parents have children of school age. They were members of an organization known as the Powderkeg. They had formed it to express complaints about forced busing in the public school system. Their faces were tense; when they spoke, they spoke loudly and in tones of strong resentment. They did not want blacks bused into Charlestown or white students transferred out. They were not appeased by statements that the law required such actions. They were mindful that the mayor was seeking reelection. They did not as a group wish to parley; they were out for more than that.

Kevin White could not give to those parents what it was they really wanted, except a patient auditing of what they had to say. Saying it inflamed them further, as they cataloged injustice, insult, and injury. Heartened and also made nervous by the presence of their friends, they grew louder and more hostile as his impotence to do their bidding was again made clear to them. What began as ventilation, which he'd desired to accomplish, turned into a rally that would make the problem worse.

White was adroit when the situation changed. He asked if two women, prominent in Powderkeg, could retire with him to talk about things and defuse the situation. The two women thought that was a good idea. They persuaded the followers that it might help matters some. Grudgingly, the others said they would agree to that, and the gathering dispersed. The two women, middle-aged, white, and middle income, looked at the reporter with antagonistic distaste. They had managed something of which they were fairly proud. They had set up the confrontation that had given their angrier followers the consoling chance to be heard, if not assuaged. They had given the mayor an opportunity to observe firsthand the animosity they were doing their best to control. Now they were prepared to haggle with him, but they did not wish their successes to be nullified by bad public relations. What their followers had said, after all, whatever its sincerity and however genuine, was the sort of talk that had been called "racist" in the past, and excoriated. They told the mayor that the reporter must be excluded from their conference.

The mayor saw their point. He met it head-on. "He's not from the _Globe_," he said of the reporter. The women withdrew their objections.

The mayor emerged from that morning of negotiation in a mood of pardonable self-satisfaction. He had endured personally the abusive complaints of constituents reviling him in an election year in frustrated expression of their outraged revulsion for impositions made on them by others. He had been castigated personally for the decisions of U.S. District Court Judge W. Arthur Garrity, Jr., over which he had no influence or control, and threatened with retribution at the polls for them. Retaliatory racial violence was alluded to; the mayor knew what personal damage that could do to his career, incidental to its potential for immense harm to the city. He had been in short unfairly treated, by any reasonable standard, but by subjecting himself to that hostility he had gained something of real value.

What he had gained was the resentful consent of the plenary session of the Powderkeg to the closed bargaining with the ladies. He had used that meeting to swap agreements that were within the power of the parties to perform. By enduring threats and insults provoked by what Garrity had done, White had obtained reduction of Charlestown's demands to claims that he could grant and would satisfy in return for Charlestown's promise to keep the peace. The ladies of the Powderkeg said they would do their best to prevent violence, and he thought that they could bring it off. He said that he would provide recorded music in the school after classes ended for the day and see to the provision of more weekend activities, such as swimming and dances. Neither he nor the ladies explicitly adverted to the fact that activities held outside of regular school hours would by their timing tend to exclude black students being bused to Charlestown High from other parts of Boston, since the buses would depart before the music started. Neither of the parties mentioned the fact that the Charlestown kids being bused to schools in other sections would be back when the fun started and would thus be able to mingle socially with their neighborhood friends as though they had been still enrolled at Charlestown High. Nobody said anything about the probable effect of the ostensibly innocuous program improvements upon the stated aim of demolishing racial barriers among the city's youth, contradicting via activities outside of school hours the objectives sought by the busing orders that had disrupted the school day. They were all too smart for that.

Pleased with himself for that morning's political workout, Kevin H. White postponed lunch for a few hours and went back to where he lived, his home neighborhood on Beacon Hill, where the fair was under way. En route on foot from his car into the blocked-off street, he shifted from the mode of skillful politician doing what he thought a Boston mayor should do, cajoling real commitments that would have some real effects, into the campaigning mode of the supplicant for votes. The gray lightweight worsted suit coat came off, to be suspended over his left shoulder by his left forefinger through the hanger hook. The rep stripe tie, dark blue and red, came down on its knot to the second button of the blue oxford cloth shirt—the collar button was undone. The cuffs were unbuttoned and the sleeves rolled up twice on his forearms. At work on members of the crowd, he extended his right hand forward for the hesitating clasp of the citizen. On more receptive subjects, the left arm swiveled the coat down, so that it media-veronicaed across the pavement like a bullfighter's cape, the left hand moving up, palm upward, to grasp the voter's right forearm while his right hand pumped away. The tanned skin around the happy, bright blue eyes crinkled quickly and deeply, and the fast smile broke across the mouth. Out from behind the white teeth came the nicely cadenced "Hi, howayas" for the totally unknown, the automatic "Good tah seeyas" for the ones who looked familiar, and all the while his eyes were scanning, looking for the contact that, on the streets of Boston, at least, promises safe passage. He wasn't scared, exactly, just sort of apprehensive.

He had reason to be. His principal opponent in the primary and almost certain foe in the November general election was Joseph Timilty, a state senator from Mattapan with firm credentials for the job and a movie star's appearance. Timilty had taken careful advantage of murmurs to the effect that Mayor Kevin White was hooked up with the Mafia. Those mutterings had been played up in the underground newspapers, the *Phoenix* and *The Real Paper*, and had received exposure, too, in the *Globe* and on television. There was published opinion that White was a liar and much innuendo to the effect that he stole. Just as the pedestrian peers through the driver's windshield, looking for the contact that says he will be safe, White scrutinized the strangers for expressions of mistrust, evidence that they disliked him or believed he was a crook. One or two such, of course, wouldn't matter much, but if many ducked away from him or would not meet his gaze, he would know he was in trouble and that would bother him.

He was therefore vulnerable, as he had not been in Charlestown, where the citizens were angry. Hostility on Charles Street would be proof against his brains and skills, and incurable by talk. One who recoiled from his handshake might have many reasons. She might just dislike the mayor, or all politicians. He might be reserved and shy, avoiding human contact as a policy of his. She might think White was corrupt or a distant relative of Timilty's by marriage. All that White would know for sure was that he had not met a friend. And when he did meet someone friendly, unless he paused to ask, he would not even know if his friend voted in Boston.

Similarly, those who met him were not gaining much. Brief campaign encounters like that told them almost nothing. An exchange of commonplaces—"Think the Sox can do it?" "Nah, they haven't got the pitching; it's the same thing every year"—would accomplish little. It would not inform a voter what the mayor had done in Charlestown; it would not advise the mayor that the voter really favored school desegregation or believed it would be wise now to curtail urban renewal. He went into those encounters knowing them to be charades, but performances that could wound him if he seemed afraid of them.

This dissonance between what politicians do with power and what they must do to get it cripples all our governments and depletes those who would run them. What we need in this age, at least, are proficient bargainers, people who have acquired skills as mediators and arrangers. Wheeler-dealers, if you will, who do not mind disparagement. What we elect are shapers, as such folk are known in baseball: players preoccupied with looking graceful at their work, striking poses, winning applause, making easy stuff look hard, and eluding the tough chances. Politicians cut the best deals, but campaigners get elected.

Some candidates combine great skills in both configurations. Edward M. Kennedy is one such paragon. He achieved his Senate seat in 1962, the beneficiary of intensive tutelage in the campaigner's mode, which he had undergone in his brother Jack's campaigns. Once there, though, he became a politician, and he flourished in that study as a man who could work deals. People of effect and power in the U.S. Senate do not get it by glad-handing; they get it by making trades and proving that their word is always good, never asking for too much or giving it away. Learning those principles, though, Kennedy did not forget his mastery of campaigns. Years ago, on a wet chilly night in Morgantown, West Virginia, tired out and petulant before he made a speech, subsisting on a few bites of cold pizza that had not been good when warm, Kennedy displayed that virtuosity in a pure *tour de force*. He appeared for Harley Staggers, who was seeking reelection to his seat in Congress. When Kennedy, weary and irritated, went into the hall, the miners and their families forgot the congressman. Roaring out a welcome of deep nostalgic affection for the last surviving brother of the man who had electrified them back in 1960, they made him forget in return that he didn't want to be there. He began to speak with passion and received their passion back. It seemed as though the very wallboard trembled with that speech and the reaction of the people listening. Kennedy, when he is on, makes speeches in the same way Gunther Gebel-Williams trains the tigers for the circus. I do not recall what he said that night, but I later voted for him to be president; many others would have but for one night in a car.

Candidates who possess both skills are very rare. Jimmy Carter could campaign, but he could not cut deals. Richard Nixon made much money playing poker in the navy, and he kept that shrewdness and deceptiveness when he won his offices; for him, winning was the hard part, which was why he tried to cheat. Campaigning, Nixon looked like he was bluffing all, deceiving his enemies into thinking he held aces, misleading his partisans into believing he had fours. Gerald Ford proved clumsy as an unelected president conducting politics; seeking election to it, he showed no talent for campaigning. Ronald Reagan is superb winning elections; it's what he does afterward that gives him so much trouble. Few candidates do even one thing well; almost none do both.

Kevin White's aptitude, however great it was, was in holding office, not in seeking it. Like Richard Nixon, his first substantial triumph at the polls in 1967 (I discount his victories in four statewide races for secretary of state; the winner of the Democratic party nomination almost invariably wins at the polls) was in large measure attributable to the nature of his opposition. Nixon lost to JFK, a formidable adversary on the hustings, but narrowly defeated Vice President Hubert Humphrey's bid as standard-bearer of a divided party that was sulking, behind a brooding lame duck president who resented his succession. Nixon humiliated George McGovern, who combined mediocre campaigning skills with a genius for disorganization. White fared best against the retreaded attack launched against him in 1971 by his vanquished opponent from 1967, and thereafter he declined in absolute strength despite gaining two more victories. His good fortune was the persisting absence of a stronger campaigner from the fields in which he ran; it made his deficiencies as a candidate, as opposed to an officeholder, handicaps that he could overcome.

He overcame them by the exercise of the same acuity he demonstrated as the holder of the office. Unlike Nixon, who beat Humphrey despite the ill feelings that the media had developed toward him long before their contest, White luxuriated in the benevolence of those who covered him, first in his early days as a candidate for mayor, then as winner of the office. To a very considerable extent, the media wanted him to do well in the office, because they feared and despised the lady who'd opposed him. It was as though a nice Richard Nixon had run against a bad Richard Nixon; those reporters and editors who were personally cool toward Kevin White were icy toward his foe. White was smart enough to cultivate the high regard in which they held him and cute enough for quite a while not to endanger it. He maintained a discreet silence about agreements that he struck with developers of large parcels of real estate, whose big contributions to the revitalization of the downtown area were regularly purchased with tax exemptions in the millions. He did not boast, on that August Sunday as he ran for his second term, that he had exchanged promises of extracurricular resegregation of Charlestown High School with the ladies of the Powderkeg for their pledge to discourage civil unrest. What he did was put on shows of style, duende, and panache—entertaining monarchs at the Parkman House mansion; making sure the

Rolling Stones were able to perform in Boston notwithstanding the fact that one of them, Keith Richards, had been busted on a drug charge in Rhode Island that concert night; welcoming occasions for great civic celebrations and then carrying them off.

That showmanship worked nicely for the first eight years or so. It worked, in other words, for as long as those upon whom he practiced it were amenable to it. Then, as they got restless, his substitute for the skills of a campaigner began to deteriorate, and he did not have another one with which to replace it. For quite a while after that dry rot set in; he was able to get by, but his eventual downfall was inevitable. He lacked that collection of personal characteristics that bring popular and immutable public devotion to a candidate and will carry him through almost every disaster he can suffer or bring upon himself. He did not have charisma.

The uneasiness he showed at the Charles Street Fair that August Sunday was some evidence of that condition and his own awareness of it. He could not attach importance to the flesh-pressing he did. He was out there in the sunshine doing what he was supposed to, trying to pretend that it was dignified, seeking to persuade other human beings (presumably equipped with their own abilities to reason) of the almost palpable falsehood that he was elated to see them, to shake their sweaty hands with his and mingle perspirations, to gaze with fond good humor on their sweaty, flustered faces. When he tried to do such things, he didn't do them well; he could not work wakes.

When the candidate is a politician of perceived ability, and he is one of a field whose abilities as politicians—officeholders—are perceived as being meager, and when none of the field has messianic powers that will unite the mass of voters, the media enjoy creative powers of their own. If the voters cannot choose their leaders by the magnetism that they show, then the voters can be guided by the media they heed.

If the voters can be guided, then the media will guide them. If the media choose well among the indifferent campaigners, then the voters will elect a smart and savvy politician. If the media choose wrong, as they did with Jimmy Carter, then the voters will elect a prepossessing bungler. Kevin White was chosen well by the media. He performed well, as their choice, for the voters who concurred. Then the man wore out his welcome and the media withdrew. Thereupon he performed badly, and then he withdrew himself.

Somehow this does not seem like the way it should be done.

STYLE VERSUS SUBSTANCE

Turn up the lights. I don't want to go home
in the dark.

—O. Henry (William Sydney Porter)
Last words (1910)

1

THE MANNER of the mayor's leave-taking from the 1983 election showed how much polish and elaboration he and his milieu had given to each other in his sixteen years in office. His predecessor, John F. Collins, had divulged his intention to retire in 1967 in some offhand remarks delivered by the way at a press conference scheduled to deal with other matters that had not panned out for it. White's farewell was comparable in execution, style, complexity, and mystery to memorable retirements tendered by the city during his reign to others of its living legends who had ended long careers in its esteem. Arthur Fiedler of the Boston Pops, which he claimed to have invented, had what seemed like a whole season of hosannas, nearly enough to satiate even his gargantuan ego. Charles Munch left the Boston Symphony with more restraint, of course, but it was still an occasion, and the city recognized it. Bob Cousy of the Celtics started his last game in tears, "We love ya, Cooz" echoing down upon his bowed head from the rafters of the Garden. John Havlicek, the Cooz's teammate, in due course played to a tribute. Bobby Orr of the Bruins left town out of season, his as well as the Bruins, or he would have had one, too. But politicians checking out of Boston offices did not get celebrations until Kevin changed the rules.

I

Not unless they were en route to higher offices at 1600 Pennsylvania Avenue, in Washington, D.C.

It was fitting White should do that. He had invented celebrations as Fiedler invented the Pops, at least as far as staid and stodgy, dour old Boston was concerned. His Bicentennial Observances had set a standard for us. Tall ships paraded in the harbor under skies of crystal blue, led to our review of them by *Old Ironsides* herself, her cannons belching salutes while bands played and thousands cheered. Arthur Fiedler and his Pops that night played "Stars and Stripes Forever" outdoors on the Esplanade, the night skies over them erupting with fireworks as the cheers broke out again. The queen of England came to Boston, and she was but one of several. And each year, on New Year's Eve, if lacking ships and queens, Boston under Kevin White staged First Night celebrations, causing those who lived nearby to think of the city as special, dipping into concerts, dances, stage shows, and more displays of fireworks as a privileged, ordained people. People led by Kevin White, who therefore deserved praise.

The difference, of course, between the planned enthusiasms that had been accorded to his predecessors in retirement from the limelights of the city and the breathless attention that the town accorded him when he made public his decision to step down was that they did not orchestrate their departures as he did his own. The handicap that limited (if any in fact did) the formal announcement of the end of the White era in the city was that Kevin White lacked a good Kevin White to stage it for him. A satisfactory outpouring of gratitude and fondness should be choreographed by a third party able to pose credibly as an unselfish actor seeking nothing for himself, seeing only that the proper homage is forthcoming for the venerable hero. The mayor is supposed to name the streets, the parks, and the auditoriums after other sterling citizens. It isn't seemly for him to be noticed darting feverishly among the decorative plants, positioning musicians and rabble-rousers to set up a great commotion of acclaim for his skill in their organization, then appearing to feign blushes of discombobulated modesty when they commence to shout their paeans. For a man who had made a deserved reputation of himself in his four terms as the real master of the public's ceremonies, Kevin White's administration of his own abdication was a potentially awkward situation.

He handled it with the aplomb of a true professional. In doing so, he demonstrated forcefully, if tacitly, how very much he'd learned and taught about the media and its capabilities since 1967.

Back then the candidates and the reporters had played a passive game, neither one bothering the other much. Only when the great world itself fortuitously provided an occasion that, if handled properly, could redound to a candidate's advantage, was there any interaction. There is as great an inclination toward indolence among reporters as there is in any other group of salaried workers whose compensation is not obviously tied to the amount of enterprise that they devote to their labors. In 1967, Lyndon Johnson was still president and we were still in Vietnam. To reporters it was arguable, though far from certain, that tenacious pursuit of the truth and vigorous disclosure of its disparity from what was uttered by Lyndon Johnson and his generals might in time lead to fame, reputation, and riches for the correspondents who conducted it. The risky option to strive for such distinction was restricted to those people who were covering the war. Therefore, except for those assigned to stories or to beats that had some piece of the war coverage included, there was no premium upon aggressiveness to stimulate political reporters to dig into people or events.

Most reporters, like most laymen, tend to see only those things that they expect to see and to find significance only in those events (e.g., natural disasters, assassinations) and persons (e.g., charismatic leaders with enormous followings, swashbuckling outlaws of any description) that overwhelm the mind. In late 1966 and the first part of 1967, "knights of the keyboard" (as Ted Williams used to call reporters scornfully), without some prospect of personal gain to inspire them into more strenuous inspection of the world around them, paid virtually no heed to Kevin White's embryonic campaign for the mayor's office. They had not been given any reason to look for it in his three public offices on the eleventh floor of the Little Building at 80 Boylston Street, across from the Boston Common. It is probable that if he had pined for their attention he would not have gotten it. The mayor at the time was John F. Collins, and in that startlingly recent and anomalously naive time, his immunity from electoral challenge until the primary scheduled for September apparently sufficed as reason to ignore the preparation of what might very well turn out to be a most formidable challenge.

This media lassitude gave Kevin White the latitude of secrecy. Within a day or two after all the returns were in for the statewide election of November 1966, he set up his campaign team for the 1967 mayoralty race—quietly, with no back talk. The media galvanized no foes for him in that expansive leisure, as they surely would today. White was reelected to a fourth two-year term as secretary of state with a plurality of 750,000 votes, the largest of any victor in that campaign. In a Republican landslide he could take his time to muster his advisers, contemplate his situation and their counsel in the tranquillity of five days spent alone in the sunshine of Aruba, and have everything neatly in place for his bid when it came time to float the trial balloons in January of the city's election year. The media of those days did not care that he had taken two rooms for conferring in the then Sheraton, now Copley, Plaza. Nor were they interested in his preference for rusticating in the Caribbean without the conjugal companionship of "his decorative wife, Kathy," as the *Globe*'s society reporter Marjorie Sherman could describe her in those days before women's liberation. (*Globe*, 4/11/67, p. 21) Candidates in those days did not find their strategizing hectored by rude onlookers, whose kibitzing and cynical asides were printed up the next morning for the amusement of the multitude and the information of the enemy.

The importance of that permissiveness was considerable. Among White's three chief advisers then was Theodore Anzalone, a tough, smart North End lawyer who had been with him from the beginning of his political life, doing what he could (which was a lot) to aid in his four victories as secretary of state. Anzalone served as director of corporations in that paper-shuffling records office. Then thirty-seven, the same age as his candidate, Anzalone offered White shrewd counsel in his efforts to secure support from South Boston, Back Bay, Charlestown, and Beacon Hill, because he knew how to gather information and cement alliances in Wards 1 through 14. But his background and his gut instincts were products of the defiantly rambunctious North End, and that was where he operated his law offices, too.

Anzalone's clientele was drawn from that predominantly Italo-American part of Boston. Several of his clients were men whose names had long been quite familiar to law enforcement officers. They were assumed to be members in good standing of the honored society that in in 1967 would acquire new infamy as *La Cosa Nostra*, or *LCN*, that being the cumbersome term Joe Valachi had employed to beguile the president's Commission on Law Enforcement and the Administration of Criminal Justice, among others. Given the reflexive tendencies of media and public to assume that every prosperous Italo-American businessman perforce is a mafioso, and that every lawyer merits complete identification with his clients, it was virtually certain that Ted Anzalone would be perceived as a *consigliere* authorized to represent the interests of "the Mob" in any and all councils called by Kevin Hagan White. It took about eight years for that equation to unfold in full public bloom and perfume a White candidacy. The allegations poisoned his third campaign in 1975 and contributed substantially, if indirectly, to the vengeful changes that he made in his approach to government after that vicious contest. Its seeds were right there in plain sight in 1966; it was just that nobody paid much attention to them then.

What did interest the *Globe* as 1967 dawned was the potential effect of election politics upon ambitious programs of urban renewal then well under way. The old West End had been torn down amid predictions, later validated, that the middle- to high-income tenants who replaced the old neighbors displaced to make room for the high rises in Charles River Park would never achieve status as the same sort of close-knit community. That type of concern served both to invigorate and to discourage fetal mayoral ambitions believed to lie within the breast of Boston Redevelopment Authority (BRA) Director Edward J. Logue, the carpetbagging genius of rebuilding, who was lured from New Haven by the businesslike blandishments of John F. Collins. Those who exceedingly admired the transformation of the old Scollay Square into the plaza and the new city hall installed in its place, bordered by the curvilinear office buildings One, Two, and Three Center Plaza and by the towers of the state and federal offices ascending to the west of it, were enthusiastic about the notion that the man who had accomplished these wonders for Collins might be persuaded to succeed his patron. There was room, too, for the proposition that this passing of the torch might not require wholehearted endorsement by Collins, who had been thrashed in the 1966 Democratic primary contest for the senatorial nomination, losing out to Endicott Peabody (Peabody then went on to lose to Edward W. Brooke in the November disaster). Collins's popularity was plainly not at its highwater mark.

Ian Menzies was saddled by the *Globe* with the unenviable chore of stating a perspective on that political situation, the meaning of life, and other trifles for the 1967 New Year's Day editions. He did as legions of his professional predecessors and successors have done in like circumstances: he resorted to a great effusion of balderdash. Menzies wrote that "over the years it has been the people of Massachusetts who have supplied the leadership and the media [that] has helped them focus on the issues." Menzies foresaw for the enlightened Boston voter demanding tasks ahead. "The city," he said, "still stumbles, still plagued by the need for more housing, torn by racial imbalance in the schools, beset by transportation problems, suffering from dirt and neglect in too many areas outside the showpiece plazas."

"What will happen," Menzies agonized, "in Roxbury-Dorchester, with an estimated 70,000 Negroes, some 10 percent of the city's population?" *Blacks* then was still a racial slur, sort of; *Negroes* then had yet to become one. "Boston escaped racial violence last year," Menzies said, perhaps suppressing a small shudder, "and still has a reservoir of Negro goodwill, but for how long?" Menzies saw but one hope for avoiding an apocalypse, the sort of cataclysm that had devastated Chicago, New York, and Los Angeles: better management. He implied it would not come from John Collins: "This should be the year, the first of four years, to close the elusive gap of tired-out management, to seek younger men who delight in challenges, to remove obstruction from the part [*sic*] and make government work exciting and vital." (*Globe*, 1/1/67, pp. 1–A6)

There was no evidence that Kevin White or anyone competing with him for mayor back in 1967 paused to consider whether gaps in management that were elusive really warranted a great deal of concern about ways of closing them. If such problems did occupy his mind, he did not make them campaign issues. What he was fretting about was his long-term career, and he arranged for disclosure of his preoccupation to the *Globe's* readers. Through a backgrounded think piece that was planted with the *Globe's* Timothy Leland, White disclosed his view that he had reached a personal dead end in the office of secretary of state. He saw no exciting future in perennial tenure as the holder of the biggest of the little statewide offices to which Massachusetts voters, being chiefly Democrats, automatically elect and if possible then reelect the Democratic candidate. Being mayor, he advised Leland, would enable him "to make headlines" and "to raise money for a gubernatorial bid." (*Globe*, 1/3/67, p. 13)

That sort of a disclosure may seem odd to people who observe politics outside of Massachusetts, the bold-faced declaration that the office sought is valuable chiefly as a launching pad for a still higher office. In the abstract it would seem to constitute an invitation to the voters to give the backs of their hands to the bumptious fellow, boasting at the outset that he's too fine for the post he's asking them to give him. In Massachusetts, though, it's *de rigueur* for every candidate who wishes to dispel all reservations about his dedication to, and his fitness for, the secular but holy game of politics. It amounts to his serving of the notice that he's like John Kennedy, another shining young man who is destined for the stars. Boston politicians seek to tap the proprietary attitude that Boston's voters feel toward favorite politicians. Those who backed JFK's bid for James Michael Curley's seat in Congress basked in the assurance of their prescience when Kennedy became the president of the entire United States, for he was theirs (Thomas P. "Tip" O'Neill took Curley's seat when Kennedy advanced to the Senate back in 1952, and as Speaker he still nourishes that sense of participation that his followers in Cambridge feel in his eminence). Every candidate who's smart recruits foot soldiers for his Boston campaigns by making strong suggestions that their early loyalty will bring them days of basking in reflected greater glories he'll win as their champion.

It is fantasy, of course, but it is fantasy that Kevin White and most of those who have fought with him and against him in the politics of Massachusetts have taken as the solemn truth. Musing after his withdrawal from the 1983 campaign to the question put by Kirby Perkins of WCVB-TV of whether his four terms had left him with any large regrets, Kevin White admitted he had one. "That there wasn't something more," he said, and went on to lament that all he had been was mayor. He said that he thought people who assessed his career in later years would wonder about that, wonder why he hadn't managed to go farther.

His pique, if somewhat amusing, was understandable in the political context in which he has spent his adult life. He had, after all, decided to hang up his spikes amid a clangor of cell doors closing on minor subalterns of his administrations: fourteen of them in sixteen years had been charged with shaking down contractors, employing the U.S. mails to secure disability pensions by means of fraudulent representations, or lying to grand juries inquiring into Kevin White's campaign practices. The United States attorney, William F. Weld, had vigorously taken up the criminal investigation files left to him by Edward F. Harrington, his Democratic predecessor, who in the eyes of several in the Massachusetts trial bar had departed utterly from his judgment in seeking Kevin White's increasingly sparse scalp. The *Globe*, joining tardily and with some reluctance the band of journalistic harriers baying after him as early as eight years before, had called for his withdrawal from the race, or his defeat if he persisted in contesting it. There was a plethora of candidates, several of them of such stature as to justify the wit's description of the competition as "Kevin and the Seven Dwarfs," but the list included two or three formidable foes who had the money and the followings to make his try for a fifth term a very dodgy thing.

There was a widespread sentiment to the effect that his withdrawal had been his cagiest act in a career that featured many of them, a neat finesse of certain political disaster at least, a prudent plea bargain at most, which might remove the impetus from the U.S. attorney's pursuit. To describe that strategic retreat as a cause for ambivalent nostalgia for higher offices that never came to be smacked somewhat of a disingenuous arrogance remarkable even for Kevin White, who has been credited with the invention of hauteur and arrogance. But none of that addressed the fact, which was that Kevin White had by the manner of his abdication plainly demonstrated what enormous skill he had brought to and developed in his sixteen years as mayor of Boston.

The news that he had for the people of Boston on the evening of May 26 was short and simple. It contained nothing that required that he deliver it in five uninterrupted minutes starting at 6:55 P.M. on Thursday night, over each of Boston's three commercial VHF television stations. Because it was his statement of withdrawal from the fray, it had no possible utility as a clarion summons to his legions of supporters or his wincing but still generous contributors. No matter how he made it, whether insulated and composed, measured and equipped with complete sentences by a TelePrompTer, or naked, raving, and distraught atop the tower of the Customs House at noon, the principal result of what he had to say would be that he would not demand another term as mayor of Boston.

If dignity and no harassment, not even the crass heckling that the radio and television reporters mount despite advance instructions that the speaker won't take questions, had been all that worried him, a one-line written statement from his office to the pressroom there at City Hall would have sufficed. If what truly obsessed him was the use of the occasion to remind the voters and the critics that he had done much to deserve their respect and admiration, he could have arranged an interview for broadcast, print, or both quite easily with friendly inquisitors who would have guaranteed civility and probably a good deal more. But none of those alternatives, no matter how fine-tuned, would have ensured he would totally control a media event that he could all but warrant would be sure to dominate the news that night, not to mention the two days that preceded it and the four days that followed it.

He did that by dispatching his press secretary, George Regan, to buy that five-minute block from channels 4, 5, and 7 on May 25. The station advertising managers were told only that the mayor wished to purchase the time in order to deliver a political announcement. Neither channel 4 nor 5, claiming audience rating shares that enabled them to charge about $10,000 each for that most desirable time segment, nor channel 7, which was able to get only about $3,000 for that same interval, had any compunction whatsoever about turning an honest dollar off the mayor's correct perception that his choice of time would get him the attention of just about every living person with a television set in the greater Boston area that night. The motive that impels commercial television station managers to endure costs that they think heavy for production of news programs, which are difficult to mount and are always being ridiculed in print, is that of profit. They secure those profits by selling pieces of those programs to folks who wish to sell soap or peddle themselves and think their chances of success are better if they make their pitches to the kind and number of viewers who draw up their chairs each evening to watch the news at six o'clock.

The mayor's homey talk, though, was a little different from those addresses that the station managers usually agree to air in exchange for that kind of money from their advertisers. There isn't a great deal of spontaneous interest in the audience in the actual word contents of paid broadcast messages. For most viewers, one suspects, there isn't any interest at all, and it is only by the merest chance that someone sitting down to watch the news at six o'clock learns to his delight that there has just come on the market a much better way of washing his soiled toilet. What the mayor had in mind was different because it was itself *news*, and the mere fact that it had come into his mind, why, that was *also* news. Actual news that those harassed station managers, priding themselves upon their coolness under fire, could relay to their own reporters for transmission to the viewers of the evening news that very same night in the warm New England springtime, two full days before the mayor's little message would be aired.

The mayor, by clearing his throat, as it were, made the media equivalent of a three-cushion billiard shot, one that left his metaphoric cue ball resting just where he desired it to be when he made his second shot forty-eight hours later, by actually saying something. The news that Kevin White was going to make some news thus dominated the entire workweek.

May, in Boston, is also probably about the best time of the year to make the news, if your purpose in disclosing it is to obtain maximum dissemination of it. In springtime the bad weather is pretty much over, which augurs against the possibility that your little gem of a news item will get buried under footage and column inches about what happened in the blizzard that arrived on the same day. The Red Sox, who in New England have the power to cloud men's minds, have not yet gotten far enough in the race for the pennant (assuming that your year happens to be one in which they possess the personnel and resolution to win more than they lose) to cause anyone to hyperventilate for more than one day at a time. The Celtics do assert a respectable claim upon the springtime attention spans of Bostonians, but they'd gone belly-up in '83 when the mayor began his gavotte. The Bruins had put up a game fight and lost, and anyway they lost their hold on Boston's collective imagination when Bobby Orr left town some years ago. There had been one considerable murder trial (in Cambridge, involving Everett policemen charged with homicide in a drunken riot in a Chelsea hot-pillow motel; some of them were convicted, too), but that was over. It was too early for the folks who live in Boston and around it to be thinking mostly about going to the beach and they had had six weeks to repress all their anger about income taxes paid in April. The only major holiday in sight was Memorial Day, which does not compel storekeepers to put out lures or shoppers to descend in hordes upon the plazas around Boston, and nobody schedules any major parties for that day. Graduations were about over, the wedding season was a couple of weeks away, so to all intents and purposes there wasn't a damned thing going on. No matter what season the mayor picked for his announcement, he would be vulnerable to a demotion on the marquee of events by fire, flood, or acts of God, an unexpected missile crisis or the death of some young hereo or acknowledged messiah, but insofar as he could make allowances for predictable events that would steal all his thunder, he had chosen masterfully.

His timing during that month in the springtime was equally proficient. By making news at the beginning of the week, about ten days before Memorial Day, he made it likely he would hog all the attention. There being nothing much around to gobble up the local public interest, his tantalizing act would fascinate the commentators in the papers and the pundits to the virtual exclusion of all other topics. All they would have would be the stark fact that the mayor was about to make some sort of an announcement, and the obvious inference that at least he thought it was important. For all they knew, he could have been preparing a short homily on ornithology. But a shortage of instructive information almost never hinders an opinion maker who is desperate to fill a column or a modest chunk of airtime. Such persiflage would of course conduce to heighten the perceived public interest in the matter, and Kevin White, carefully absenting himself from Boston without leaving firm word of his destination, could confidently bet that the suspense would carry through the week.

By Thursday, when his tape would be broadcast, the media with his cordial assistance had worked themselves into a near frenzy of frustrated curiosity. This afforded him the *gratis* chance to obtain incidentally a measure of revenge for all the mean things Peter Lucas had sneeringly published about him in the Boston *Herald*. White permitted Lucas to secure from him by telephone what the columnist could only have interpreted as an assurance that His Honor was about to declare for reelection, so that Thursday's *Herald* bannered WHITE WILL RUN and backed it up with Lucas's bylined story attributed to a close pal of the mayor's. (*Herald*, 5/26/83, p. 1) The day after White's tape had splattered that headline in crimson over Lucas and Rupert Murdoch's editor, Robert Page, Lucas was so upset that he published what White said to him, including White's boyishly conspiratorial shared giggle with the writer: "We'll screw the *Globe.*" (*Herald*, 5/27/83 p. 2) This was not a very nice thing for the mayor to do to Lucas, but then Peter had made routine sport of him under the epithet of "Kevin DeLuxe," riding him unmercifully for his lavish tastes in travel, entertainment, and official transportation, and it would have taken the forbearance of a saint, which even White had never claimed, to eschew that lovely opportunity for getting even.

Coming on the heels of that painstaking preparation, White's reflective oral essay on the progress Boston had made since—and, impliedly, because—he became the mayor was an affecting presentation. His audience, after all, received it with a respect and attention that its members do not ordinarily accord to more intrusive bellowings by pompous and ambitious politicians who have fouled up their accustomed television programming. There was likely very little fidgeting and getting up to visit the bathroom while Kevin White's professionally made tape rolled his sonorous cadences out over New England. For that brief interval, if for no other during his whole tenure in the office, Kevin White enjoyed the undivided attention of those whom he addressed. He continued to enjoy it on Friday morning when the papers came out summarizing and interpreting his speech. Through the whole long holiday weekend, lasting until Tuesday morning, May 31, Kevin White was still the focus of the Boston media. No candidate, to be sure, but still the center of attention.

It is tempting to dismiss his *tour de force* with the observation that it is ironic to find such virtuosity limited to the scope of a message of resignation; just as our parents and our moral teachers taught us, it is wrong to succumb to temptation. It is wrong in this instance because that championship manipulation of the media, performed by a politician who had found himself hamstrung in his recent efforts to control virtually any other aspect of his public life that was important to him, represented his prudent retreat, not his abject surrender, in the face of powerful opponents who had arrayed themselves against him. He did not say that he was quitting politics; he said the time had come to move on toward some new challenge. That at the very least left open to him the option to declare a candidacy for some other elective office, and even a *pro forma* announcement would stay the operation of the state's law that would otherwise escheat to the Commonwealth an estimated several hundred thousand dollars in accumulated campaign funds. At most, it excused him with dignity intact from a most unpleasant fight that he was picked to lose, and at the same time, he was putting to U.S. Attorney Weld the troublesome question of whether it was desirable to seem to persecute a politician who has withdrawn from the occasion of his alleged sins. And in the process of accomplishing those far from negligible betterments of his personal and political situation, that interlude reminded nearly everybody of his genuine achievements as the mayor of Boston, just in case what he had done had slipped out of their minds. It is not wise, when evaluating a man who at thirty-seven took his office rudely from the grasp of one just ten years older who was quite reluctant to relinquish it, and who had held it for sixteen years of turmoil during which he generally prospered, to assume that he dwindled in that tenure. He had learned what was important.

Tell me, Muse, of the man of many wiles.

—Homer, of Odysseus
The Odyssey

2

IN BOSTON, Kevin White was a beacon for the media throughout his entire career as mayor. Initially this was probably attributable more to the nature of the office than to any remarkable personal characteristics. The mayor of Boston is a powerful figure, made so by the city charter which adjures him to rule, not merely reign. Only a very retiring person indeed could hope to occupy the office without simultaneously undergoing the unremitting scrutiny of the press, and if he did not exert himself to reward the attention, he would soon find himself ridiculed for his preposterous modesty. Such a person, of course, would not be likely to achieve the office in the first place, and certainly would be ejected from it promptly, with few tears, at the end of the first term, if for no other reason than for nonfeasance as the dominant official of the city.

That sort of attention, the lot of every politician who becomes well known enough to warrant more than casual mention when a major controversy or elective office opens up, necessarily affects the subject. He becomes cagey, if he knows what is good for him. Puissance in elective politics is curiously fragile, obtainable perhaps by him who reacts brilliantly to luck and then works very hard to see to the consolidation of his gains, but frighteningly easy to dissipate by too much nonchalance. When Edmund Muskie reached for the Democratic presidential nomination back in 1972, he stood upon a senatorial pinnacle of power achieved by a long and diligent career in public life. From there, in Manchester, New Hampshire, he climbed upon a flatbed trailer to denounce the publisher of the *Union Leader*, William Loeb, who had chastised Muskie's wife, Jane, for talking dirty on a campaign plane. The candidate was angry, overtired, and not in full command of his emotions. He had something of a tantrum in the softly falling snow, and with all the people looking on and all the reporters listening, Edmund Muskie cried. That transient moment of real human anger and frustration, perhaps one of the few sincere displays of true conjugal affection to be found in all the welter of them staged by candidates since American elections were invented, cost Muskie the nomination that until then had been his. He was portrayed as weak and possibly emotionally unstable. Oddly, very little of that condemnation was retreaded eight years later, when by then Elder Statesman Muskie was cajoled out of retirement by Jimmy Carter to preside over the State Department shattered by the attempt to rescue the hostages in Iran. It was astonishing how much Muskie had matured.

The thoughtful candidate, aware that more than enough hazards lurk for him no matter what he does, therefore begins early to train himself against the real, spontaneous outburst. He curbs his tongue, no matter where he is or how trustworthy his companions may profess themselves to be (Kevin White may have carried this to an extreme, making no effort whatsoever to disguise his refusal to share sensitive political intelligence with his own wife, an admission that by rights ought to have won him a measure of obloquy from the conventionally uxorious among the Boston media, but that somehow passed almost without comment). As David Stockman learned to his dismay when William Greider shared with readers of *The Atlantic* the misgivings that the White House budget director had about the Reagan administration's economic plans, the sanction for untrammeled candid conversation is a public reputation left in ruins. The candidate, of course, will ostentatiously and heartily profess to accept at face value invitations to take part in discussions off the record, expressing his full confidence that those who promise solemnly that they will never tell are men and women of impeccably chivalric trust. Having so professed, he will treat them as mendacious, scheming knaves, lusting to betray him on the evening news the instant that he lets slip something juicy, and take extreme good care to disappoint them.

He will, that is, if he has plans to prosper. Carl Sandburg and Walt Whitman, among others, have celebrated this Republic's robust and rambunctious spirit, heedless of demure proprieties and scornful of meek leaders, but there's another, contradictory tradition which enforces seemliness upon our public figures. Richard Nixon chided Harry Truman for employing mild profanity, to some public effect. Agriculture Secretary Earl Butz stupidly repeated a coarse joke about blacks within earshot of newspapermen who hated him and his old boss, Richard Nixon, for which lapse he was hounded from office. When Henry Kissinger's reputation was severely damaged by the evidence turned up by Seymour Hersh, alleging that the secretary had among his other sins acquiesced in the slaughter of thousands, there was room in the discussion to debate whether Nixon had called African leaders "jungle bunnies." Ronald Reagan's secretary of the interior, James Watt, learned nothing from this and was driven out of office. No antic impulse can be safely indulged by the prudent politician in the current dispensation. He may not tell an ethnic joke or express impatience at some individual action as the typical reaction of any member of a given race, country of origin, or extant religion, even if he laughs when he is saying it. Nuance of tone, inflection, or gesture vanishes between the utterance and its publication. He must at all times take care

to comport himself conformably to our neo-Victorian, censorious, sanctimonious, and fraudulent pretense that all men
are created equally nice, and make jokes only about the
weather.

The candidate, therefore, renounces his enjoyment of the
First Amendment's cheerful freedom to allow his wits to
romp with much the same solemnity as the devout novice
making vows assures his God that he will not give in, not
once, to any sexual urges. The candidate does not get quite as
good a deal, there being in his contract no provision for full
room and board together with a great life in the hereafter as
reward for his self-discipline. But then, perhaps in the abstract, the sacrifice he makes is not so great. It can be argued
from the paucity of real wit in what candidates have said over
the years that nothing they may have stifled in addition could
have been much better. Still and all, it would be nice to know
for sure, and it would be reassuring to have some proof, that
our candidates do harbor the same sense of humor that occasionally improves other human commerce.

The practice of that pinching vow transforms the candidate into a calculator. On his own motion he says nothing
that he has not pondered carefully for several days or more
and has had inspected by his advisers for unintended slights.
The preparation of announcements of such relatively mun-
dane boons as urban redevelopment assistance grants is not
quite as elaborate procedurally as the drafting of nonaggres-
sion treaties between nations, but it remains one of careful
attention to detail, painstaking flattery of all who had or
hope to have some stake in their administration, and ritualis-
tic celebration of the great achievements. In less commodious
circumstances, when the candidate is engaged not in making
a set piece announcement but in fielding questions from the
media or the odd private citizen, he enjoys less time for reflection and is more prone to make errors, but he generally manages to frame his answers vaguely when he cannot contrive

actual judiciousness. After a few years of it, the candidate will usually acquire enough polish to risk in his riposte some evidence of the emotion that his split-second assessment of the situation tells him would go over well with his listeners. The politician who has been around for a long time and enjoyed a good deal of success is in fact a world-class word association player, manipulating those who listen to him much as the older Frank Sinatra sloughs the higher notes in old songs, now above his grasp in youth, his art so perfect and complete it seems no art at all.

This rote legerdemain comes at a very stiff price: the candidate's real intellectual and emotional existence. It can be cynically asserted that the fellow who embarks upon a career in elective politics is pretty much a faker and a poseur anyway, or else he would not have the stomach for it. That theory holds that no man actually devoted to his wife and children would select a line of work in which success is reserved solely for those who most shamelessly neglect their wives and children, all the while proclaiming hypocritically their familial devotion. Neither, it is argued, would a man who was not out to steal create so much noise declaring his own honesty. The bleakest outlook is that politicians do not become skillful liars; rather, it is the most skillful liars who achieve the most success as politicians.

The difficulty, though, with this pan-cynicism, is that the vast majority of politicians, including most of those who are the most successful, somehow seem to survive their careers without much more than the occasional minor smirching, and most escape even that. It is very hard for anyone who has known a few politicians reasonably well to claim that they have not compromised themselves or their ideals at some point in their public years but quite impossible to surrender to the notion that this makes them somehow into ignoble creatures who deserve disgrace. This is the vicious aspect of the public orthodoxy which requires candidates to profess moral, ethical, and intellectual perfection; it implies that the alternative is utter degradation. To avoid being branded as a rogue, therefore, the candidate must canonize himself a saint, and he thus begins upon his course of flummery in order to discharge the obligation to demonstrate his integrity.

Kevin White in 1967 confronted the primary chore that since 1932 has loomed forbiddingly before every politician seeking a plurality of voters from an economically heterogeneous community: how to placate simultaneously those enraged by levels of taxation and those infuriated by inadequacies of revenue. At least by 1959, when White's predecessor John F. Collins won his first term, the concept of the government as redistributor of income had filtered down to the municipal level from the national level where Franklin Delano Roosevelt had established it in 1933. Conflicts under way in Boston when White cast his appraising eye upon the new city hall in 1968 were available in numerous disguises, ranging from the residues of Protestant-Catholic religious animosities to white and black racial hostilities. But fundamentally they all belonged to the genus of economic class warfare.

They remain so today. The likelihood is that they will remain virtually unchanged when Kevin White's heir has left office. Boston is a microcosm of the national antagonism between those who pay the taxes, which is to say the predominantly white middle class, and those who benefit from the disbursement of the taxes, which is to say those who are employed by the government and those who derive their support from it without formal employment by it. To say that Boston was in this condition of low-grade tension when Kevin White took office, and remained in it when he departed, is to level no charge of futility against him or any other human politician who held office anywhere in the United States under similar conditions since the end of World War II, because there isn't anything he could have done to put an end to it. There is no palliative for the resentment that develops when the government enforces laws and regulations that are meant to divest one group of its earnings in order to divide the proceeds up among the members of groups that have not earned them.

Sensibly enough, Kevin White did not begin his 1967 campaign by directly addressing this problem. He opened with an advertisement that purported to recruit campaign workers, a ploy intended to attract a few foot soldiers but chiefly meant to gather the political equivalent of groupies: fairly large numbers of people who have time on their hands, not a great deal on their minds, much surplus enthusiasm, and vague longings to be part of something that will be exciting. Their function is to create the appearance of wide popular appeal by the candidate, so as to impress still less attentive citizens with his specific gravity as a potential leader. The candidate who calls for workers really hopes for followers, people who will wear buttons and wave signs at rallies, stand at intersections with placards, plaster bumper stickers on cars parked in supermarket lots, and cheer loudly whenever the great man is exhibited in public. Especially when there are television cameras aimed at the exhibition. It does not take a great deal of thoughtful substance to attract such followers, the principal blandishment being the promise that the leader will furnish the poor souls with victory they will be allowed to share, the chief evidence of its good currency being the large number of other drones just like themselves who are seduced by it. In Boston's case, Kevin White did not seek to provide much substance. He alluded to parks and to policemen, two subjects of which nearly everyone is in favor, and he acknowledged that the city had become so unattractive to some residents that they had decided to move out of it. White said he would put a stop to that.

It was in that wistfulness *cum* boldness that he verged upon the issue that is bulletproof against all manner of political attack: how to reconcile the economic classes struggling against each other in the city. Kevin White put it in terms of race.

He did that, to be sure, with extreme delicacy, speaking very gingerly about the problem that disturbed him. Making his first formal announcement for the office of mayor on February 15, 1967, he reported that 100,000 people had moved out of Boston in the previous ten years. He said they were motivated by "a crisis of confidence among Boston residents in their city." This "debilitation of 25 percent of the city population since 1955," he said, not pausing to explain how he had arrived at that percentage, or even just what it was a percentage of, was "central to all questions about Boston's future, its loss of representation in the legislature, in the amount of taxes paid by its citizens and the selling price of residential property and in the blight of the city." Those, of course, were effects of the exodus, not causes of it, but he did not pause to explore that nice distinction. "The stark and irrefutable fact," he told those assembled at his Sheraton Plaza press conference, "is that people are leaving Boston in such unprecedented numbers it can only be described as flight."

Rashly, retrospect suggests, White laid the best part of the blame for this deplorable situation at the feet of the incumbent, John F. Collins, and Collins's predecessor, John B. Hynes, thus inviting if not actually demanding those who heard him to conclude he would contrive to change the trend if he could be the mayor. At the time there was some arguable tactical advantage to be had from this approach. Collins had not yet announced his retirement from office, and White wanted to intimidate him, if that were possible, with the prospect of defending himself against charges that he was the chief reason why his voters were getting out of Boston. "The last two administrations," White said, "have laid plans and in part constructed great new buildings. There has been a revitalization of spirit in the business community. But the truth is that a great city is not only a place to work, it is a place in which to live and raise a family, and it is precisely here that we have failed." Referring to the migration as evidence of "acute disenchantment," White promised to the "alienated voter in Boston" the encouragement that he would need to feel qualified to participate in city government, then made racial harmony the linchpin of his candidacy: "If we fail to foster and sustain our human relations, then any other achievements will mock our efforts for the future." (*Globe*, 2/15/67, pp. 1–47; 2/16/67, pp. 1–6)

Three days later, its interest evidently piqued by White's citation of those unattributed figures, the *Globe* printed some other figures indicating that the candidate had rather underestimated the dimensions of the problem. The paper said that in ten years the city's population had declined by 171,869, from 788,195 to 616,326. In 1959, eight years before, 329,498 had been registered to vote in Boston; when White spoke, 294,000 were on the rolls.

Sixteen years later, taking bows for his tenure in office, White included in the inventory of his accomplishments the claim that he had reversed those population trends. He made the claim very carefully, saying that when he came into office people were moving out of the city, and that as he left his post people were moving in. A more forthright presentation would have put it this way: When Kevin White first ran for mayor, many Boston residents were moving out of permanent residency in the city because they evidently did not wish to bring up children there and had somehow gathered up the money to buy houses in suburbia. Very few, in 1967, were coming into the city to establish permanent residences. As he prepared to leave office, sixteen long years later, most of those with the means to escape from the city had accomplished their intentions. Others, buffeted by what happens to wage earners in an uncertain economy, had not had the opportunity to leave, and over the course of time their children grew to the age at which the principal motive for the move was no longer impelling. While they weathered those depressing years, other people without children, or with children and the private means to shield them from excitements they might anticipate in Boston's public schools, did move into the city— the 1980 census recorded a population hovering around 650,000. But neither in numbers nor in variety did those newcomers compensate for the people who had fled.

More accurately, therefore, White might have claimed that his tenure had coincided with the transformation of the city from a battleground between the poor and lower middle classes, on which members of the upper class quite regularly trespassed to the further irritation of the principal combatants, into a much neater joust between the same two contenders now relieved of all those annoying interruptions. The ranks of the Caucasian middle class remained heavily diminished. The ranks of the minority lower classes had been markedly increased. The number of prosperous white people without children of school age had grown also, but they tended to remain aloof from lowdown politics.

Accuracy, of course, is not required of political pronouncements. This is because such remarks ordinarily address subjects of great complexity. Boston is preeminently such a subject.

Sweet is the scene where genial friendship
plays
　　The pleasing game of interchanging praise.

　　　　　　　　　　　—Oliver Wendell Holmes
　　　　　　　　　　　"An After-Dinner Poem"

3

THE POLITICAL COMPLEXITY of Boston is partly attributable
to its confining geography. Some 650,000 people live within
the city limits. About 570,000 people hold regular jobs in that
same territory, which requires daily visits by some 333,000
who live elsewhere in the 2.73-million metropolitan population. Boston is not only the largest city in the Commonwealth; it is the capital of the state, and it is for federal and
other purposes the central city of five New England states
(excepting Connecticut). All of those people, reinforced by
the transients who arrive and depart in such droves from
Logan Airport as to make it the sixth busiest such center in the
United States, create a great deal of civic commotion, no
matter how peaceful their private intentions in hiving together in this manner.

They do this in two fewer square miles than are occupied
by the summer-swollen population of perhaps 12,000 that
contrives to make Nantucket Island seem so crowded in July.
Boston consists of forty-seven square miles of real estate, so
arranged by the Creator and linked by human transportation
systems as to make no major part of it readily accessible to
any person located in a different part. San Francisco, employing about 622,000 with a resident population of about
674,000 on approximately the same amount of land, is vastly

easier to traverse, notwithstanding its considerably steeper hills, and not just in the winter months, either; getting around Boston is pure hell even in fine weather. The snows of winter only make it worse.

Because it is so time-consuming and frustrating to enter the city, leave the city, or move around the city once you have overcome its daunting barriers, those who live and work in it tend not to frequent any areas except those where they work or live. Public transportation, something of an oxymoron in Boston, is grudgingly, inefficiently, and (on some lines) dangerously offered by the Massachusetts Bay Transportation Authority, a device of the Commonwealth's invention that is not answerable to the mayor or the Boston City Council. It consists of decrepit old streetcars, fragile new streetcars (Light Rail Vehicles) manufactured by Boeing Aircraft on its first disastrous and penultimate foray into LRV construction, rump-sprung diesel buses belching black smoke in fair imitation of a used-tire incinerator, and two varieties of subway trains—old ones which afford no more than perfunctory seating accommodations, and new ones which have reasonably comfortable seats but do not run reliably in wet, cold, icy, or snowy weather. The Boston Parking Authority hazards the guess that most of the 333,000 who enter Boston each day to go to work do so in automobiles, one to a car. The same authority believes that the downtown area, where most of the jobs are, offers no more than 31,000 legal parking places. This means that 90 percent of those determined to lead regular hours while combining work in the central city with residence outside the city cannot find a place to park. The Boston Parking Authority collected $20 million in fines and other charges from such people during 1982, and projected a net of $29 million in 1983, the increase being attributable to improved computer harassments of scofflaws.

The general consequence of this combination of infuriating circumstances is that longtime habitués of Boston will upon close interrogation prove to be expert only upon conditions that prevail in the neighborhoods and districts where they work and/or live. Those drawn by ambition or homesickness to Back Bay by work or housing in the Prudential Center area do not know much about what's going on in the financial district, let alone in blasted slums of Roxbury. Those whose business is located in Brighton or Allston cannot be depended upon for cogent exegesis of the conditions current in South Dorchester. Those who are black shun certain white neighborhoods which they rightly fear, while those who have white skin keep a good distance from black enclaves where street people throw rocks at the cars of interloping strangers. It's sort of fun to think of Boston as the sunny citadel beside the Charles where witty and well-mannered folk from many tribes convene in raucous rue to lament the malfeasances and misfortunes of their ill-starred but beloved Red Sox, and that image of the hospitable kingdom does have some validity. Still, it does not quite suggest the genuine meanness that pervades the competition for advancement, for advantage, and for preference in most arenas of human commerce in the city, especially contests in politics. For that at least, a rough idea of its layout and makeup is needed. What follows is a collection of sweeping generalities intended for that purpose and no other.

—Charlestown is the most northerly part of the community, of which it has no business being any part at all. It is bordered on the north, east, and south by water. To the west it touches Cambridge and Somerville, both of which muddle along without political connection to Boston, over there on the south bank of the Charles. Nevertheless, Charlestown sits there with its Navy Yard, its 1980 population of 13,400 (down by some 2,000 from the 1970 census), overwhelmingly white (13,100) and overwhelmingly Irish (5,100 claiming single Irish ancestry), surly in its unwavering assurance that its riparian isolation from the seat of city government amounts to a guarantee that it is getting screwed at City Hall, no matter who is sitting in the mayor's office.

Charlestown, like all the other settled neighborhoods of Boston not subject to immigration by nonwhite settlers, was growing old when Kevin White first ran for mayor (the 1970 median age was 27.9 years, about the city average of 28.1) and has persisted in growing older faster than the city as a whole. The median age there in the 1980 census was 30.7, an increase chiefly caused by a net loss of about 2,200 in its population 19 years of age and under. Those who moved out of Charlestown during Kevin White's heyday as mayor appear to have included a disproportionate number of parents with young children. Those who moved in, including opportunistic young professionals attracted by low-priced homes of architectural excellence needful of repair, plainly did not choose the community for its promise as a place in which to rear large families. Those families that remained or moved into Charlestown lived among households earning a median income of $15,700 per year, about $400 below that of the city as a whole.

When Kevin White's consolidation of his power as the mayor was or should have been complete, in 1970, seventy-six black people lived in Charlestown. After ten years of his diligent efforts to diminish racial animosity in Boston, twenty-six blacks remained there. This shows both that most of Charlestown's blacks did not put a great deal of trust in Kevin White's sincere strivings to improve the lives of black people who might choose to live in Charlestown and that they were prudent. It was and it remains a very dangerous place for black people, assuring that at best the black man will feel most uneasy, and with good reason. Black sailors ordered to the Navy Yard do not prowl Charlestown after dark. Unless they are extremely stupid, they travel in pairs on its streets in broad daylight.

Historically, Charlestown by means of the exploits of

many of its native sons has gained a reputation as a center for bold criminal entrepreneurs. Its bank robbers and leg-breakers have won wide respect for their fearlessness and reliability, and its hijackers, perhaps benefiting from Charlestown's proximity to the trucking depots of Chelsea and the easy commute to Boston's waterfront, are justifiably renowned. So also its tailgaters, who prey upon the people who steal the freight first (and have nothing in common with the tweedy chaps who savor martinis and enjoy crustless sandwiches from wicker hampers in the autumn sunlight on the grass by Harvard Stadium before the game with Yale every other year). This sort of activity appears adequate to satisfy the community interest in collective excitement; for the past thirty years or so, Charlestown has not fielded an impressive political cadre or mustered behind a native standard-bearer.

—To the east of Charlestown, across the tidal and estuarial basin where the Atlantic, the Charles, the Mystic and the Chelsea rivers flow together, East Boston crouches in sullen defiance also of the governmental headquarters unit. Its principal feature is Logan Airport, deemed by Eastie's 32,000 residents (down in 1980 from about 39,000 counted in 1970) to be a fractious and expansionist excrescence of a government contemptuous of private citizens. The largest single ethnic group by far is of Italian ancestry, some 17,000 residents claiming unmixed blood of that origin. Eastie's median income is about the same as Charlestown's and is earned in the same sort of blue-collar trades. Some 4,900 persons of the 7,000 who fled East Boston between 1970 and 1980 vanished from the age group under 19 years of age, suggesting the same sort of young-parent exodus that the Charlestown figures manifest. The community had attracted only 326 blacks by 1970, and at the end of the following ten years harbored 126. The only issue that moves East Boston residents to significant protests, other than the racial quarrel which can be depended upon to inflame most of the settled neighborhoods of Boston, is the perceived abuse of the community resulting from actions by the Massachusetts Port Authority, which operates the two tunnels under Boston Harbor, and the airport, which depends upon them. The mayor of Boston has no control over the Port Authority; the best he can possibly manage for those in East Boston who elect him is persuasive power over Port Authority members appointed by the governor.

—To the south of Charlestown and the west of East Boston, downtown Boston juts out into the harbor like a dislocated thumb, the Charles River cutting in around it to the northwest to define the joint on that side, the Fort Point Channel giving awkward—and, at low tide, odoriferous—definition on the southeastern exposure. The Boston Redevelopment Authority collects several discrete areas into this central district, which gained some 2,500 heterogeneous inhabitants between 1970 and 1980, registering a total of about 22,000 at the end of the decade. The chief population gain was in Asians, almost 2,000 of them moving in to up the count in Chinatown from about 1,400 to about 3,400. The black population increased from 263 to 648, and the white population remained relatively steady. The median age for the district was 38.6, and the only age group to show a large increase was that between 25 and 34, some 2,200 people.

This increase reflected the narrow but powerful appeal that the housing available in the West End, North End, Waterfront, Downtown, Chinatown, and Bay Village neighborhoods exerts upon current and prospective residents. The high-rise apartments of Charles River Park, erected on land reclaimed from the old West End over the intense objections of established, predominantly Jewish, middle-class, and lower-class inhabitants, attract retired people with comfortable incomes, young professionals with improving incomes, and middle-aged survivors of broken marriages whose means are adequate to shelter the uncoupled spouses in relative and

genteel anonymity. The residents of the North End are stragglers of the Italian immigration wave that jammed the area
around the turn of the last century. They remain either by
choice of convenient prosperity or lack of means sufficient to
enable them to move and are now mingled against their will
in rebuilt brick apartment houses with less prosperous young
professionals who proclaim their relish of the old-time ethnic
neighborhood ebullience. The renovated stone warehouses
and wharf buildings along Commercial Street, together with
the condominiums made from the high-rise apartments built
as Harbor Towers in the early 1970s, house the same sort of
trendy, well-to-do childless couples, unfettered husbands and
divorcées, well-kept mistresses, and wealthy semiretired couples who for reasons of fashion, commerce, scenery, or convenience find the waterfront languorously suitable. Except for
the unpolished Italians who provide the local color in the
North End, and the aging *mafiosi* who preserve their customs
of long standing by persisting in convening there to transact
their business affairs, none of these varieties of resident has
more than an aloof, speculative interest in city government or
a desultory curiosity about it.

The Asians who have gathered in Chinatown since the
city under Kevin White began to pay a bit more attention to
it, knocking down the old red-light district—known with
reason as the "Combat Zone"—and sponsoring new medical-
facility construction hedged about with low- and medium-
cost housing, show rather more potential for political impact
than positive results to date. Many of the newcomers are
Vietnamese and their acceptance by the entrenched Chinese
population has not been without incident.

The homosexuals who have gravitated to the high-rise
apartment building at Tremont on the Common, and even
more so to Bay Village down behind the theater district on
the edge of Chinatown, have achieved more political lip service than significant effect upon the city government. "Fag-

bashing" was a troublesome but far from epidemic problem, and it has been discouraged. Boston's straight majority has a century-old tradition of tolerating deviant behavior within elastic limits, so while it is fair to say that homosexuals have taken only a few mincing steps in the Hub, it is also correct that they did not have much ground to cover and no real need to attempt great strides. (Homosexual advocates dispute this, which of course is the sort of thing that advocates *per se* do.) In the 1984 elections, David Scondras ran for city council as a homosexual and won.

The people who live in the central district, or downtown part of Boston, then, resist grouping other than by place of residence. Except for the Asians they are pretty much deracinated, unresponsive to traditional claims of ethnic origin, religion, or family roots. The two characteristics that they have in common are comfortable means and the mobility that goes with independent incomes or the salable skill that enables its possessor to earn good money almost anywhere. For them the Grange Hall or the auditorium in the basement of the church has been replaced by any bar that serves burgers on seeded rolls, a choice of blue cheese or a bacon strip on the side, and one trip to the salad bar included. Any joint with ferns and Miller Lite on draft will do to meet old friends or pick up new ones, perhaps with a dividend of a chronic genital infection. These people are the politician's dream: they don't want anything from him, and since their tax bills are concealed in their rent or condo maintenance bills, they generally have no idea what they're paying to keep more demanding citizens docile. To a considerable degree they contrive to live not only as though the New Deal never happened, but as though there had never been a need for it. White pretty much ignored them during his reign, and he was correct in doing so.

—Beacon Hill with some success reminds the architectural observer of London, except steeper. The Boston Redevelopment Authority melds its statistics in with those of Back

Bay, which makes demographic sense but tends to deprive both enclaves of deserved distinctions based upon style and ambiance. The people who live on the Hill may have about the same amount of money in their pockets as the people who resemble them in attire, age, and cultivation and live down on the flat west of Arlington Street and the Ritz, but they behave quite differently. Each deserves separate inspection.

Viewed in gross, Beacon Hill inhabitants appear to be a swarm of ADA types who rely upon new blood migrating in from Cambridge to refresh the breeding stock without leavening the liberal ideology. A patronizing sense of intellectual and hyperkinetic *noblesse oblige* informs their strenuous exertions to preclude the possibility that someone may come to cherish an idea not yet approved by John Kenneth Galbraith or his designated vetter. The origins of contemporary Beacon Hill types are extremely various but understood to have become irrelevant as of the date when the moving van unloaded the brocaded love seat on West Cedar, Mount Vernon, or Pinckney Street. Then, like the pedigree steeds registered each year by the Thoroughbred Racing Association, the newcomers are considered to have been newborn as well, fully accredited white Anglo-Saxon Protestants, raised decently upon the incomes of trust funds amassed by shrewd ancestors who secured their profits in the China trade and fully equipped to make any known religion of their childhood indistinguishable from civil Unitarianism.

In this homogeneous disguise, the Beacon Hill voter is constrained to be obstreperous. This obligation was especially severe for those who were in place or arrived after Kevin White of 158 Mount Vernon Street let it be known to a few friends after his thumping reelection as secretary of state back in 1966 that he planned to be mayor. To many of the younger residents indigenous to Beacon Hill at the time and since then, that was an announcement of surprise and delight, an implied vindication of innate superiority which they had long suspected clearly demonstrated of themselves by reason of their choice of residence. He would be, and to a degree he was to less cultivated sections of the city, fitted out much like a missionary of correct thought from Beacon Hill. He was the well-groomed emissary whose domicile was proof sufficient that an Irishman could acquire some manners and a certain *savoir faire*, together with a set of ideas and grace in their presentation that would do Beacon Hill quite proud. There is no evidence that any of this nervous lapel straightening, coaching in adenoidal accents, or earnest tutoring in the approved ideas ever made Kevin White guffaw. There is a great deal of evidence that he took every bit of it quite seriously. From the beginning he acted as though John Kennedy's approach to politics had established the controlling code of etiquette and conduct for the up-and-coming Boston politician. This attitude, which he imbibed on Beacon Hill, after Tabor Academy and Williams College, did not always assist him.

—At the western end of the Boston Public Garden, Arlington Street provides the crossbar for a T-shaped intersection at the eastern terminus of Commonwealth Avenue. Between Arlington Street and Massachusetts Avenue, eight residential blocks long and four across, is the Back Bay. The Boston Redevelopment Authority's statistical collection of its residents with those of Beacon Hill is reasonable if income and life-style are factors that distinguish one neighborhood from another but not so defensible if the criterion is political yeastiness. Together, the two neighborhoods gained just about 10 percent in population between 1970 and 1980, adding 2,674 to reach a total residential population of 30,212 at the start of this decade. Ninety percent of that population is white now and it was white in 1970; the black population counted 664 at the beginning of the decade and 1,284 at its conclusion. Hispanic residents totaled 604 in 1970 and 937 by the time 1980 rolled around. And while the city as a whole was growing older during that period, the median age increasing from 28.1 to 29.9, that of Back Bay/Beacon Hill went up dramatically, from 23.7 to 28.6. It was never cheap to live in that area, but the dawn of the era of conversion to condominiums made it really pricey, putting it well beyond the reach of those just starting out to make their piles. The net gain of roughly 2,700 residents came despite a loss of 2,530 residents under the age of 24; 5,788 newcomers between 25 and 44 more than made up for them, bringing with them very few young children for enrollment in the Boston public schools.

They moved into a renovated swamp. Filled in to furnish the underpinnings for this admirable exercise in metropolitan living, the district is crowded with townhouses, graceful old hotels now rejuvenated into high-ticket condominiums, and dignified apartment buildings inexorably following the same schedule of transformation. The well-to-do people who inhabit these buildings appear to suffer from no herding instincts when it comes time to express political preferences, and within recent memory they have not exhibited any interest whatsoever in developing a community political identity. It may be that all tacitly agree this would be crass behavior. More likely, most who live in the Back Bay have so little need of government improvements in their lives, at least on the local level, that they perceive no real reason to band together to lend force to their demands. Residents of the Back Bay do not make public demonstrations of support for much of anything of less global importance than, say, the protection of large seagoing mammals and the reduction of storehouses of atomic weapons, and when they are exercised they make their points as individuals. For this courteous behavior, however anomalous it may be in this generation of commotion, they deserve much praise.

They do not receive such praise, at least from City Hall or those campaigning for its occupation. Politicians as a rule are not a grateful bunch.

—The South End looms to the south of the Prudential Center, on the other side of Huntington Avenue. It used to be a very fashionable place to live, quite as trendily built up with Federal period townhouses as the Back Bay but much quieter. That was a long time ago. The buildings more or less survived the neighborhood's debacle after World War II, when it went straight down to hell in a hand basket, but by 1970 it had become a fetid, dangerous, hellhole of slum. There were stout boards on those graceful old bay windows and holes made by stones in the stained glass around the paneled doors.

In the next ten years, the South End's population increased by about 4,500 residents. Whites, totaling 10,714 at the beginning of the period and 10,662 at the end of it, went from 47 percent of the population to 39 percent, even though their actual number dropped by only 52. Blacks, adding about 2,100 residents, went from 39 percent in 1970 to about 41 percent. The major change numerically was in the Hispanic population: about 7 percent of the 1970 neighborhood population, it grew by 1,802 and at the end of the decade totaled 3,443, about 13 percent of the growing neighborhood.

The composition of the South End changed in age as well during that period, declining from the 33.4 median of 1970 to 30.4 in 1980. Major population increases came in the age group between 25 and 44; 4,510 new residents were in that category. There was a 28 percent increase in the number of available housing units during the decade, nearly ten times the rate for that of Boston as a whole; it added 3,042 units to a 1970 supply of 10,719. The BRA's figures for 1970 report a median income of $6,122 per South End household, about 67 percent of the citywide $9,133; in 1979, when figures were next collected, South End households averaged $14,571, while the city average was $16,062—the neighborhood was still trailing but had improved to about 91 percent of the city average.

That betterment was chiefly attributable to the arrival of large numbers of young white people with strong yearnings for fashionable townhouse living and insufficient capital to secure it in Back Bay or up on Beacon Hill. Persuaded of the extremely questionable premise that man is naturally perfectible, and beguiled by the idea of obtaining a genuinely beautiful home at a fraction of the price it would command on Commonwealth Avenue, they marshaled their assets, hopes, and dreams and started moving back into the area. Acquiring either great expertise with tools for woodworking or business relationships with craftsmen who really did know how to use such implements, they commenced a great hammering and sawing in the South End, peeling the boards off the windows and the cheap, flaking paint off the walnut and oaken doors. Competition for scarce on-street parking began to include Volvo station wagons and old Mercedes sedans that had not been stolen elsewhere and abandoned by the thieves, among the clapped-out junkers and tarted-up pimpmobiles, but that actually belonged to the new residents. There was much well-publicized talk of "gentrification" of the neighborhood, the invented term serving to reinforce the grimly held conviction of these refined young marrieds that they could in fact bring up their children in the slums and watch them attend the same fine universities that had prepared the parents for the rewarding professional careers and inculcated the unrealistic attitudes that had brought them to the South End. This enabled the high-minded to endure the taunts, assaults, batteries, burglaries, rapes, and odd murders committed upon them and their children by swaggering young black men who seriously disliked them, their honky pretenses, their physical presence in the South End Community (as newcomers like to call it), and regarded them as purveyors of nearly factory-fresh merchandise available for quick and easy resale to support importunate drug habits.

This volatile mixture causes the South End to produce two varieties of political diversion. Both are noisy. The whites make earnest clamor for more city money to improve the streets outside their homes, so that the thoroughfares will not clash with the restored interiors. They also think it would be nice to light the out-of-doors brightly at night and order large numbers of policemen to patrol it, so that the law-abiding gentrifier can climb the stairs to his bedroom on the third floor without pausing on the second to pick up a handgun in case some predator has gotten through the skylight. A feature of these petitions is invariably the claim, made with great solemnity, that the desired amenities will conduce to the improvement of the lives of all economic classes living in the South End, notwithstanding the fact that the plain purpose of a good many of the requested changes is to curtail the criminal business that has thrived there for so many years. Politicians, including Kevin White, make soothing noises and don't do very much about the demands, which is sensible enough.

The blacks, while all this backchat is going on, take a more sternly realistic view. They are all for the neat things the whites would like to see, but they do not delude themselves with the quaint notion that polite solicitations for the goodies will secure them. When Kevin White announced for mayor, back in 1967, Melvin H. King, then also thirty-seven, was engaged in a fierce power struggle to regain his post as the head of the United South End Services (USES) organization, very aptly acronymed. A fierce-looking black gentleman who until his 1983 campaign for mayor affected the dashiki as his uniform of approach to the moderate white community, King has been plagued all of his political life by the refusal of liberal whites to stop interfering in black matters and let black people deal with them. True, King's public programs for addressing black problems always begin with the receipt of large amounts of tax money chiefly put up by the whites, but King is a child of his generation, his mind conditioned by the gleaming promises of John F. Kennedy and the wildly unsuccessful Great Society projects of Lyndon John-

son, his résumé uncluttered by much work experience un-
funded by the government. King has not gotten rich ramrod-
ding government schemes to get his people off the welfare
rolls and onto the taxpayer lists, but he has made a living in
that line, doing that and lecturing about it after he has done
it. It is understandable that he reflexively reverts to that
mode when invited to submit plans to correct some annoying
circumstance.

King's problem, back then, was Herbert P. Gleason, later
to be Kevin White's chief corporation (city) counsel. Gleason
was the chairman of the USES board, which King had
ired by spending USES money without bothering to confabu-
late first with its members. King made much of the fact that
Gleason was a resident of lily-white Needham, which shares a
boundary with Boston's West Roxbury section but little else
with the city as Mel King of the South End is accustomed to
viewing it. King's hole card in the struggle, which he won,
was that unless the city made some strenuous efforts to clean
up the South End, he might not be able to assure its administration that his followers would remain peaceful. This articulated precisely the sort of apprehension that the *Globe* had
voiced in its New Year's Day homily. There was an obbligato
that tended to resonate with the sound of polite extortion, but
that was overlooked.

By 1983, when King bottomed his mayoral candidacy
upon a drive to register large numbers of blacks eligible to
vote but theretofore uninterested in doing so, the threat of
black uprising had lost its power to intimidate the influential
members of the white community. To account for this felici-
tous development would require citation and analysis of hundreds of factors, few of which were brought about or influenced significantly by Mayor Kevin H. White or any other
politician operating in Boston. More to the point of this exercise, perhaps, is the fact that White reacted very skillfully and
quickly to those changes, making such adjustments in the

flow of federal money, and in its administration, that blacks interested in politics in Boston had always to calculate how their lot might be improved if somebody else were helped to defeat White. That calculation in 1970 had to be based upon the likelihood that about 16 percent of the city's population could muster enough votes to control an election's outcome, and in 1980 upon how much roughly 22 percent of the city's diminishing population could accomplish by themselves, if they all stuck together. Neither prospect could have inflamed a candidate in his right mind with prospects of victory as the black standard-bearer. Furthermore, in 1967 and again in 1971, Kevin White's major opponent was Louise Day Hicks, and no black voter facing a choice between White and Hicks was likely to see much need for agonizing. Nevertheless, White might have squandered the support he enjoyed from black voters during his sixteen years in office, to the point at which it would have gone to a careful opponent who could seem to promise more; he did not. His decision to retire from office undefeated constituted something of a puzzlement for black voters; registering in unprecedented numbers, they did not immediately flock afterward to endorse Melvin King but said they were undecided just about as often as white voters did when they were polled. In October when they voted in the primary election, though, they voted 95 percent by color.

—Albany Street, running northerly from Massachusetts Avenue to the west and along the Southeast Expressway, terminates the South End at the old Boston & Maine Railroad yards. Those yards, now the site of the Boston City Incinerator and the wholesale meat market, butt up against South Boston. Further north, Southie borders the Fort Point Channel, which was cut to facilitate commerce between the seaport and the railhead in the nineteenth century and now lies virtually useless, stinking and ugly in the sun. Southie occupies a thick peninsula with two prongs extending into Boston Harbor. The northerly one is partly the U.S. Naval

Reservation, including the South Boston Naval Annex. The southerly one is residential, arcing out into the water to enclose Dorchester Bay on its south side.

Southie has a bad name, partly of its own choosing, as a rough and strident place where the natives would prefer to give a stranger a fat lip instead of the right time of day. It is also assumed to be completely Irish, principally because for more than a century it has been the place where Boston's Irish have gathered on the day Boston sets aside to celebrate the departure of British troops from Boston during the Revolution, which happens to be March 17, to hold a parade in honor of St. Patrick.

That assumption of pure Irishness was correct a good many years ago, but it is not correct today and it was not correct when Kevin White first ran for mayor. John Joyce, operator of Joyce Brothers Service Station at the intersection of Old Colony and Dorchester avenues in South Boston, expertly clarified that matter for the *Globe* back before St. Patrick's Day in 1967, addressing his remarks to a proposal to rename Dorchester Street "St. Patrick Boulevard." A native of Southie, Joyce said: "That name change would have been a good idea, twenty years ago, but the Irish have moved out of the district. They've gone to the suburbs. Every year the Irish population has grown smaller in South Boston. There are many fine Polish and Lithuanian families now. There's a Puerto Rican colony on D Street. Also a number of Cubans. Saint Patrick was a great saint. I'm Irish-American and personally I like the idea. But South Boston is no longer strictly Irish. Times have changed." (*Globe*, 3/7/67, p. 20)

What had not changed with the times and the ethnic character of Southie was its strong sense of community identity. So far as I am aware, South Boston is the only section of the city with its own custom-made anthem, "Southie Is My Home Town." Its lyrics boast of the flippancy and mouthiness of its residents, their truculence toward bill collectors whom it warns to anticipate falling three floors down when dunning third-floor residents in the three-deckers and reminds of the hard marble tiles in the hall.

It has a certain mucker's insouciant charm, a grinning bravado, which asserts that anyone who comes from Southie is superior to anyone who comes from any other place, simply by reason of that geographical accident, the strut and the defiant braggadocio that are adopted to console the swaggerer who doesn't have a damned thing in the world except his youth and strength, both of which are dwindling before his very eyes. Edward J. McCormack, nephew of the late Speaker of the House, John W. McCormack, vanquished in his bid as the attorney general of the Commonwealth and a real comer in Bay State politics to wrest the senatorial nomination from Edward M. Kennedy in 1962, once escorted reporters on a tour of South Boston High School. Ushering them into the library of the school, he described it as the least-used room in the building; he said he had visited it but once before he was yanked out and dispatched to the Jesuits, who then ran Cranwell Prep in the Berkshires, in order that he might learn something. He drove his point home by selecting a book at random from a shelf and blowing across the top of its pages. A cloud of dust lifted at his breath. What John Joyce said in the yard of his service station back in 1967 was correct so far as it went; the Irish had moved to the suburbs, those who had been smart enough and lucky enough to make it. Those who remained then and who remain today are those who have been left behind, and now as then they reserve their deepest resentment for those of their ethnic heritage who have gotten out.

That is something to be kept in mind when thinking about South Boston's reaction to what Judge W. Arthur Garrity, Jr., of Wellesley commanded the Boston School Department to do in order to achieve racial balance in the schools: forced busing. It also explains why Louise Day Hicks, daughter of

Southie's much admired Judge William J. Day, after whom
Day Boulevard along the beaches of South Boston was
named, commanded loyalty in her prime as Southie's own
chief champion of neighborhood schools. So great was her
appeal that she was said to have 40,000 voters who would
follow her off a cliff. It is very easy to be quite contemptuous
of the more vocal people who still live in South Boston, and
that careless, supercilious cruelty is accordingly indulged by
otherwise mannerly people who would never think of sneering about blacks or ghetto-dwelling Jews. The people who
lived in South Boston back in 1967 and those who live there
today know this, and they bitterly resent it.

The statistics provide little consolation for those residents
of Southie. Some 8,100 of its residents moved out between
1970 and 1980, a 21 percent decline in a community of about
38,500 which included 373 of the 388 blacks who had been
bold or unfortunate enough to have been caught living there
at the beginning of the decade. The Hispanic presence upon
which John Joyce remarked in 1967 did not increase as he
might have expected; 116 of the 276 Hispanics recorded in
1970 had left by the time that census takers reappeared in
1980. Southie got older during that decade, the median age
increasing from 31.4 to 34.2. At the end of the decade there
were 5,672 fewer children of school age in Southie than there
had been at the beginning and about 2,400 fewer residents of
the child-bearing ages between 19 and 54 (the Irish tend to
marry and to father children late in life). Of those who remain, 12,440 told the 1980 census takers that they were of
completely Irish ancestry; the next largest group of single ancestry were the Italians, who reported 1,660. For decades,
Southie has been a place to have come from, and those who
have stayed behind do not like that.

—At the northerly, narrow tip of the railroad yards and
the cul-de-sac of the Fort Point Channel, Dorchester begins,
occupying a great deal of land for a section of a small city.

With Southie to the east and Roxbury to the west, the section extends all the way to the Neponset River and the boundary with North Quincy to the south. To the west its putative boundary is Blue Hill Avenue, with Roxbury on the other side on the north and Mattapan on the south, but the racial composition of the area has changed so much in the past twenty years or so that those traditional borders have ceased to carry much real relevance. It may help to rely upon the numbers here to see how one neighborhood has split, to the point at which it is no longer recognizable as a single section of the city.

By 1980, there were 24,168 fewer people living in Dorchester, North and South, than there had been ten years before, when about 107,000 had lived there. More than 39,000 whites cleared out; nearly 19,700 blacks moved in. By 1980 census takers could find only about 83,000 people in the two neighborhoods. North Dorchester in 1980 was 17 percent black. South Dorchester was 28 percent black. But, since the easterly neighbor of the two Dorchesters is water, and the westerly boundaries (starting at the north and heading south) are shared with the South End, Roxbury and Mattapan, that apparent white majority did not exist in the real world. The two Dorchesters and the other three neighborhoods mustered about 204,000 residents in 1980—105,367 of them, 52 percent, were blacks. For the 16,520 whites who resided in North Dorchester and the 39,178 in South Dorchester, still burdened with the notion that one's place of residence is first identified by parish— "I'm from Saint Gregory's"—and then by neighborhood, such as Dorchester, with "Boston" being added to the disclosure only in the event that the listener is someone from very far away, and obviously quite unsophisticated, the perception was that of representing a minority.

As is the case in South Boston, those whites who remain residents of the Dorchesters are overwhelmingly of Irish stock: 20,221 told the 1980 census takers that they had no

other blood in them, meaning that if any of their Irish forebears had selected mates outside the Hibernian fold, they
were either not aware of it or were ashamed of it. No other
ethnic group with white skin even approached that number.

The depletion of the population of the Dorchesters during
1970–80 was remarkable for its distribution over the entire
span of generations. The net loss of 24,000 included 13,872
under 19 years of age, residents whom one would expect to
live with their parents and attend the public schools. Those
who were reaching, passing through, or had completed the
usual child-bearing years between 20 and 44 showed a net
loss of about 4,500 residents. But emigration did not tail off as
the events of the 1970s impinged upon the older residents:
about 6,000 between the ages of 55 and the grave vanished,
and there were no plagues or other natural catastrophes affecting only older people to account for that decline by natural causes. Those reductions are not statistically calibrated for
race, but the figures that are broken down by race for the
entire changes of the population in the Dorchesters warrant
the inference that most of those who left and were not replaced were white people.

The principal distinction between the two Dorchesters is
money. In 1970, the median income for North Dorchester
households was $8,513; that for South Dorchester was
$9,739; that for the city as a whole was $9,133. By 1979, that
disparity had widened: North Dorchester households reported family incomes averaging $14,939, while those in
South Dorchester reported $16,601; the city median was
$16,062.

I surmise that South Dorchester's relative decline in comparative prosperity in the city—from 106 percent of the average Boston income to about 100 percent of it—is attributable
to that exodus of young families whose superior earning
power enabled them to move out of South Dorchester. North
Dorchester's percentage of the average city income remained

almost constant during those ten years—93 percent—
probably because its 1970 black population of 3,842 didn't
change very much (it was 3,978 in 1980) and was establishing
itself economically—South Dorchester's black population
more than doubled, from 7,218 to 16,488, and the new arrivals tended to pull down the averages.

Split, demoralized, and addled as it is, white Dorchester
understandably fails to manifest a coherent political personal-
ity in Boston politics. When Ronald Reagan's staff advance
men chose the Eire Pub on Gallivan Boulevard in South
Dorchester for his surprise visit during a trip to Boston in
1983, they by implication depended partly upon the hospitality of that Irish working-class neighborhood to a Republican,
and they were right in doing so. Forty years before, I think,
his reception might have been somewhat chillier, but white
Dorchester today is nowhere near as enchanted by liberal
Democratic politics as it was when JFK was running. Policies
developed out of those exhilarating days have done a lot of
damage to a settled neighborhood and the ways in which its
people looked at things, and when it comes to politics these
days, they fall back upon the old and proven ways. First, you
determine which of the contenders with a chance of victory is
likeliest to make sure that your boy gets a job with the city,
and then you put a sign up for that fellow in the yard of your
three-decker. White Dorchester doesn't go for the Kennedys
today. When the only obstacle to the construction of the JFK
Library in Cambridge was the relocation of the MBTA trolley
yards to Dorchester on a patch of unused land, Dorchester
residents turned out in numbers large enough to sink the notion easily, thus putting Mayor White in the position that
some theorize cost him the vice presidential nomination in the
1972 McGovern campaign. Rumor has it Edward Kennedy
never forgave the mayor for siding with the voters in
Dorchester, who will never forgive Kennedy for endorsing
forced busing.

Black Dorchester as a sector gets but scant attention. Its voters are wooed by appeals to their racial interests, not by promises of what the candidates will do for their down-at-the-heels neighborhood. It's lumped in with Roxbury and Mattapan.

—Roxbury borders Dorchester on the westerly side and, with Mattapan on the south, is almost entirely black. When Kevin White announced for mayor in 1967, there were 90,000 black people in Boston, more or less, over half of them having arrived since 1962. The *Globe* guessed that blacks were 60 percent of the population of the South End, Roxbury, and Dorchester. (*Globe*, 2/19/67, p. A-2) The city's public school enrollment was 26 percent black, and it was predicted that nonwhite enrollment would hit 50 percent by 1972 (by 1982, public school enrollment figures in Boston put the non-white majority at about 70 percent).

It is very difficult for upper-middle-class whites to describe life in those two black districts of Boston today. This is partly because they have been trained for the past quarter century or so not to utter remarks about black people that suggest that any of them are in any way responsible for the predicament in which they find themselves, or for the anti-social actions that they take in a putative attempt to escape from it or express their rage against it. It is also because no sensible upper-middle-class white person traveling between downtown Boston and Milton to the south voluntarily takes the most convenient and direct route between those points, Blue Hill Avenue, because Blue Hill Avenue, a four-lane divided boulevard for most of its long, straight course, runs right through Mattapan and Roxbury. In fine weather and in slightly inclement conditions, at first only during darkness but now during the daylight hours as well, gangs of black youths congregate around the intersections where the traffic signals halt the cars from time to time, and make determined efforts to acquire the valuables of white persons riding in those cars by smashing the car windows with large stones. White drivers and their passengers who resist this informal program of redistribution of their wealth have been dragged from their cars and beaten so severely as to require long periods of hospitalization. One such victim also required an undertaker.

Having in mind then that the white observer adds miles to his commute between the city and its southern suburbs by prudently selecting circuitous routes between those points, and that the adventures of the few white strays or passionately reckless palefaces who do not observe such precautions regularly reinforce the dictates of that prudence, it can be said with mingled confidence and revulsion that Roxbury and Mattapan are hostile territories. In recent years there have been efforts, mostly led by black churchmen, to galvanize the law-abiding blacks who live there into organizing crime patrols and demanding greater police control of what goes on in those districts. Blacks in the Sonoma Street neighborhood just north of Franklin Park, a block away from Blue Hill Avenue in Roxbury, have welcomed law enforcement campaigns to disrupt its burgeoning traffic in heroin, for example, and have not protested when the media branded the street as certainly the most lawless in the entire city. It may be that these grass-roots efforts will in time serve to restore a measure of ordinary peacefulness to those districts, sufficient at least to permit a white man to consider passing through it without immediately causing his kinfolk to ponder having him committed for psychiatric observation. Nevertheless, before Kevin White sought office space in City Hall, those two slums were isolated, quarantined zones of the city, and they remain so to this day.

Their progress to that sad estate had first been noticed around 1955. The decline of population that so bothered Kevin White in 1967 had been manifested on the parish rolls of St. Joseph's Roman Catholic Church in Roxbury, where five years before some 3,000 chiefly Irish-American families had been listed. In 1955, the parish census toted up about 2,000 families. In 1967, 250 of them remained and the church was going broke. Right Reverend Monsignor Russell J. Collins, pastor of St. Joseph's and also chairman of the Archdiocesan Human Rights Commission, professed no perplexity about what had happened to it. The people had "escaped the problems of the city," he said. "They have turned their backs on it." Among the commision's long-range plans, he told the *Globe* (2/11/67, p. 1, *et seq.*), was one of "encouraging suburban parishes to provide low and middle income housing in their own areas." In order, presumably, that they might transport to their new surroundings in the suburbs precisely those folks who had given them such strong interest in departing from the city. If the idea ever caught on, there's no evidence of it.

The Jews of Boston had been engaged in doing the same thing as the inner-city Catholics during the years that preceded Kevin White's first try at City Hall. Fifteen Jewish congregations had packed up their Torahs and departed from the city between 1955 and 1967. Some 70,000 Jewish families had been dispersed from the Roxbury, Dorchester, and Mattapan areas. Rabbi Samuel Korff, president of the Association of Synagogues of Massachusetts, had removed his Congregation Kehillath Jacob from Mattapan to Newton. Temple Mishkan Tefila, overlooking Franklin Park, had declined from a regular 1,000 attendance at Friday night services to emptiness fourteen years later and moved as well to Newton. Rabbi Abraham Koolyk of Congregation Beth El Hereth Israel on Fowler Street in Dorchester said his 1,000-family congregation had repaired to Newton because Boston schools had deteriorated so severely. (*Globe*, 2/12/67, p. 63) Whatever the prime reason, an estimated 90,000 Jews had left Boston in the ten years that preceded Kevin White's announcement.

Those who had fled had been energetically and effectively

political. Election eves in Boston had for decades closed at the
G&G Delicatessen on Blue Hill Avenue in Mattapan, with
candidates appearing to shake hands one last time. The solid
God- and black-fearing citizens who had wrenched themselves out of their homes and moved out of town took with
them the long-cultivated political savvy they had acquired
over decades, broke alliances that they had contrived over the
course of many years, left to wither the measures of influence
they had devised for themselves, and abandoned politically
blasted geography, nothing more, to the succeeding blacks.

It is hard to find convincing evidence that those unedu-
cated blacks who thronged the city when John Collins was
still mayor have achieved much political improvement since
then. Their heralded effort to establish a black Unity Bank &
Trust Company collapsed in a modest scandal which opened
with stern remarks by auditors and admissions of extreme
mismanagement. There were revelations that the black community, however hard-pressed it had been to amass savings,
had not seen fit to entrust them to the black bank. The majority of the relatively few black voters in the city spent the years
between 1967 and 1983 marking ballot spaces next to Kevin
White's name when the mayor's office was contested, understandably enough when the alternative was Mrs. Hicks of
South Boston, reasonably enough when it was Joseph Timilty,
another white man whom they had no reason to believe
would treat them better than White had and might, as some
suspected, treat them nowhere near as well. In 1983, when
the blacks did register and vote, they voted as a bloc for a
hopeless cause.

The blame for this persistence of powerlessness of the people who reside in Roxbury and Mattapan can be avoided and
imposed at endless length by any number of disputants with
the zeal to worry all of those old bones once more. The fact is
that today there are not enough blacks registered to vote in
Boston to constitute an absolute majority in a city election.

They can muster at the most about 30 percent of the electorate, enough to extract promises from reasonable candidates so long as keeping those commitments would not serve to infuriate the white majority of voters enough to cause them to vote *en bloc* against the promisor. Given the pervasive white suspicion that what legislatures, courts, and pious do-gooders have done for blacks has come well nigh to ruining the city for those whites who can't leave it or don't want to, there is not much latitude for the white candidate to display generous compassion toward the blacks who live in Boston.

—On the west side of Roxbury, curving away to the south and west from Massachusetts Avenue, where the western edge of Back Bay lies, Jamaica Plain, Roslindale, Hyde Park, and West Roxbury enclose the well-to-do and separate the town of Brookline, and border on the similarly well-fixed towns of Milton and Dedham. To the northwest of West Roxbury is Newton, where the Jews of Mattapan and Roxbury took refuge in their Hub diaspora of thirty years ago. In the exodus from Boston that appalled Kevin White in 1967, Hyde Park and West Roxbury each gained 3,000 families. Those two districts by themselves had 56,000 eagerly eligible voters to claim his attention and that of his opponents. Jamaica Plain and Roslindale had less, but those they had were of the same variety.

Those communities offer green space, a reasonably good facsimile of medium-sized community living, and a range of housing starting with three-deckers like those found in Dorchester and ending with comfortable upper-class residences in the six-figures bracket.

Those sections—economically relatively homogeneous, staunchly Catholic, predominantly Irish-American, highly politicized, and easily aroused into a community posture of belligerent defensiveness against anything perceived as threatening to their serenity—were then and remain today the sources of enormous strategic problems for candidates seeking votes in Boston. Seductively they offer by themselves almost enough votes to assure victory in any city primary election. Fatally, the demands they levy in exchange for those votes amount to a pledge of suicide for the candidate in his appeals to the other sections of the city. These are the nests of the "aginners," those suspicious, fickle folk of negative intellectual preferences whom Kevin White occasionally in exasperation calls "the Hyde Square Brick-Throwers Association." They are notable for cynicism, what is known as "Irish go-wannism" ("G'wan, if it was any good, they wouldn't be giving it to us."). They do not trust anybody that they do not know, and those whom they know they believe they have unmasked as the untrustworthy, treacherous devils that they are.

It is hideously frustrating to attempt to deal with individuals who think like that and almost impossible to treat with entire communities that are dominated by such individuals. Because those districts have such blocs of voters in them, though, the Boston politician has no choice other than to bite clean through his lower lip and do the best he can to win their precarious allegiance, knowing full well that the very fellow who grins widest at his face and claps him hardest on the back tonight before the softball game at Legion Field in Roslindale will stab him deepest in that same back tomorrow night on the way out of mass at Sacred Heart. And furthermore, he will do it purely for the fun of it, thus inspiring less imaginative friends to envy his wit and make their own attempts to emulate it the next night down at the saloon. The best that any candidate can hope for, working the high-numbered wards in Jamaica Plain, Roslindale, West Roxbury, and Hyde Park, is that in the contempt that voters in those wards will lavish upon the whole field of hopefuls, there will remain reserved for him some lingering congeniality, viz., "Yeah, I know the guy's an asshole, but I think he might help us." That is not much for a man to hope for, but it is enough to get him a nice fat plurality, and that is what he's after.

It is the animosity of those four sections that the candidate in Boston fears when he is importuned by black leaders to pledge unstinting devotion to the desperately needy black people who reside in Roxbury and Mattapan. The risk that he will incur malice in Jamaica Plain, Roslindale, West Roxbury, and Hyde Park is perhaps not as great as it is in South Boston and those areas of Dorchester that have reacted most strongly against forced integration of the schools, but the effect of it at the polls is considerably more intimidating because there are so many watchful, angry voters in the southwestern districts. If Edward M. Kennedy had to depend upon the people of those districts to deliver the plurality he needs for election, he would have to temporize on racial issues when he visits them. Since he does not have to depend upon them to reelect him, Teddy Kennedy finesses the potential awkwardness by not calling on them very often, and that is just as well because he is not popular in those precincts.

Those sections in 1980 totaled 133,513 residents, about 85 percent of the population they had claimed ten years before. Some 111,712 of them were white, about 84 percent. In 1970, those neighborhoods had reported 148,136 white residents, about 94 percent of their total population. Hyde Park, its black population burgeoning from 127 in 1970 to 3,864 in 1980, was the only one of those neighborhoods to undergo such an influx; the newcomers to Jamaica Plain included some 4,812 Hispanics, with another 800 or so moving into Roslindale. The reduction in the white majority's percentage was clearly not attributable to a massive invasion by blacks and Hispanics; it was brought about by the net loss of around 36,500 white residents.

That net loss seems to have been related in large measure to the strong reluctance of white families to submit their children to the procedures instituted for the racial desegregation of the Boston schools. There was a net loss of some 18,000 residents between birth and 19 years of age, during which years residents normally prefer to live close to their parents and ordinarily attend school. At the same time, 8,558 residents entering or passing through the child-rearing years of 2 to 54 left without being replaced. Of those residing in those sections in 1980, 31,145 boasted pure Irish ancestry—no other single nationality was even close.

Economically, the four sections reported median incomes in 1970 of $8,907 in Jamaica Plain to $12,285 in West Roxbury, when the citywide average was $9,133. In 1979, when the average Bostonian wage earner gathered in $16,602, Jamaica Plain had slumped to $14,122, but West Roxbury was averaging $23,451 (Kevin White and his pals on Beacon Hill and in Back Bay were pulling down about $32,686 apiece, though, so there was still room for resentment on Center Street in West Roxbury).

—Newton and Brookline divide the northern border of Hyde Park by nearly two miles from the southwesterly extremity of the Brighton district of the city. Brighton's northern border is the Charles River, narrow, slow, and only recently reclaimed from brackish, stinking swamp sludge with the use of lots of tax money. Brighton harbors many students who attend Boston College, most of which is in Newton, and affords them the opportunity to see how middle- and lower-middle-class renters and homeowners in a mostly Catholic community manage to get by. With its neighboring section, Allston, to the east (nobody, including the U.S. Postal Service, is exactly sure where Brighton ends and Allston begins, but there is general agreement that Brighton is the bigger chunk of the mixed residential and light industrial area), Brighton was numerically affected only slightly by the population convulsions endured by the rest of Boston between 1970 and 1980. The total population of 64,657 increased by 1,607. About 3,800 whites departed. Some 1,524 blacks came in, making the 1980 total 2,673. Asians added 1,817, for a total of 3,112, and about 1,100 Hispanics left them with a potential voting bloc of 2,911.

Politically, this meant almost nothing. With the Fenway-Kenmore Square neighborhood, Allston-Brighton is a refuge for transients in the city, totaling in 1980 about 96,000 people who took very little interest in the operation of the city. Fenway-Kenmore, convenient to Boston University, reported a net loss of 2,123 residents in that decade, losing inhabitants in every category except the 20–34 age group, which gained 1,700 new arrivals. Allston-Brighton, surrounding the eastern edge of the Boston College main campus, now the largest Catholic university in the United States, and affording lodgings to Harvard students who cannot quite swing the levies charged by the landlords in Cambridge, lost heavily from all age groups except those between 20 and 35—11,227 of them showed up to claim permanent addresses. *Permanence* in those sections of the city until 1983 meant that the person who asserted it had not yet decided where he would like to settle down when he completed his studies for his degree: the chances were that it would not be Allston-Brighton or the Fenway-Kenmore area, and until 1983 almost everyone involved in Boston politics was agreeable to receiving that view without any argument.

•

What is probably of central importance, when contemplating just how various the city is today and the daunting magnitude of the task challenging any politician who would seek his mandate from the whole of it, is that for all the bluster which has been devoted to Boston's character and grand plans for its betterment, it has not changed very much at all. The purveyors of those plans include Kevin Hagan White, and he should be very proud of that. It speaks well of his stewardship.

"If everybody minded their own business,"
said the Duchess in a hoarse growl, "the world
would go round a deal faster than it does."

—Lewis Carroll (Charles Lutwidge
Dodgson), *Alice in Wonderland*

4

FABLES about Boston's provincialism, like most stereotypes,
have a solid basis in reality. If entire communities may be said
to suffer from advanced cases of narcissism, Boston is long
overdue for therapy. The invariable if tacit presumption un-
derlying general statements made about the city by her residents and self-appointed spokesmen is that what delights or
dismays them about Boston is unique to her. Prudent politicians, if they are alert enough to question that belief, keep
their skepticism to themselves. Its lack of conformity to reality is therefore seldom challenged, and Kevin White before
and after he became the mayor left it pretty much un-
touched.

The emigration from the city that alarmed him so in
1967, and that still distressed him enough as he abdicated city
hall in 1983 to cause him to claim he had stemmed it, when
the most he had done was to alter it, was a feature common
to the cities of the northern tier of the United States in the
years that followed the Korean conflict. Boston did not differ
from Detroit or Albany in undergoing that sort of desertion,
and its inception was not caused by racism, either. Later, to
be sure, racism became one of the motivating factors in decisions to evacuate the inner cities of the north, but what provoked the fad in the first place was the unexceptionable desire

to improve one's living standards, coupled with the economic boom of the growth years that burgeoned after almost two decades of war. The suburbs that surround Boston today may be embarrassed by their numbers of tri-levels and raised ranches crowded onto lots of one-third acre or less in the days before the local zoning boards wised up to what new owners of abandoned farmland had in mind for their late acquisitions. But those tracts are not denuded of trees anymore. Maples and pine trees were installed by the new homeowners when they arrived thirty years ago, and those trees are in the full leaf of maturity each spring. The suburban schools now being closed, as towns regroup in the ebb of the postwar tide of babies, include a fair number of structures less than twenty-five years old. The suburban parishes that used to do most of their business in baptisms and first communions now have a brisk trade in weddings. The mayoral statesmanship of John B. Hynes in the midfifties and John Collins after him, starting in 1959, did not affect by increase or diminution the rate of departure from the city that filled up the Boston suburbs. It took place because a lot of Boston's residents concluded that the suburbs offered better family accommodations, and their finances had improved to the point at which they could afford to secure those advantages for themselves. Those whose hunger for a better life stopped short of being strong enough to send them to the Sun Belt, far away from the damned snow and all the other high-priced problems of New England's winters, moved out to the suburbs without reference to the identity of policies of the man who happened to be mayor of Boston.

As perhaps befitted the men who had been and would be mayors of this solipsistic city, neither Hynes nor Collins, nor White who came after them, manifested publicly a strong acknowledgment of that fact of their powerlessness to affect that migration. This, too, is a standard feature of contemporary urban politicians: ravenous for any praise that they can glean from having been in office when some betterment, however accidental, happens to the city, they appear at least thereby to accede to the disagreeable concomitant responsibility for whatever may go ill.

On the face of it, this practice looks pretty stupid. The history of larger northern cities since the end of World War I has contained a lot more gloom than grounds for great elation. A man of rationality, confronted with the obligation to take blame for regular disasters as the price of hogging all the credit for the infrequent successes, would be well advised to duck the odium and let the applause go. Yet, so far as I've been able to ascertain, no politician of recent vintage has sought to accept that option.

This anomaly persists not because all pols are by definition stupid, although they will almost always prove on close examination to have rigorously conventional mind-sets. It is because what appears in the abstract to present the most realistic and secure adjustment to reality—frank admission that the occupant of the mayor's office in fact enjoys very little genuine ability to improve substantially the lives of most of his constituents—is not recognized by media. *Newspapermen and broadcast journalists, however they disparage politics and politicians, evangelically believe and profess the same profane creed: Government, in one form or another, is and ought to be the central and overriding fact in the life of every citizen.* News of government, local, state, and federal, always comes first in the paper, and it dominates the evening news, unless God or Mother Nature intervenes with some calamity. Absent a major disaster or the escalation of international politics to the next level, which is war, editors and broadcast news producers construct their reports on the foundation of what government has done that day. At least 30 percent of the daily paper is concerned with politics, and broadcast journalism's bias is at least as pronounced in that direction.

There are two ways, at least, of viewing that concentraton. It can be argued cogently that since the New Deal, government has so expanded its oversight of everyone that the decisions made by those in charge of it in fact do represent the most important aspects of the life of every citizen. Whether governmental influence redounds to the benefit or detriment of individuals, in determining its importance as a subject of the news, is therefore irrelevant; what matters is only that the government is the most important factor in most people's lives and thus merits the most intense scrutiny. The flaw in this reasoning, of course, is that it is circular—governors on every level rely for the perceived importance of themselves and their decisions upon reportage of those decisions by the media, at the most appalling length and in excruciating detail, and when the media accord this homage to them, the iterative process is well under way.

The second way of estimating the legitimacy of media concentration upon politics and politicians is from the viewpoint of that diminishing but still vast majority of Americans who do not depend upon government for much beyond the defense of the coast and the carriage of the mail (and who irritably in recent years have of necessity reduced that second dependence considerably, thus contributing handsomely to the prosperity of Federal Express and the other private outfits that actually succeed in delivering promptly what is entrusted to them). To these people the enormous government bureaucracies and their obstreperous and putatively controlling elected supervisors are a blasted nuisance and a hideous expense. For those who hold down jobs in private enterprise, provide for the support of their dependents, and harbor no ambitions to injure their neighbors or to seize their property, virtually all news that comes out of government is bad, unless it is irrelevant. Like the legendary resident of Maine who declared he would never vote because "that just encourages the bastards," the unreconstructed private citizen endures rather than devours the abundance of news that he gets about the government and those who aspire to run it, and he finds very little difference between what is presented to him as the news and what is unabashedly proffered to him as political advertising. From that point of view, media emphasis upon news of politics is illegitimate because it constitutes the means by which the reporters and politicians synergistically combine to secure each other's power.

When John Collins announced, on June 6, 1967, that he would not be a candidate for reelection, the news that he made for fully private citizens was bad. He raised his voice in a maelstrom of civil unrest. Refreshed by a short vacation in Ireland at the end of May, Collins had returned to confront first a school committee overdraft of $226,000 in pay raises for truant officers, janitors, supply room personnel, and secretaries. Louise Day Hicks, seeking his office, remained on the school committee that spring, and she had a lot to say about its treatment of "the little people" who worked for the school department and might be expected to cast votes in the election. Also before Collins was widespread exasperation in the Codman Square section of Dorchester, where the MBTA proposed to expand its yards for storage of the rolling stock, until then parked in its yards in Cambridge, so as to free up that real estate near Harvard for the proposed John F. Kennedy Library. The good residents of Dorchester did not feature that notion at all. And just in case Mayor Collins wasn't entertained enough by those items on the public agenda, the Mothers for Adequate Welfare (MAW) decided to stage a sit-in in the Grove Hall welfare office.

MAW was a rump group of women on the dole of Aid to Families with Dependent Children, virtually all of them black and residents of Roxbury, the number of whom appears never to have exceeded 300 persons. The gravamen of their complaints was that they did not get enough cash on welfare, they disliked the presence of cops in the welfare offices, they were not received with respect when they came in, and they lacked a committee—with a majority of members on welfare—to hear grievances. Their demonstration in the welfare office provoked the increased attendance of police and the interest of unemployed and unschooled black youths in the neighborhood, a combination that proved volatile. Official reports quoted in the *Globe* (6/3/67, p. 1) put the crowd between 300 and 700 civilians, some of whom threw rocks at the policemen. The policemen construed this as a riot, which seems understandable enough, and took steps to quell it. Those steps in turn were received by the mob as a signal to start breaking into stores, starting fires, and looting. On June 4, Fire Lieutenant Joseph Donovan of Ladder 4 in Dorchester was shot in the hand (and alleged by the *Globe* to be on the danger list), and two young civilians were hurt badly enough to require hospital attention—one was stabbed and the other had a fractured skull.

Full credit for the rioting was variously placed: "If the police don't get out of Roxbury," said a young mother holding an infant in her arms, "this rioting is going to go on forever." But others attending the same meeting that night in June at Grove Hall's St. Hugh's Roman Catholic Church said peace in the area was at the option of the young civilians: "It's the kids' bag." (*Globe*, 6/7/67, p. 1) Black adults with reputations for responsibility in judgment said the young people in Grove Hall had gone out of control in three days and nights of rioting that had left forty-seven injured and a number of buildings in flames.

Perhaps still smarting from his loss the previous autumn of twenty-one of the city's twenty-two wards in his unsuccessful quest for the Democratic senatorial nomination, Collins, against the background of those two emerging school and racial problems, succinctly stated the truth on June 6 when he withdrew from the upcoming campaign, saying: "I am not going to have a political future." (*Globe*, 6/6/67, p. 1) Interestingly, though, neither he nor the *Globe* (in its admittedly "premature" editorial evaluation of his tenure the next day) remarked the impregnability of those two new civic problems to any genuine corrective efforts Collins might have undertaken. The financial difficulty, comparatively small but typical of the school committee's airy attitude toward fiscal responsibility, was beyond the mayor's control because the committee enjoyed statutory fiscal autonomy (since legislatively repealed). Collins was powerless to prevent the Hicks majority on that board from distributing gratuities in the form of wage increases to department support personnel. The much greater problem of the Grove Hall disturbances, among the first in a long, hot summer that would headline the Algiers Motel killings in Detroit and disturbances in 103 U.S. cities (by wire service reports), making soldiers commonplace auxiliaries to civilian law enforcement officers, displayed the vulnerability of the community to extortion by means of incitement to riot. That, too, Collins was impotent to change. He articulated no recorded frustration at those circumstances. The *Globe*, declaring its intention to hold him answerable for "critical unresolved problems facing him" until his term ended with the year, explicitly included "the current crisis in race relations" as tops on the city agenda (*Globe*, 6/7/67, p. 20), thus at least implying that he could relieve it.

That sort of habitual thinking, with its smug hubris to the effect that elected officials have the capacity first to palliate and then to cure all problems, obliterates the distinction between those that are amenable to change and those that are proof against all practicable efforts. As the *Globe* noted in that same pontification, in its estimation there was "no denying that Mr. Collins took a city that was flat on its back and got it up and moving forward" during his eight years in office. "When he became mayor, the tax base was shrinking, the city was not far from bankruptcy, and civic leaders were talking glumly of the probable need for a commission form of government. Today, Boston is in the midst of a building boom of unprecedented proportions." The *Globe* then applauded Collins for having instituted "the nation's finest urban renewal program." (*Globe*, 6/7/67, p. 20)

This elided the facts that the actual investments had been made by private financiers and federal grants, enriched by tax concessions and zoning permissions, which at most had amounted to encouragements of intents formed outside of city government. John F. Collins had created little of that. Barry Hynes, the city councillor who would withdraw later that summer from the race to succeed Collins when he found he couldn't raise enough campaign funds, had become a candidate to reclaim the job his father, John, had held in part because the family resented Collins's claim of authorship of projects that Hynes had started. Collins, Hynes felt, had merely presided. To list Boston's structural progress as a Collins accomplishment was as unjust as to debit him for the unrest in Grove Hall. Nevertheless, that was how the *Globe* totted up accounts that day: Nagle's Law—complex matters are not susceptible to simple explanations—is not enforced in politics or the reporting of it.

White, issuing his first position paper of the campaign five days later, took his cues from the conventional wisdom. Collins had won office despite opposition from Boston's financial leaders, then as now known as the Vault. Its members prefer to call it the Boston Coordinating Committee. Holding meetings in the Boston Safe Deposit and Trust Company offices, self-selecting themselves from Boston's banks and businesses, they in 1959 had preferred John Powers, Senate president, who had also sought to succeed Hynes in 1959. Collins had wooed them away from that misplaced loyalty, and his reward had been what the *Globe* guessed to be about $1 billion in building investments. (*Globe*, 6/11/67, pp. 1–42) Unprepared for, or unapproving of, the Collins abdication, businessmen and bankers polled by John Becker's research firm for the *Globe* were described on June 7 as grudgingly preferring White to all the other candidates who had by then announced. Collins still claimed fealty from 32 percent who had control of major venture capital, but White at 22 percent was comfortably ahead of Hicks at 13 percent, and nobody else in the field of mayoral hopefuls received more than 4 percent support. Evidently either sharing the *Globe*'s sense of a necessity for new priorities in city politics or shrewdly wishing to appear that he did, White availed himself of the luxury of assuming the investors would back him, having nowhere else to go but to Louise Day Hicks, and struck a posture as something of a populist.

His showpiece in that position paper was the promise of a Neighborhood Services Department, which would employ "coordinators of community projects, grievance officers for individuals or neighborhood groups, and will be reporters of human needs to all levels of government." These tribunes of the people, which as White envisioned them strikingly resembled ward heelers of bygone and disparaged days of machine politics, would add their advice to his plans for upgrading the police, building new substations, and increasing wages for the men in blue, while at the same time he essayed to "push school building programs and select sites based on educational needs." (*Globe*, 6/8/67, p. 8) John V. Lindsay in his successful campaign as New York City's mayor had promised to open thirty-two annexes in the neighborhoods and did not appear damaged when the city council held him to just three. White was following that suit.

The beauty of that sort of whey-faced earnestness is its widespread appeal to those volunteers and voters who have real stakes in elections, i.e., money for themselves. Clients of the government, seeking jobs or those job substitutes that provide income with no dreary work involved to women who've been fertile, care deeply about outcomes of city elections. Civil service has eliminated much of the anxiety that used to pervade city government when the old order changed, because those who have secured jobs under it can no longer be fired. Still they retain an interest in the plans of the successor, much preferring someone who proposes to raise salaries for city employees to someone who sets out to cajole votes from those who just pay taxes, by pledging to hold city budgets down. Those, too, who are outside the city government and quite resentful of that fact find most agreeable a candidate who says he has plans to create new layers of bureaucracy and thus numerous new jobs for which early partisans may expect preference, especially if those jobs don't sound too tiring. Kevin White's first detailed paper mentioned very easy work and left no doubt about its purposes.

"Obviously, the people of the city judge Boston not only by its skyline but also by its services. They are not different from people anywhere, they want what they are entitled to—a decent environment. They rightly believe that a city capable of attracting hundreds of millions of dollars to revitalize downtown Boston where people work is equally capable of attracting private and public funds to influence new life into the neighborhoods where people live.

"Boston," White said with a straight face, "needs people programs to match the building programs." (*Globe*, 6/12/67, p. 9)

So far as the public record shows, nobody seriously quarreled publicly with White's first Edenic vision of the city. Any critic with the brain of a nematode must have perceived when White uttered all that balderdash that he was advocating spending that would require tax increases. Boston, like the other towns and cities of the Commonwealth, then depended heavily upon taxation of real property to fund its government. Real estate development wanes and waxes in inverse proportion to the tax rate in the city because rents and mortgages vary in direct proportion to that rate. Investors contemplating the erection of new office buildings for rent to normally intelligent tenants do not embark on vast projects in the expectation that the tax rate will go up like some variety of rocket, leaving them with vacant space no sane man will lease. If they are persuaded that such tax hikes are in store, they defer or curtail severely their plans to replace old office space, which in time leads to the reduction of the city's real estate tax base and to fears of bankruptcy, which John Collins had faced down by placating the Vault. White, who would leave office four terms later making almost the same boasts of downtown rejuvenation that accompanied the Collins withdrawal, set out seeking election ostensibly in conflict with the interests that would finance those additional new buildings.

The Vault members took no umbrage when he flung that gauntlet down. Neither did they offer much encouragement to Beacon Hill Republican John Sears, who might have seemed on the surface more cordial to their views. Séars could not win. The Vault, as it always did, kept a low public profile, but in private, off the record, and with circumspection, its participants supported Kevin White. They did this because they were smart and they correctly appraised Kevin White as being smart as well. They had something in common with him, too: they all feared Louise Day Hicks. If he had to say some things that grated on their ears, and if his victory would mean the institution of a new political machine, that would still be better than the prospect of what a win for Louise Day Hicks would mean.

I beseech you, in the bowels of Christ, think
it possible you may be mistaken.

—Oliver Cromwell
Letter to the General Assembly
of the Church of Scotland
August 3, 1650

5

MRS. HICKS thus ran for mayor up against a cabal of opposition which feared to admit the extent and the reason for its emnity toward her, lest publication of its animus and the motives behind it inflame those who might not support her into becoming her devoted partisans. The official competition that she faced, chiefly from Kevin White and former BRA Director Edward Logue, would remain barely civil through most of the campaign. City business leaders would have risked apoplexy if that had been necessary to preserve their taciturnity about prospects for the city should she be elected, thus pushing silence to the verge of near mendacity.

The media were less restrained. From them she got something that approached overt hostility. Even for a city that takes its politics most seriously and is quite accustomed to strong passions being aroused, Mrs. Hicks's first run for the mayor's office was a strenuous experience.

She did not look like a demagogue with great potential. She was stubby and overweight, middle-aged, and had a fussy hairdo that was very shiny black indeed. She had at least a double chin, and wattles that vibrated when she talked. Her voice was high and reedy, suitable for parliamentary supervision of meetings of the Ladies Sodality but hardly promising as a means of rousing the rabble. Yet perhaps partly because her very unattractiveness served to remind establishment observers of successes achieved by those two loutish redneck southern men, Lester Maddox and George Wallace, Hicks was able to inspire great fear in men who under other circumstances would have smiled at her indulgently.

Globe management manifested that fear quite disgracefully. Assigned to her campaign were two city hall reporters, Elliot Friedman on nightside to report in morning editions and Joseph A. Keblinksy to hold forth on dayside for the evening papers. Fleshing out their coverage of her formal announcement was then general-purpose columnist, now worldwide free-lance tennis guru, Bud Collins.

Keblinsky on the first of May set the scene for Hicks's Sheraton Plaza party to be held that night by writing that she'd be the first woman to seek the mayor's office (she was not—Frances Curtis had run briefly in 1925—and the *Globe* had to correct that). He said also that hers was the first such gathering to offer free food to attending supporters, which was rather a backhanded way of saying that she wasn't selling tickets. He dwelt at some length on her friendship with John Powers, whom he described as her mentor and a two-time loser for the mayor's office, thus inviting readers to link Mrs. Hicks with the odors of state house chicanery that had clung to Powers's candidacies. (*Globe*, 6/1/67, p. 1)

Friedman the next morning played the party pretty straight. "My chapeau is in the ring," the candidate had said, and he went on to summarize her position as one of "Boston for Bostonians." He reported that she opposed all federal aid that carried with it federal oversight of funded programs; that she thought tax exemptions for private institutions ought to be repealed; and that she advocated city income taxes for nonresidents of Boston who earned their livings in Boston.

She said repeal was the only solution to the city's problems in obeying the law that prohibited racial imbalances in the schools. (*Globe*, 5/2/67 pp. 1–6)

With that announcement speech, attorney Louise Day Hicks, daughter of Judge William Day of South Boston, demonstrated that she was a lousy lawyer unacquainted with decades of binding precedent laid down by the Supreme Court of the United States. She also showed herself to be a blissful dreamer when it came to predicting what the Massachusetts General Court, its legislative branch, would do if asked to repeal the imbalance law. Her proposals to refuse aid from the federal government would have beggared Boston in a year, without interfering in the slightest with federal authority to hold its civic institutions up to scrutiny. Her suggestions to tax institutions that have been historically exempt, e.g., schools and churches, would have run afoul of the Bill of Rights, if they had stood a chance of being expressed in a law. Any candidate for public office who proposes that the city should enact a payroll tax on Boston workers implies by his proposal that he has never seen the undeveloped territories just outside the city limits of Boston, and that he has not reflected on the implications of his notion for landlords of Boston office buildings. Mrs. Hicks's first salvo clearly established her status as a candidate with one issue, to which she alluded only delicately with her remarks on the imbalance law. She was on the side of whites who did not want their children bused around the city so that some observer visiting the Boston public schools would see just as many white faces as he saw brown ones eager for their learning for the day. The issue before she spoke was whether Boston was the voting residence of enough whites, who felt the same way, to decide the mayor's election; that was the issue when she was finished.

Keblinsky obviously thought the matter needed something more than mere reportage. He said the cake presented to the guests was "covered with off-white cream frosting . . .

beautiful to behold as was Mrs. Hicks of the Boston School Committee.

"She was wearing," he wrote for the afternoon editions, "a peacock-blue outfit trimmed with sequins, blue shoes, a pretty black hairdo and white gloves which waved dramatically and kept saying [*sic*]:

" 'Boston for Bostonians! My chapeau is in the ring.' "

So excited that he seemed to overlook either the obvious news value of those talking gloves or else the slovenliness of his own diction, Keblinsky went on to allege the twenty-four-inch cake was "almost as big as a football field," which seems most unlikely. "The audience," Keblinsky wrote, "was mostly women. Mink stoles were in the majority." Feigning breathless ignorance of what office she would seek, he said: "The world was eagerly awaiting her declaration." Reporting her proposal to secure new revenues from those living outside of the city, he wrote: "For the thousands of non-residents who come here to their daily jobs, they will have to pay a payroll tax once Mrs. Hicks ascends the mayoral throne—by golly!" Keblinsky said the candidate's brother terminated her interrogation by print journalists and led her off to do a television interview, "before the reporters' questions got too technical." (*Globe*, 5/2/67 P.M., pp. 1–16)

For Bud Collins in that same edition, some allowance may be made. His fine prose was published as a column of opinion, in which one is not obligated to strive for even-handedness. Collins didn't. He compared the lady to "Cassius Muhammad Ali Clay" and called her "the new champion of champions, an essential compote in aqua silk standing nearly six feet in aqua pumps. She was immaculate, glittering with rhinestone earrings, and sequins on her dress, her hair well-coiffed and very black—not from olive oil, which is a Republican drink." Timely wit gets a little labored as the years go by—then Massachuestts Governor John A. Volpe had said that his hair stayed black as he grew older because he drank olive oil. "I don't drink or smoke or tell lies," Collins quoted her as saying, while the band played "Louise." "That is what you are going to be hearing for the next six months," Collins predicted. " 'Louise' in one form or another. Although the underground said Mrs. Hicks's campaign song would be 'White Christmas' it is 'Louise' and the time may come when a musician won't be able to get a job in Boston unless he knows how to play and sing it." (*Globe*, 5/2/67, p. 39)

The next day the *Globe* took editorial notice of Mrs. Hicks's candidacy. Under the headline CHAPEAU IN THE RING, it predicted that her candidacy would enliven the campaign. "The tea party candidate," it said, "may well turn out to be the one to beat." (*Globe*, 5/3/67, p. 18)

She was clearly the one to beat, and that fact was taken by altogether too many in the media as some sort of a personal affront. This was in large part attributable, I think, to the variety of people that dominates delivery of the news of politics.

Ordinarily the news of government is prepared for announcement and accepted for publication by males who tend to resemble one another greatly. They are relatively young, thirty-five at the outside, and they are sort of rough-and-ready pals. These men—there are female members of this *de facto* society now, far more than there were in 1967, but the few unstated rules remain about the same—permit themselves a perplexing exception to their general code of tolerating all behavior short of the atrocious. For what seems to them to be good and sufficient reason, they feel and express contempt for lower-middle-class white people who fiercely believe in the old verities. Reporters and their in-house counterparts in political campaigns, the men who furnish the reporters with the daily provender of campaign schedules, statements, and exclusive interviews with candidates, early on acquire the habit of professing privately amused contempt for those who strive for office and for those who seek to influence their conduct when they get it, and they apply this astringent but still private cynicism right across the board. This is an important part of the unstated macho code, and it serves its ostensible purpose of at least reminding the newsman of his duty to keep his sentiments out of his reportage.

It is kept privately right across the board, that is, until the subject comes across as someone who claims injury to himself as the result of some program with egalitarian pretensions. Proponents of religious principles that sophisticated persons have declared outmoded or oppressive of the underprivileged; members of the American Legion or the Veterans of Foreign Wars; persons whose abstinence from alcoholic beverages arises not from medical necessity but from promptings of their consciences and who proselytize others to abstain for the same reason; people who fear truly that the property they have worked and sacrificed to get will be depreciated or indeed made worthless by some government program put forward as improving of the public good: such folk are unlikely to be mercifully treated by reporters assigned to observe their behavior. It is almost as though there is a clear exception to the code of public tolerance, under which exclusion from its benefits is provided for those who were strident in the advocacy of views now considered quaint.

This means that an arrant poseur, such as Jesse Jackson, can survive for years without tonal rebuke in all the news reports about his self-aggrandizing and hypocritical efforts to promote himself, so long as he can contrive to put up a plausible pretense of acting to advance racial equality. It means a John F. Kennedy can get away with private sexual liaisons that obviously compromise the efforts of the Department of Justice, under his brother's direction, to investigate and prosecute chiefs of the Mafia, because JFK meandered with élan. It means that a Reverend Martin Luther King can enjoy what amounts to an informal immunity from disclosure of indiscriminate sexual indulgences, because his cause is rightly perceived as just and righteously considered to be more significant than his priapism. The now suspect rationale for this deference used to be that what a public figure did in private was not to be circulated for the public's information unless and until his behavior commenced to interfere with his ability to perform the duties of his office or got his name on some police blotter. The deficiency in that reasoning is that every affect short of arrest required of the informed reporter a close judgment call of whether what the great man was about had gone so far as to impair his judgment or his independence of action, and in retrospect it seems clear now that those calls made when JFK was fooling around with Judith Exner, Sam "Momo" Giancana's moll, were grievously mistaken.

More disturbing still was the obvious explanation for the error of such reportorial judgments. Ben Bradlee and other journalists who knew of JFK's misconduct did not divulge it because they liked the guy and they admired what he claimed as his purposes in politics. So far as I am aware, no journalist has yet come forward to admit with sheepishness that he knew something shameful about Richard M. Nixon but concealed it from his editors because he liked the guy. So also we may comfortably assume that there's no real dirt on the skirts of the Reverend Jerry Falwell's preaching garb that equals what was clinging to the hems of Martin Luther King's robes; the media dislike the Reverend Falwell and would hang him gleefully if they had the goods on him.

There is no way to eliminate, by institutional fiat, the influence of the reporter's affections upon what he serves up for the paper or the evening news broadcast. Doctors strive not to deliver treatment varying in quality according to their personal reactions to their patients; they do not succeed in this noble undertaking. Lawyers grind their teeth and promise they'll defend the most obnoxious of their clients just as tirelessly as they protect the interests of their oldest and most loyal of supporters, and they don't. Butchers cut meat and mechanics repair cars with greater or lesser concern for their work according to their feelings toward their customers. The only defense that an editor possesses, and thus the only one available to the reader or the viewer who receives what he publishes, is the understanding that the report may be incomplete if its subject is likable, or couched in terms to ridicule him if he isn't.

Generally speaking, reporters are predisposed to dislike noisy women, and in 1967 this was more so than today. Mrs. Hicks was an uncommonly loquacious woman. That predisposition was rebuttable in those days, as it is today, by a careful selection of topics by the woman making the noise. She did not exercise that care. Had Mrs. Hicks essayed in 1983 to argue for the Equal Rights Amendment, or government funding of abortions for indigent women, her reporting auditors most likely would have refrained from publication of snide comments about sequins on her dress. Mrs. Hicks in 1967 could have secured the same sort of courtesy from the *Globe* by adopting a position strongly favoring desegregation of the Boston Public Schools, up to and including forced busing. Bud Collins and Joseph Keblinsky would still have considered her appearance laughable, but they would not have made it clear to the reader that they thought scorn the appropriate reaction; they would have kept still about it. Since she did not elect to propound what the *Globe* thought was a responsible and moral position, she was denied the ordinary courtesy of a respectable report of what she said.

It is difficult to be sure whether it improved her cause or injured it, that plain bias against her and what she said in the pages of the *Globe*. The temptation is to say that the *Globe's* treatment of her achieved no effect at all, reinforcing the devotion of the 40,000 or so voters who would have followed her off a precipice, confirming as well the antagonism of those who despised her as a vicious bigot. To indulge that temptation is to presume a great deal about her followers and the strength of their resolution: that it was so great from the outset of her campaign that no public abuse of her could diminish it in any way—or, conversely, make it more passionate. It is to say as well that all of those who started off opposing her were so convinced of the correctness of their choice of someone else that they could not be influenced into supporting her as the plain underdog in an unequal contest with the *Globe:* this does not say a good deal for the independence of mind upon which many of such people pride themselves. And it requires the assumption that the *Globe* persisted in demeaning her without hoping or expecting thereby to affect in any way the outcome of the voting still to come, which is imputing rather more of whimsy to the paper's editors than they will usually admit.

Therefore, reasoning that the *Globe*'s attitude had some effect upon the vote that Mrs. Hicks rolled up, that the *Globe*'s intended effect was to affect her adversely, and that the majority of *Globe* readers who went to the polls in that election did not pause to weigh for themselves all of the implications of the *Globe*'s shrill coverage, it seems probable that this employment of First Amendment rights redounded to her detriment, as its employers intended. In the event, at any rate, Mrs. Hicks lost the election in November, and that was what they had wanted.

The manifest sense of urgency in the *Globe*'s program for that outcome suggests something of the magnitude of support that Boston's regular observers thought the woman had. Since the Massachusetts legislature had passed the racial imbalance law nearly two years before, Mrs. Hicks had been a fixture of the headlines in the city. Section 37C of Chapter 71 of the General Laws of Massachusetts, inscribed on the law books in 1965 in the persisting hangover of grief plus idealism that had washed over the Commonwealth with the murder of President Kennedy in 1963, at its inception affected only two communities in the Commonwealth: Springfield, which had

Boston's racial problems on a smaller scale, and Boston. Then, at least, no other towns or cities in the Bay State had enough nonwhite children of school age to appear to present an imbalance problem, that being statutorily defined as coming into being when enrollment of a given school became more than 50 percent nonwhite.

That legislation, voted for in righteous joy by reps whose districts counted far more knee-jerk liberals than real black people, on its face appeared to be a gratuitous, showboating gesture. The decisions of the Supreme Court of the United States were plain enough for anyone who cared to look at them. If the public schools of a community were so arranged and managed as to separate the white kids from the blacks, then the blacks were not receiving education of the same (presumed high) quality as the white children. Inasmuch as public education is afforded and conducted by authority of state and local laws, that amounts to governmental action that denies equal protection of the laws to some persons solely on the basis of their race and color. That is a violation of the Fourteenth Amendment to the Constitution of the United States, and it is not permitted.

Section 37C by its terms therefore officiously, self-righteously, and, in the long run, uselessly served only to accelerate the commencement of public turmoil that would probably result when, as, and if black parents who resided in the city became incensed enough about the education the children were receiving to bring suit against the public schools, in the federal court. Indulging in a bit of speculative hindsight, it seems likely that such litigation, claiming violation of the Constitution of the land, would have required the judge who heard it to find facts favoring the plaintiffs and to order the members of the Boston School Committee to commence corrective action. What the state statute accomplished, when it mandated the elimination of imbalances and declared such corrective measures to be goals that education should pursue, was to instigate an interim skirmish in the state courts that would serve for the next seven years to crystallize and calcify the racial conflicts in the two largest cities of the Commonwealth. This meant that the Boston School Committee was contesting racial issues in the state courts during the last half of the 1960s when the national programs of Lyndon Johnson's Great Society and the mutinous disruptions over war in Southeast Asia had made riotous ferment the hallmark of major cities.

That state litigation offered an advantage to the Boston School Committee that it would not have enjoyed if its policies and actions had been challenged at the outset in the federal courts. Inasmuch as blacks opposed to segregation in the schools were suing in the state courts to enforce a state statute, the committee was enabled to defend itself in part by challenging the validity of that statute under the Constitution. The committee did so, putting forth the argument that the state statute was defective because it failed to distinguish between imbalances that had occurred by chance and those that had been willfully created by a governmental body, in this case the Boston School Committee. This embrangled all involved in an arcane discussion of whether the state statute was intended to confer more rights upon the citizens than they had enjoyed under the federal Constitution, and if so whether it might not remain unsatisfactory because it held a governmental agency responsible for creation and correction of a situation that it had not in fact created.

The Massachusetts Board of Education was thus brought into the picture. This, too, complicated matters. Under state laws, which controlled disbursements of state aid to local public schools, the Massachusetts Board of Education was required to ascertain whether those school systems were complying with the state laws governing their operation. If the board found noncompliance, it was obliged to withhold all monies set aside for such systems. Boston had been counting on some $23 million from the state to build new schools, which the city really needed. This meant that the efforts of black parents to achieve state court enforcement of the state imbalance law had the effect of reducing the cash flowing to the Boston School Committee, which had been notorious for decades for its prodigality with funds.

Mrs. Hicks, although not chairman of the Boston School Committee, led its 4–1 majority through the first two years of the struggle over the imbalance law (the sole vote of reason on the school committee, as the *Globe* and most white liberals saw it, was its quondam chairman, Thomas Eisenstadt. He was an engaging young chap with expansive views of his own future in the city's politics, who went on to become the sheriff of Suffolk County—he resigned from that job under criticism that he had lived in luxury on public funds). Mrs. Hicks was instrumental in arranging for the use of portable schools in South Boston, accommodating young children in the drafty plywood buildings hastily put up on vacant lots until the state authorities should see fit to release construction funds for new permanent school buildings that had long ago been promised. She was not much of a lawyer and she didn't look so hot, but she was adroit in making sure the voters stayed indignant and had no doubts about whom to blame.

With the aid of her three backers on the school committee, she made several nominations of those culpable. John J. McDonough, taking office back in January of 1967 as the chairman of the Boston School Committee, confessed he had "come to the position that we cannot solve the problem of racial imbalance in Boston without the help of the suburbs." (*Globe*, 1/6/67, p. 11) The suburbs, of course, beyond taking some 250 volunteer black kids privately bused out to their schools daily from the inner city, were not noticeably eager to participate in this grand scheme, nor did McDonough or the lady in all likelihood believe they would be. But Mrs. Hicks, who had won more votes than anybody else who sought elec tion to a city office back in 1963, knew something about politics, and about resentment, too. The *Globe* lost its temper editorially on January 25 of the new election year and called her and William O'Connor of the school committee "scofflaws." (*Globe*, 1/25/67, p. 14) It declared she was not committed to a sincere effort to comply with the imbalance law, as she certainly was not.

This sort of back and forth in the limelight which had fallen upon her under the imbalance act made her credible when she cited to the *Globe*'s Robert Healy "tremendous pressures on me to enter" the mayoralty race. (*Globe*, 2/5/67, p. A6) She said that this pressure came from policemen, firemen, mothers, and businessmen, who desired a leader for the people of the city and believed that it had long been run by people who didn't live in it. Healy, a reflective and dispassionate observer (who lived in a South Shore suburb), reminded his readers that she had a strong following of people who admired her service on the school committee, and he said, correctly, that her candidacy would change the campaign radically, centralizing the issues. "Mrs. Hicks," Healy wrote, "would become the central figure in the contest. . . . What she stands for would be the central issue in the campaign." That issue Healy disingenuously affected to see as the tax rate. Mayor Collins had predicted that if the Massachusetts Board of Education stood firm in its refusal to release the $23 million in aid for the public schools, it would hike the tax rate by some $16.40. "Mrs. Hicks represents the status quo," Healy said. "And a vote for the status quo could add $16.40 to the tax rate." (ibid.)

Healy's allegation, though, was not precisely correct. What the woman purported to offer was a return to the *status quo ante*, what it had been in some relatively recent time that appeared to have passed by 1967 without anybody really noticing. In that golden age, now dilatorily regretted, the Irish in the city had consolidated their control of it, and nothing had occurred since to disturb their possession. Elliot Friedman in the *Globe* on May 7 attributed that view to two city councillors whom he did not name. He said they said she was in the same tradition as James Michael Curley. "He was the symbol of the antis," Friedman's faceless onlookers said sagely, "people who are anti everything going on at the time. Anti a lot of things: blue ribbon committees, closed employment doors, the self-righteousness of the privileged, the arrogance of the establishment, anti-Yankee, a feeling that the Irish are still on their knees.

"It's a tradition so abrasive," Friedman quoted them as saying, "that reason is left out.

"People today in their 40s and 50s in Boston learned their way of living 20 years ago and the abrasiveness is still there.

"These people look at Mrs. Hicks," he continued, without bothering to say when the other unidentified councillor had stopped speaking, "and say she's got the courage to stand up to the papers, to the establishment, to the whole system, and that's the basis of her support." (*Globe*, 5/7/67, p. 19)

If, as I suspect, those were mostly Friedman's broodings, meditations perhaps first inspired by a chance comment from some other reporters or an unusually insightful conversation with a politician he bumped into at City Hall, they were not the less perceptive for the disguise that they wore. To a degree, every Boston citywide election is an experiment determining whether an irreducible and surly quarter of the eligible voters will be allied temporarily with enough malcontents who have been splintered off from other interest groups to form a coalition that will elect a protest candidate. Those sullen, hypersensitive, defensive Irish blue-collar voters remain where they are, convinced that they have never gotten a fair shake, never will, and cannot help it, waiting for the reinforcements to arrive from those who dislike the bankers, the doctors who perform abortions, or the airport managers who devise flight patterns that bring noisy jets over their houses while they try to sleep. And the candidates lick their lips nervously, covetous of the strength of that voting bloc, tempted by the knowledge that it is almost certainly enough to weather a primary, frightened off by the awareness that its attraction will surely alienate the rest of the electorate.

Mrs. Hicks was the first such candidate to reason that racism was the new factor that would rally those reinforcements. The hope of her awkward campaign was that bigotry was the nearly universal solvent that would do away with differences among Italian voters, Polish voters, Greek voters, and swamp Yankee voters, motivate however many Jewish voters remained on the Boston register, and unite all of them behind her as the champion of ethnic purity. That reasoning accounted for her birdlike cries about preserving neighborhood schools; so long as the schools got their enrollments from families within walking distance of them, those schools would be white in white neighborhoods, black in black neighborhoods, and proof against all change. That reasoning, too, was the message carried by her signal of "Boston for the Bostonians," and her fatuous proposals for commuter taxes; those were not merely defiant principles that she was expressing, but codes devised to alert all members of the lower middle class to the outrageous enrichment that day-hoppers had gleaned from the city. And it was most emphatically the true meaning of her boasts about support from the policemen, firemen, schoolteachers, and school personnel; Irish or not, they were people who had locks on lifetime city jobs, and the potential black invasion of those payrolls would mean a calamitous disruption of their secure tranquillity.

That aspect of the torment, which the public schools of Boston were to suffer throughout all of Kevin White's four terms as mayor, was nonchalantly disregarded where it was not deliberately downplayed by those who were involved in those struggles. For the consumption of the public outside of the city, the matter was invariably treated as a contest between those who sought in good faith to distribute all available advantages of Boston public education evenhandedly to all students, without cognizance of their complexions, and those who meanly opposed that millennial idea. In the courts and in the halls of government, *de facto* segregation of the schools was debated by those who denied it existed, when it obviously did, and those who deplored its existence, as though white kids in the city's schools were being educated far more diligently than the black kids were, and that this disparity was the result of free-floating racism. That pretense was rubbish then and it remains rubbish to this day.

The fact of the matter was that few enrolled in the Boston public schools in 1967, with the exception of those students who had gained admission to the Boston Latin Schools and Boston English High School, were receiving competent instruction in all subjects. This was because the vast majority of their instructors lacked the competence to furnish such instruction, the books and equipment to advance it, and the physical plants necessary for its delivery. That was why the Jews of Mattapan had left the city.

It was true then, of course, that the dwindling cohort of capable instructors was cosseted by the committee and its school superintendents in the award of teaching assignments, so that the good teachers tended to be sent where the good teachers wished to go, and those good teachers tended to apply for slots in white classrooms. It was therefore true that the few students who received quality instruction were almost entirely whites, and that blacks participated in virtually none of that scarce commodity. Still, the overwhelming reality of the city's public schools was that their principal function had long since ceased to be the education of the young and had become the employment of the unambitious, undistinguished, and incompetent. When the buses were stoned by irate adults in Boston, the real issue was jobs.

So long as the school committee retained full control of Boston schools, it would retain also the appointive power to distribute teaching jobs. If blacks gained any part in the control of the school system, whether through the legislature or by application to the courts, they would inevitably gain a share of those precious jobs. That was what Mrs. Hicks feared, what her close supporters feared, and what she sought to communicate to those who hadn't thought about it.

Mrs. Hicks was protecting a severely damaged institution. The damage had not been fully perceived. It is useful, in the furor over public education that has recurred in the nation from time to time since Sputnik went up back in 1961, to reflect on the changes it has undergone at the hands of the national economy. Those strict and rigorous public schools, which their alumni in their middle years remember with chagrined admiration, were the occupational accomplishments of a generation different from the one that today dominates that public system. Men and women between forty and sixty today went to school and were thought by those who had chosen to be educators because that was the entry profession for smart offspring of the lower middle class. These teachers, who knew their subjects and demanded that students learn those subjects from them, by and large were the first members of their families to get education for themselves beyond high school. Many of them had to be content with two years at a normal school. Those who went on to earn bachelor's degrees were very often the first members of their clans to bask in the heady title of "college graduate." It was a neighborhood event, back in the 1920s and the 1930s, when some kid who had played ball right beside the other kids now pounding a police beat or on night shift at the fire station posed on the front steps in his cap and gown, with his college degree furled in his hands. College for the people who taught us was still quite a privilege, not just something that you did for four years while you tried to find yourself. Education for them was something to be admired, exciting and unquestionably worthwhile.

Nevertheless, the possessors of those cherished degrees had to demonstrate to the still skeptical, and envious, that their acquisition of them could be practical. Education was no good if it meant that you couldn't make a living.

In the Depression and its lingering aftermath before the start of World War II, that was not an easy matter, even for a young man or woman with a college degree. There was no expanding computer industry then, gobbling up math and physics majors as voraciously as colleges could turn them out. International commerce was in the doldrums, depressed into stagnation during those uncertain early years of its development into the huge field of employment that it offers today. There was no demand for graduates who had studied foreign languages, economics, or marketing. English majors, of course, were as useless then as they are now, and that applied also to history majors. Until military conscription obviated the need for a young man to worry about his employment for the foreseeable future, just about the only professional field that was wide open was teaching in the public schools.

Teaching was not in those days—or the days right after World War II when new college graduates fresh minted by the GI Bill emerged to swell the ranks of first-generation professionals, eager to get on with postponed lives and deferred families—the faintly ignominious career selection that it was to become later. Public schools offered low pay, to be sure, but low pay that was virtually guaranteed. When communities went broke in the Depression, their teachers received scrip, but when things improved the wages were made up. People did not get laid off in education as they did in other lines of work. The hours during the school year permitted industrious faculty members to hold second jobs, and the long summer vacations invited them to augment their salaries with seasonal employments. Health benefits were instituted as insurance programs evolved. A pension was assured at age sixty-five or seventy—not a large one, but one that was dependable. The public schools would not go bankrupt when their employees got old. In those days before rampaging inflation, when banks paid 3 percent on savings deposits and levied 4 percent on mortgage loans to purchase houses going for $8,000 or so, that was an attractive package for a young person whose family did not control a company, a law office, or some other enterprise that deemed heredity an assurance for advancement.

It was not until the late fifties that the term *schoolteacher* acquired overtones of mild disdain, its pronunciation by the ones who were engaged in teaching gradually coming to include embarrassment, its usage by those who had rejected that job possibility usually including the prefatory "just a." Those in the second and third generations of college graduates from their respective families, if they contemplated teaching at all, envisioned doing it after "going on" to the Ph.D. and delivering their wisdom on the college level. By then the educationalists had annexed hegemony of the field, instituting all manner of requirements that the novice teacher first ingest a lot of foolishness dispensed in courses about methodology, together with much half-baked nonsense labeled *child psychology* and other such claptrap. These educators were the more ambitious teachers who had swerved away from satisfying their naked ambitions by taking the traditional course of advancement into school administration and had become theorists. As theorists, they assured that they would excel in new fields by inventing them, along with a serviceable pseudo-jargon, and then making rules for everybody else.

The result was that Schools of Education cropped up on college campuses like weeds, while normal schools expanded their required curricula from two to four years' full-time work, very little of it having anything to do with teaching math to people who intended to teach math. Liberal arts students were barred from considering careers in education unless they would submit first to the tyranny of the nitwits who had devised the meaningless courses, but few liberal arts undergraduates with much intellectual pride were interested in doing that. In the universities, it came to be agreed that Schools of Education were where dizzier coeds and males tending toward slow-witted should matriculate, the former to rely on luck for the capture of husbands who would save them from applying whatever it was that they might learn by some accident, the latter to elude the grasp of draft boards for another four years, while hoping something better would turn up. The people that those schools released as certified for teaching in the public schools were the chaff of those who entered as freshmen at their universities four years before, poorly motivated, poorly educated, with poor images of themselves as functioning intellectuals.

When those people drifted into the employment market, it was avid for their bodies and in no mood or position to question their credentials—which had been acquired, after all, in bovine obedience to standards established by the very people who were evaluating them. The sixties and the early seventies saw the long crest of the baby boom roll through the public schools, and recruits to baby-sit that horde, if nothing else, were desperately needed. Whether they were themselves literate was an issue that approached irrelevance and therefore was not regularly raised. Besides, those who occupied the hiring offices were gradually becoming people who had accepted the same ersatz substitute for academic education that the applicants proved they had endured by the diplomas they brandished. Furthermore, the severe inadequacy of their own educations, which left them unable because unfit to teach properly, would not be grasped fully by outsiders still in full command of their wits until the pupils who would be subjected to this prechewed twaddle escaped from the secondary schools all but incapable of reading simple English sentences or doing basic sums. There was a lull of some fifteen or twenty years, therefore, which allowed all to remain serene while the feckless postulants of educationalism grew older in their service, succeeded to administrative slots, and in the meantime released a whole generation of new graduates marginally equipped to function in an increasingly demanding and complex society.

During that period of blissful ignorance, cultivated in the schools and unseen by society at large, people of the ilk of Mrs. Hicks thought they perceived in service as members of the Boston School Committee a potential for political advancement so enormous as to fairly dazzle them. There was in those days no compensation in the form of salary or wages for the time that school committee members put in at their jobs. Then as now it tended therefore to attract the sort of candidates who have always outnumbered by far those motivated solely by some *noblesse oblige* sense of public service: people who believed that there were other things in life that were perhaps even more precious than money, such as, for example, power.

Most of those who vied for school committee positions were jockeying for higher office, obscure lawyers who believed that at the very least the money spent on campaign posters would remind potential clients of their law degrees, furnish them with plausible excuses to enunciate in public their considered views of the right thing to do on civic questions, and very possibly win them the hearts and minds of silent but uneasy masses of the voters who would then propel them into statewide office. Or at least the mayor's office, anyway. Discontented dreamers bored with drafting wills and divorce libels, annoyed that their learning had not brought them fame and rich rewards, envious of smooth-talking advocates who had their names and their pictures in the paper all the time, greeting visiting potentates and making State Street banking moguls perform to their bidding. These candidates spent time and money fairly lavishly to capture offices that did not offer any cash return.

What those offices did confer was the hiring power, the ability to make or break the career plans of young people whose backgrounds and upbringing had convinced them permanently that to "get on the city" was the sole feasible route open to them that would lead to a long lifetime of contentment and financial security. Even at midcentury and after it, more than one hundred years after the potato blight struck Ireland and impelled the first wave of her people to depart for Boston and a diet that would support human life, notwithstanding the fact that the applicants had those college diplomas which attested to their education far beyond the dreams of the ancestors who had cut peat for the cottage fires and cursed the British soldiers through the smoke, the specter of eventual privation still haunted the Boston Irish, as it does today.

When the Irish first arrived in Boston, there were no jobs except menial ones that offered no tenure, and not even a strong man or woman could be sure that he or she would always have work and thus bread upon the table. That real fear of unemployment created a persistent anxiety which accounts for much of Irish success in American politics, local, state, and national. Only those jobs that the government dispenses could be captured by the sheer force of hardworking numbers who lacked capital. Commerce, banking, and professions: those paths to advancement and assured financial safety were all closed to applicants who started with no money of their own. But city hall and the state house, in time even the presidency, could be taken by those people if they worked hard enough and stuck together, and in time that came to pass. And, when those bastions were seized, their occupants could dispense jobs, jobs that could never be taken away from those who got them, jobs that would provide the pensions that would keep them safe and dry when they got old, jobs that would make it possible for their children to get the education that they needed to make money in business, practice medicine and law, and maybe even acquire dignity. *Patronage* is not a dirty word for those born of those immigrants; its pejorative connotation was veneered upon it by those who were comfortable enough not to need the jobs that patronage created and whose parsimony with the opportunities outside of politics had made the resort to politics necessary in the first place. The Boston School Committee controlled patronage.

That patronage, and the loyal gratitude of its beneficiaries, was the predicate of Mrs. Hicks's candidacy. Reductions In Force (RIFs) taken since she first ran for mayor have left the city with about 4,000 teachers on its payrolls today, collecting an average wage of about $25,000 per year—the amount of that mean salary is disputed by the administration and the teachers' union, but the figure is a reasonable approximation. When she announced, close to 7,000 instructors were on the rolls, with probably about four times that number of support personnel behind them. The two cadres, including many janitors, school nurses, truant officers, and secretaries who had benefited from the salary increases her committee had voted earlier that year, were the bedrock of a potent organization. If there were, say, 35,000 employees of the public schools, and if three-quarters of them lived in Boston, and if each of them claimed at least one dependent whose vote could be relied upon along with the wage earner's, she could expect to begin with some 56,000 votes—more than 20 percent of those registered—either committed to her cause or leaning strongly toward it. White parents incensed by busing, much better aware of where she stood on that issue than they were well-informed about her inability to affect its eventual outcome in the manner that they wished; cops and firemen, plus the bureaucrats, who might deduce from her treatment of teachers a strong indication of how as mayor she would treat them—these enormous groups of voters might well be amenable to following the example of the teachers at the polls. If they did, then she was home in the September primary. Nobody then enrolled in the contest could expect to conquer her, if she could get the backing of that coalition.

In the springtime and the summer, that was a promising strategy. Beneficiaries of patronage do not concede the slimness of distinction between them as clients of the city treasury who must make a pretense of work, and welfare recipients whose income does not demand job attendance. As the riots spread across the nation, and the blacks were blamed or boasted of their part in starting them, Mrs. Hicks stood as a beacon for the Boston Caucasian who feared and hated them. For her, though, the dilemma thus became one of ensuring that the hatred overmatched the fear. For Kevin White, Edward Logue, Christopher Iannella, and the stragglers who remained in the race until Labor Day, it was just the opposite: how to harness the fear without undertaking simultaneously the impossible chore of eliminating the hatred.

Publicly, both camps—Mrs. Hicks's against everybody else's—chose to do nothing, and plenty of it, which might serve to suggest neither of them had even recognized the contending attitudes. They had, though, both of them. Mrs. Hicks retired to her oft-stated confidence that her backers knew where she stood on school issues, justified in her belief that they would infer from her attitude toward busing her probable opinion of programs to improve black access to city jobs. White said very little about issues, devoting his time to lambasting Edward Logue, while hoping against hope that those still emotionally tendentious toward Mrs. Hicks's candidacy would devote some thought to the likely consequences of her election. The media, with what approached unanimity, muttered now and then about the polarizing effects of the wrong result in the final election. Notwithstanding their unshaken belief that the candidates in all elections owe their first responsibility to address the issues forthrightly, the media made no strenuous efforts to obtain such remarks from the candidates or any real complaints of the failure of the candidates to volunteer their views. Between the fear of black uprisings (which would without any other stimulus warrant the concerned white in casting his vote for the candidate least likely to provoke them, Kevin White) and the hatred for blacks who fomented the disturbances (which uncomplicated would prompt the resentful white voter to back Mrs. Hicks unstintingly), there was no comfortable resting place for the observer who had any stake in Boston's future. All that the media could do was issue regular and bland reminders of long-standing debts of justice, together with placating homilies urging calm and peace, and hope that the consumers were sophisticated enough to perceive what was unstated. This was that a victory for Hicks would so alienate the blacks that they might decide to dismantle the city; as events fully reported from other cities showed, not even soldiers could prevent them from accomplishing such a program.

For those whose personal and direct interest in the future of the city was not the preservation of $16,000-per-year teaching jobs, but the prospect of attempting to rent forty floors of prime office space to major corporations, or the even greater gamble of obtaining financing to erect such skyscrapers, that real possibility was a horrid nightmare. Everything that had been done by Collins, and by Hynes before him, to rebuild the downtown section had been based upon the expectation that large companies would be receptive to locating at least regional headquarters in the middle of Boston. Armed rebellion would set back considerably the efforts to realize those profitable dreams. The men who had counted on those profits therefore calculated who best could be designated to secure peace in the streets, and they were prepared to allow Kevin White as that person to express himself somewhat extravagantly when he went to garden parties.

White therefore laid the foundation for his early image as a liberal on racial and so-called public interest questions as the preferred spokesman of shrewd men who saw such ostensible populism as the best guarantee of capitalist prosperity. If he promised much to the blue-collar voter—and he certainly appeared to do that with his pledges of close consultation with the neighborhoods, more cops and firefighters, and, of course, all those new streetlights the voters never seem to have enough of—and if he was warmly welcomed in black neighborhoods where Mrs. Hicks was feared quite as sincerely as she was at meetings of the Vault, that would be quite satisfactory. The important thing, the overriding interest, was seeing to it that the city remained quiet after the election and for the foreseeable future. Kevin White looked like the candidate most likely to achieve that goal.

Politics is perhaps the only profession for which no preparation is thought necessary.

—Robert Louis Stevenson

6

ESCALATING INSTABILITY has been the major feature of American big-city politics since the early 1960s. This, I think, is attributable principally to the occasionally desperate manner in which frustrated would-be brokers of black political power have reacted to the failure of their studiously planned efforts to copy Irish strategies that captured city governments as the century began. The result has been city government that lurches back and forth between relatively pacific periods, during which incumbent mayors with reasonable assurance of reelection choose to seek it—and are either returned to office or ejected from it after comparatively dignified contests with opponents greatly resembling them—and intervals of considerable disorder brought on by the decision of incumbents to retire from office, for whatever reason.

Incumbency, notwithstanding its profligate dissipation in the hands of Jimmy Carter floundering for reelection to the presidency in 1980, remains a powerful advantage in the possession of one even dimly aware of the media's willingness to revalidate its owner every day as the rightful holder of the office: "the Mayor," thus relegating his opponent inescapably to the status of "the Pretender." When an incumbent who is not under indictment, has no publicly recorded drinking problem, is not known to practice bizarre sexual amusements, and has a grasp of rudimentary party loyalty decides to seek reelection, he is almost certain to achieve it. The mayor's office is very much like credit: he who has it now has a much easier time getting it tomorrow than does he who does not have it and can only claim that he would like to have it and will exercise it more judiciously than the incumbent.

That fact is not a secret. It is widely known to people who have ready cash to donate to that candidate who promises the best return on such investments. The expectation of return is usually the motive for the investment: the most comforting assurance of that desideratum that is hoped for is experience of happy returns made on past investments. Any candidate can make a promise of encouraging downtown development, taking a hospitable attitude toward a program to rebuild the roads, or seeing to it that the zoning board will not stand in the way of innovative projects; an incumbent can point to his past graciousness toward similar vast undertakings and inquire rhetorically how his would-be successor could do better by the donor. Money ordinarily being the lifeblood of politics in this television age, as less of it was back when a full coal scuttle swung the votes of a three-decker, this means that only a very magnetic rebel or a man of great independent means and much wistfulness can finance a contest with a fellow who's already where the rebel or the hobbyist would like to be. An incumbent who has not disgraced himself and retains wit enough to commit no extraordinary gaffes in public therefore proceeds toward election like a champion at joust, shivering a spear or two with his opponent over issues that are trumped up to test his attention span, smiling a great deal and making as few new enemies as possible. If John Collins had decided, back in 1967, that he might enjoy another four years grappling with interest groups that raised their voices at him and annoyed him very much, he could probably have beaten Kevin White, Louise Day Hicks, and all the other strays who most likely would have stayed at home if he had said he meant to stay in office.

When the incumbent decides, as did Collins in that year and as White did four terms later, that he will retire from combat as the undefeated champion, the joust is called off. In its place is staged a pig pile of impressive size.

Ten seems to be the cabalistic quorum of the fields presented on such occasions; in that number, in 1983 as in 1967, will be five or six would-be mayors whose apparent intelligence, political groundwork, and attractiveness to power brokers new and old give them the warrants to be taken seriously; two or three people who might in strict meritocracies deserve office and discharge it creditably, but who lack exposure, recognition, and money; and two or three harmless strays.

Viewed as a purgative opportunity for the electorate to empty out its cluttered mental drawers and reflect for six or seven months from time to time on the purposes of government and who of the available candidates seems most likely to advance those objectives, those pig piles are probably beneficial. For the dispassionate observer who has very little personal stake in the actual administration of the city, those melees furnish some amusement, albeit not quite as much as that offered by the Red Sox. But for those who do have substantial personal interests in the city, homes located there and lives consequently vulnerable to impact by an irresponsible or malevolent administration, collateral for large investments that will return desired profits only if their management is not hamstrung by the decisions of a hostile officialdom, or jobs upon which they depend for their livelihood in a time of economic uncertainty, the clamorous contests that occur when the incumbent does not run again are extremely unsettling times.

They exhilarate only those who have nothing to lose or

who incorrectly perceive that they have nothing to lose. On all levels of elective politics, from the presidency on down to the smallest of local offices, the hardest hurdle for the candidate who would succeed an incumbent who does not yet wish to be succeeded, or an incumbent who has departed from the fray and left it to a cohort of would-be successors of whom the given candidate believes himself to be the worthiest, is to convince his auditors that his installation will somehow lead to the improvement of their lives. To do this, he must address his persuasion to a polyglot collection of citizens who, if they were fully informed and both able and willing to think clearly about full information, would in all likelihood firmly reject the abstract proposition that any single politician can in fact greatly improve their lives. The majority would reply that while their existing condition could indeed stand considerable improvement, what they fear is deterioration. Yet because defense of the *status quo ante* requires the defender to argue that the devil who is known is almost certainly to be preferred over the opposing, strange devil, to direct one's campaign to this uneasy sector of the voting population is to embrace the political variety of diabolism and concede that as disagreeable as things are in the city, they are likely to remain so. It does not cheer up the listener to argue then at him that actually things are not all that bad.

It is bracing, though, to lament the *status quo* and make ringing promises of invigorating change. The first obligation of the candidate, we should remember, is to acquire a cadre of partisans who can be galvanized to do scut work for him— posting signs that advertise him, tearing down signs that promote his opposition, opening their homes to total strangers who have muddy shoes so that the candidate can visit and talk earnestly of the great deeds he will do for them. Such recruits must believe there is something for themselves in his prospective victory, and that something does not mean more streetlights for their neighborhood—what it means is jobs and power, the real confidence that when he is elected, their man's distribution of tax revenues will include checks and envelopes with their names or those of family members on the front. He who contrives to recruit the largest and most cohesive number of such dedicated followers is the only candidate with a real chance of victory. When the incumbent is running, he has them in place. When he does not run, his successor will be the man who gets the most of them without at the same time alienating those who give the money.

When the Irish made their moves, back when the century turned, government was a much simpler matter. It was not expected to exert managerial responsibility for private enterprise, much less to compete with it. Except for those people who had actual employment with the city, no one really looked to it for sustenance. Those who were very needy did not look to government for aid or claim any rights to money for their welfare. Welfare in those days was charity, distributed to the deserving poor by condescending ladies and lords bountiful who had been appointed Overseers of the Public Welfare. Those whose businesses had outgrown their existing quarters did not importune the mayor for tax concessions without which they would construct new offices elsewhere; taxes then were not the factor that they are today, and the pool of prospective employees was in the city close to work, where the work consequently had to be.

Because city government in those days was a much less pervasive influence upon everybody, those who controlled it when the Irish rose up lacked a clarion call that would rally their loyalists in opposition. Politics for the incumbent Yankees was an avocation for all but the most intemperate. For the rest it was a pastime vaguely disreputable, much like Finley Peter Dunne's description of the vice presidency: not an offense actually, for which one could be jailed, but still somehow something of a disgrace. Those running Boston when the Irish made their bid were not as committed as the upstarts, and they were gravely outnumbered.

The blacks who began stirring in the 1960s manifested superficial similarities to the Irish leaders who had been their professional forebears before World War I and the genealogical ancestors of the Irish officeholders who controlled the government after the pioneers. Those blacks represented a downtrodden class of people who were suffering discrimination because of what they were by birth and not because of anything they had done. They were poorly educated and they did not have much money. They bred new citizens at much greater rates than their (perceived) oppressors. In time by migration and by propagation they might very well become the actual majority of those living in the city. In the meantime there appeared no obvious reason why their increasing potential voting power should not be bartered in exchange for solemn promises by the recipient that he would favor blacks. When Kevin White first ran, about 18 percent of Boston's residents were black. In a crowded field, which by midsummer had shaken out to four major candidates with real chances of winning, the fealty of 18 percent of the voters should have been a valuable counter, if it could be secured without putting off the 82 percent of Boston's citizens who were white.

In the primary, September 26, 1967, a record 55 percent of the electorate turned out, casting 156,928 votes. Nearly 129,000 who were eligible to register their views did not, notwithstanding strenuous efforts of the candidates to the contrary over the previous several months. And this was a good deal better demonstration of voter interest than what is deemed the "normal" turnout in a primary election, 40 percent of those eligible. (*Globe*, 9/27/67, pp. 1–12)

Seventy-seven percent of the votes cast went to the top four finishers: Mrs. Hicks, 43,719; White, 30,497; Republican John Sears, 23,879; and Logue, 23,026. Mrs. Hicks, with 28.2 percent of those who actually voted, had drawn from a city in which 278,562 had registered to vote the loyalty of just under 16 percent. That was less than 7 percent of those who lived in Boston, three years later, in 1970, and of course presumably included no expression of opinion pro or con by the more than 300,000 whose jobs in the city conferred upon them at least a passing right to be interested in the identity of its next mayor. White, who would be that next mayor, pulled 20.3 percent of those who voted, just under 11 percent of those eligible to have done so and less than 5 percent of those who lived in the city and would be subject to his leadership. If we make the generous assumption that there were just as many living in Boston three years after this election as there were when it took place, 641,071, we are left with the conclusion that less than 12 percent of them had drawn the battle lines for a general election that would attract international attention and would so vanquish editorial judgment at *Newsweek* as to prompt that journal to feature the specter of a possible Hicks victory as its cover story a month later under the title "Backlash in Boston." That story itself, in its turn, would become an issue in the campaign pitting Hicks and White in "racially troubled Boston," Mrs. Hicks taking umbrage at the magazine's assertion that she and her supporters, "insular Irish and Italian provincials," should be characters in a Moon Mullins comic strip. (*Globe*, 11/4/67, p. 3) She read it aloud at a rally and her followers expressed great indignation.

It is difficult to resist the conclusion, given these facts, that to a great extent the peril that threatened Boston had been conjured up by the candidates and the media that covered them. Eighty-eight percent of those who lived in the city had no part in the selection of the two opponents, either because they were ineligible to have one, saw no reason to seek one, or had voted for a candidate who didn't make the cut. To argue that 11.5 percent of Boston's voters had contrived a referendum on race in the city, as the tenor of the coverage manifestly demanded, was to attach to the issue of race vastly more importance as a political issue than the overwhelming majority of Boston residents accorded to it. It was also of a piece with the foundation belief of those who work in media that what captures their attention as the focus of the moment is and ought to be the focus of the lives of those whom they address. It is to require of the onlooker the agreement that government and the people who aspire to run it constitute the chief reality of human life, and that simply is not so.

Obviously it was especially not so for the black residents of Boston who, in the opinion of the media, had so much at stake in the outcome. In Wards 8 and 9, encompassing heavily black residential areas of the South End and Roxbury, White attracted 847 votes; Hicks drew 838. Wards 10, 11, 12, 13, and 14—Roxbury, part of Jamaica Plain, North Dorchester and its Columbia Point housing project, and Mattapan— mustered 6,457 votes for Hicks and 5,992 votes for White. White, of course, was not the sole alternative to Hicks for those voters who indeed knew where she stood and abhorred her for it. Wards 8 through 14, where the heaviest concentration of potential black voters lived, returned 7,295 ballots marked for Mrs. Hicks and 6,859 for White. None of the possible explanations for this—blacks had not registered and voted in numbers adequate to overwhelm the remnant of white voters still residing in those wards; blacks had not identified Mrs. Hicks as their mortal enemy in Boston politics; blacks had not united behind one acceptable white candidate, bargained with him before the primary, and then delivered by turning out to vote for him in large numbers in that primary election—reflects creditably upon black political leadership in the city or upon the efforts of white liberals to act in its stead.

When the general election took place on November 6, that oversight appeared to have been rectified. Only 31 percent of the 35,255 who went to the polls in Wards 8 through 14 voted for Mrs. Hicks. White emerged from them with 24,189 votes to her 11,066. Once the alternatives were reduced to two, blacks and their leadership reacted quite appropriately. But by then, of course, they had little choice. As Robert Healy had pointed out in his column of analysis the day after the primary election, Hicks had "the 'anti' vote. It was against a strong mayor, John Collins. It was against the Boston concept of urban renewal." He paused paragraphically and continued: "And it was against Negroes." (*Globe*, 9/27/67, p. 12)

In politics, local, state, or national, a choice made when you really have no choice is usually a real choice that has earlier been wasted. It creates no negotiable instruments which its makers can endorse after the election and cash in for major favors. When White finished second in the 1967 primary, he was in a strong position to haggle with the liberals. They had nowhere else to go. The trouble was that he did not know how many they might be. The sole question that remained for decision in November was the extent of their number and their dedication to the cause that he now represented as the survivor of the primary. If there were enough people in Boston who would bother to turn out and vote for moderation, he would conquer Mrs. Hicks. If the zeal of her beleaguered followers made up for the probable numerical superiority of those who preferred Kevin White, she would be elected.

In the six weeks between the shakeout election and the final in November, neither side was at all confident. This imparted to the campaign an extraordinary sense of urgency verging on hysteria. It was so great that the *Globe*, the day before the election, broke a seventy-one-year-old tradition of refraining from endorsements (lest they imply something nasty about the newspaper's coverage of the candidates involved, a profession of impartiality that would have gagged a goat in 1967) and came out at great length for Kevin White. "There is," the paper thundered, "a principle at stake in this election. In a city which once led the nation in public education and in calling for the end of slavery, it is now the principle of equal treatment for all people. And because principle rather than politics dictates its decision, the *Globe* today departs from its tradition and endorses Kevin White for mayor, and hopes that Boston voters will support him." (*Globe*, 11/6/67, p. 16)

That editorial was a mistake. The attitude that prompted it was an extravagant indulgence. The fear that inspirited the attitude had usurped reason. Kevin White, a year before, had viewed the wreckage of his party on the morning after its debacle in the statewide battles with the GOP, and he had found himself the tallest of surviving Democrats. He had reasoned then, at least by January, that as mayor of Boston he would enjoy more opportunities, and better ones, to position himself for a campaign to be governor of Massachusetts. He had not made any secret of this covetousness (though he in expedience disowned it on October 31, 1967, under challenge from the Hicks camp that he would desert city hall in time to contend in the 1970 gubernatorial contest). If he was a man of principle, the principle was that a man who has proven he can attract votes for a minor statewide office may have some substantial promise as a major statewide candidate, if he's willing to seek major local office and thus get himself some leverage with those who have some money or control the media.

Between his formal announcement for the job as mayor of Boston and the *Globe*'s decision to beatify him, Kevin White had done absolutely nothing, made no public utterance, to warrant it. He spent nearly a year talking about stemming the tide of emigration from the city, leaving it to his listeners to infer that he was talking about white working people who were abandoning it and vouchsafing not a syllable of the concomitant concern that poor blacks were thus free to occupy the emptied spaces. Under an ill-timed and worse-considered challenge to his nomination papers cobbled up before the primary by his principal rival for the *Globe*'s admiration, Edward J. Logue, White had come out strongly against "city hall politics at its worst"; he termed Logue's use of a straw, Richard Iantosca, of whom nothing had been heard before and nothing was again, "a power play" and "dirty politics that [have] alienated the Boston voter from his city government." (*Globe*, 9/1/67, pp. 1–11) As an outsider, then, White had condemned "the power establishment of the city," which did "not wish the people of this city to choose their next mayor," but he did not see fit to renounce such power if he should be the one elected. The best that the *Globe* had been able to bring itself to say of him when it reviewed the field of ten before the primary in September was that he had "campaigned hard and directly on the issues" (*Globe*, 9/21/67, p. 36), which demands the conclusion that his status as the embodiment of principle had not yet become apparent. Indeed the only change in his position between Valentine's Day of that year and the general election was that Kevin White, paladin, was now all that stood between Louise Day Hicks and the mayor's office, and the people at the *Globe* did not like Mrs. Hicks.

Interestingly, the *Globe*'s 1896 decision to quit endorsing candidates had been prompted by the Democratic National Convention's choice of William Jennings Bryan as its presidential nominee. The *Globe*'s ownership, though too Democratic to accept Republican William McKinley as a suitable alternative, found Bryan's advocacy of Free Silver too radically populist to garner its support.

> Yes, I had been chosen to Congress then from
> the wild West, and with hayseed in my hair I
> went to Massachusetts, the most cultured state in
> the Union, to take a few lessons in deportment.
>
> —Abraham Lincoln
> (Reflecting, in 1861, on a campaign
> swing made in 1848 in behalf of the
> Whig presidential campaign of
> Zachary Taylor)

7

KEVIN WHITE adverted to that 1967 campaign to define himself in several ways in later days. He did not appear to follow any orderly system in doing this, and he did not always do it, but when he was in need of an attitude or a position that would in his estimation achieve some improvement in his future prospects, he referred to that campaign for guidance. He had the incomplete eclectic's faith in serendipity. What he'd learned by accident in 1967 had caught his attention because it had worked then and consequently he thought that it ought to work again.

One big thing he thought he learned was that he straddled the electorate. On the night of that November 7, he interpreted the polling totals to an aide beside him: "The rich love me," Kevin said, "and the poor. But everyone in the middle hates me." (*Globe*, 11/8/67, p. 22) Another worker studying the tallies remarked how strong he had been in the North End and how feebly his efforts had paid off in West Roxbury: "The Irish in Ward Twenty knifed him." He would cherish that grudge for the rest of his days as Boston's mayor, always acting on the expectation that his own kind would betray him, and he would repay that debt of treachery in many slighting little ways: tardy snowplows, procrastinating road repair crews, sloppy trash collectors, and insufficient police and fire protection. All of them of course would be marked indelibly on the memories of those who did not get the jobs done in their neighborhoods. The next time out they would exert themselves to poison Kevin White's well just a little more. There is nothing quite as nasty and enduring as an Irish pissing contest, especially when all who are involved are very practiced haters.

Out of that night when 72,123 voted in Wards 16 through 20 and 2,935 more pulled the lever down for Mrs. Hicks than did for Kevin White, he elaborated approaches to the government that he trusted without reservation vastly longer than he should have. Shrewd to see what had drawn cheers down at the *Globe* and up on Beacon Hill, White had flailed his way through the last week before election setting off glorious barrages of rhetoric. He would treat with the suburbs, he assured the gaping voters, and deal also with the world. (*Globe*, 11/4/67, pp. 1–4) He would labor to secure Boston's designation as the site for the 1975 World's Fair, installing it in a new, airy city worthy of a Prospero on unused harbor islands out near Boston Light. And he would recruit a brains trust, something Mrs. Hicks had not been moved to promise.

"I think there is a tremendous amount of talent in the city's government," he said, "and I hope to encourage as much of it as possible to stay. But I'm also going to make every effort to encourage new talent into our city's public service.

"It would be a tragedy," he said, "if the next administration doesn't attempt to recruit some of the talent available in our academic institutions." He knew whereof he spoke when he said that: he was being interviewed on channel 2, WGBH-TV, Allston, home of the Public Broadcasting Service in the

Boston area. (*Globe*, 11/4/67, p. 3, report of interview 11/3/67)

This tactic showed adroit and deliberate self-mutation by the candidate who had disclosed his plans eleven months before. He had not set out to carve with creativity a new and glossy following. He's been after the endorsement of the old alliances. Starting out then, he or someone close to him had been straightforward with the *Globe*'s Timothy Leland, candidly admitting that he wanted to be mayor because Mayor White could make headlines out of reach of Secretary of State White. Once installed in City Hall, he could raise more money for a gubernatorial bid than he could filing documents in the State House. (*Globe*, 1/3/67, p. 13) His brains trust was the troika of Ted Anzalone, the crafty lawyer from the North End, White's own age, whose professional associations would give him so much grief in the years to come; Frank Dooley from Dorchester, another young lawyer (thirty-six) who had managed his campaign for secretary of state back in 1960; and Lawrence Cameron, who with Dooley had been one of White's classmates at Boston College Law School. (Cameron was forty-two, and in his position as assistant district attorney of Suffolk County could claim somewhat more experience. Later to become a judge in Boston Municipal Court, Cameron was deemed expert in vote-getting in those critical sectors of Hyde Park, Jamaica Plain, West Roxbury, and Brighton-Allston.)

Together, White and his closest advisers constituted a quartet of technocrats whose sole interest in the mayoralty race was how to win it and what use could be made of it as a vehicle for transportation to still higher office. None of them, in January, displayed any history of coherent ideology, proposed any grand programs, or expressed any commitment to abstract and idealistic goals. White was *tabula rasa* when he first ran for mayor. He was free to invent himself as he proceeded and to permit the media to shape him as seemed expe-

dient to the campaign. He went into it a living exemplar of
Mr. Dooley's definition of a Democrat: one belonging to no
organized political party, owing no more to the party of his
registration than whatever cachet it might give him among
voters who refused to vote Republican; there was but one
Republican in sight in Boston's nonpartisan election.

White emerged from that experience a newly minted liberal. He was hell-bent for good government. That is to say
that he had been so described. He had been perceived as at
least tolerant of blacks, as he had wished to be perceived because that seemed to be the surest route to election, and that
mild attitude was liberalism in a context in which the opponent was Mrs. Hicks. *Moderate* would have been a better designation for him, but political nomenclature is an inexact
branch of lexicography and he was stamped, once and for all,
a *liberal*. Affably enough, he appeared to accede to the label
if he did not actually collude in its application, which was
reasonable enough. With his eye roving every now and then
toward the governor's office, there was future advantage to
be anticipated from the appellations of *liberal Democrat* and
Democratic liberal, much too desirable an advantage to be
heedlessly spurned.

This edge existed because Massachusetts had then as it has
now a reputation for being a liberal state. The reputation is
questionable, notwithstanding the Commonwealth's singular
support for George McGovern's presidential quest in 1972
(which I think attributable chiefly to the depth of revulsion
for Richard Nixon in the state, and not to overwhelming
admiration for McGovern or his ideas), but very seldom questioned. It is taken as an article of faith. In those few remaining contests in which Republican contenders actually enjoy
some possibility of victory, the observer will almost always
find that the Republican in question promotes himself as a
liberal member of that party. Edward W. Brooke, being
black, probably had scant latitude to seek office under any

alternative label, of course, but John A. Volpe twice achieved the governor's office and Elliot L. Richardson bottomed his interrupted (in 1968) but successful career in the Commonwealth's elective politics, both as purely voluntary liberals. Henry Cabot Lodge, notwithstanding the conservative heritage left to him in the U.S. Senate by his League of Nations–hating father, remained liberal enough even after his vice presidential candidacy (with the despised Nixon at the top of the ticket) had been scuttled by John F. Kennedy and Lyndon Johnson to be chosen by the Democrats as their ambassador to South Vietnam. Leverett Saltonstall spent most of his adult life in the U.S. Senate, comfortably reelected each time out by hordes of Democrats who concurred in the belief that he was philosophically at least in the same neighborhood with them. It made good sense for Kevin White to travel under liberal colors as the mayor of Boston; he would have been a fool to reject them, and he didn't.

Neither did he seem to trouble himself greatly over details of just what this newly acquired designation might require of him. This, too, was quite in keeping with the reality of politics, as contrasted with the visions of politics preferred by people such as I, who merely write about how they are practiced. Clear-cut differences and fine distinctions are seldom to be found in purposive discussions by working politicians. Vagueness and hyperbole are greatly preferred by those who are employed in politics, the function of the rationally planned campaign being to elect a candidate and not to vindicate a system of philosophy. Anzalone, Dooley, and Cameron did not embark on Kevin White's first mayoralty campaign in order to articulate a credo that would accomplish justice for the black man or establish domestic tranquillity. Rather, they adapted his campaign to promise the latter and adumbrate the former because that seemed like the strategy most likely to bring him the most votes in November.

Nevertheless, once that campaign strategy had succeeded,

White remained pretty much true to it. He did not abandon Anzalone in victory, although it might have been better for his long-term ambitions had he found the gentleman a post other than that of chairman of the Board of Tax Assessors, a position of much potential for a fund-raiser. Cameron was content to remain in the D.A.'s office, cherishing a doomed hope that his eternal boss, Garrett Byrne, would retire from the D.A.'s office sometime before Cameron became too advanced in years to seek it for himself (Byrne didn't; he was ultimately beaten, crowding eighty, by another of his own subalterns, Newman Flanagan). Dooley regarded politics as relaxation from the rigors of the private practice of law, where he was beginning to make some money; he didn't want anything official. Consequently, White was able to fashion his administration to reflect not major personal debts he had incurred in winning office but less pedestrian and grander plans for the city as a whole. He began to develop a program of hiring the best and the brightest to operate Boston, promising publicly that their disinterested eagerness to achieve excellence in municipal government would lead to a new dawn of exciting metropolitan living for the drowsy old dowager of the Northeast, one unequaled since the heyday of Pericles. They would not steal, for stealing was beneath them. They would not sacrifice high goals to personal aggrandizement, because they were the sort of people who coveted only perfection in governance. They would make all things new and radiant, and Kevin White would lead them.

It is hard to imagine a likelier time and location for such an enterprise to prosper. Greater Boston is infested with people of relatively high intelligence. Many are born in these parts, grow up attending school here, and remain because they find the company and the surroundings most congenial. Others, born in less hospitable regions, migrate to New England in their high school and college years. Latecomers arrive to secure graduate degrees, and later comers still show up to test educations acquired elsewhere in the scientific and artistic major leagues that Boston fields.

None of them leaves. The stay-at-homes, people who were born here and grew into careers that stress intellect, remain because they are seldom offered any combination of occupation, climate, and collegiality that equals what they have right where they've always lived. Those who arrived late at the fair are not stupid enough to renounce it when they have completed studies or finished their postgraduate training. Within easy reach of New York and Washington, about as close to Europe as it's possible to get without transplanting all your stuff to Newfoundland, close by sailing in the summer and skiing in the winter, regularly freshened by the contributions of those passing through from other cultural centers, New England is about as near to paradise on earth as the most demanding intellectual snob could wish. The manpower for great schemes lives in abundance within half an hour's radius of Boston City Hall.

The defect in that manpower is the converse of its superiority; those who gravitate to Boston and Cambridge do so because their innate intelligence at an early age set them apart. They came or remained here because they were equipped to receive and understand the superior book-learning offered here. They proceeded to those studies without any substantial and direct personal experience of the world in which the waking hours are absorbed by activity the actor does not like and would not do if he were not receiving pay for it and had another source of money. Those who study; those who teach; those who after a great deal of costly study profess law or medicine; those who consult for fees; and those who devote their days to commenting on how other people behave: none of them gains from the preparation for his work or from the doing of it that gnawing and incurable, low-level repugnance for his occupation that comes early (and survives until retirement) to the person who acquires his livelihood by doing something that he would not do for fun.

That is the fundamental distinction of the people who have been fortunate enough both to be born with relatively high intelligence and to have secured by birthright, hard work, or the beneficence of strangers the education required to train that intelligence, so that its exercise acquires monetary value to somebody else. From the age of reason on, these blessed children are surfeited with ego gratifications—praise, financial rewards that reinforce the praise, repeated admonitions that the entire world lies before them for their full enjoyment, if they will only proceed diligently to tasks that they would like to do anyway. Such privileged children, when they have grown large without suffering any personal rebuttal of their own flattering estimates of themselves, encounter and are baffled by cognitive dissonance when they attempt to communicate with people who have not been blessed. Technologists and technocrats of any discipline have trouble dealing with technicians in the same fields. Technologists and technocrats are stimulated and quite frequently extremely well rewarded for what they do; technicians do what they do because they get wages for it, and no matter how emphatically they may protest pride in their workmanship, their set pay is their satisfaction.

There is thus a gulf between those who spend the first half of their lives in study and training and those who terminate their full-time, formal educations at the age of eighteen or before. Anyone who has taught adults on the college level, whether those adults were combat veterans cashing in the chips of federal gratitude or grimly determined working men and women denying themselves relaxation after putting in full working days, knows the difference between those students and their putative equals in learning for whom college followed secondary school in the same unremarkable manner as dinner follows lunch. It is commonly described as one of intensity, viz., "Older students are so much more serious." A compliment is intended, and its subjects strive to accept it as one. The fact, somewhat different, is that the older student who submits to college education does so in much the same rebellious mood as one agreeing to have root canals: he expects it to be an ordeal, and nothing in his subsequent experience suggests he was mistaken, but he undergoes it because he expects he will feel somewhat better afterward. He does not, if he is halfway realistic, expect that he will be as well off as those who finish their educations without ever having done anything else. He does not seek training in intellection in order to practice intellection; he endures the training in order to secure a college degree which will establish to the satisfaction of some personnel officer that he has been trained in intellection. Generally, the person who enters college late in life does so for the same disagreeable reason that he works during the day: to secure, in the long run, more money than he would earn if he didn't.

White, covertly glancing at the model of government by intellectuals invented by Franklin Delano Roosevelt and considerably elaborated by John F. Kennedy, sought to pattern his city administration on it without any evident notice of the dissimilarity of federal and city politics. This was a miscalculation. There is permissive space for experiment in the management of a national administration which does not exist in local management. Presidents have more freedom than mayors do.

The federal government is remote from the overwhelming majority of citizens whom its policies affect. It is geographically removed, which makes it very difficult for the individual to identify the office that is tormenting him, or the individual in that agency who has forgotten all about him and his request. It is organizationally inaccessible: the citizen who has a beef will usually grow weary of his anger long before he manages to find the agency that provoked him, let alone the scoundrel in that agency who did the actual dirty work. It is unresponsive, taking so long to act or react to any stimulus caused by the individual that time elides the connection between all causes and all effects. And because it is huge, complicated, harboring many anonymous misfeasants, malfeasants, and nonfeasants who advance their careers by protecting that anonymity, it provides insulation from reproof to those who infiltrate its lacunae near the top and in those positions of authority commit egregious acts of stupidity, corruption, or arrogance. Jimmy Carter could attempt to conceal an abrasive prima donna such as Joseph W. Califano by putting him in plain sight as secretary of Health and Human Services, and very nearly get away with it. Kevin White, delightedly installing highly qualified Robert DiGrazia of Bethesda, Maryland, as Boston's police commissioner, guaranteed himself and the commissioner years of drumfire criticism from the police force and its friends in the media, dwelling in repetitive detail upon DiGrazia's alleged superciliousness, insensitivity, contempt for the foot patrolmen, and general hatefulness. That chorus of catcalls had its origins in local resentment of an outsider nailing down a job that those in the ranks believed properly their own, and it was exacerbated by DiGrazia's manifest intention to treat black officers with special care, neither of which attitudes would have caused the slightest electoral discomfort if he'd been appointed to preside over the FBI. Heading PD Boston, though, DeGrazia was initially to Kevin White in the swift stream of Boston politics as the baby Jesus was to the apocryphal St. Christopher of the travelers' medals, a very heavy weight to carry (DiGrazia repaid that favor with interest in the 1975 election, though, carrying the mayor through the rapids of corruption charges).

He was not by any means the only one. Taking office in the late 1960s in Boston, with operational jobs in the real world of government to proffer to intellectuals, Kevin White could have luxuriated in a plethora of interested applicants. There were many in the universities and early stages of careers in law in Boston who to their chagrin had missed out on a hitch in JFK's Camelot on the Potomac; they were lustful for this unexpected reprieve from dull lifetimes devoted exclusively to minding their own business, and Kevin did look and sound as much as possible like JFK. There had been a bitter struggle in the middle sixties in the Massachusetts legislature between such liberal idealists and forces allied with Speaker John Forbes Thompson of Ludlow, the man who was the Iron Duke and that decade's horrid incarnation of nonparticipatory democracy; liberal refugees from that war (not yet with the access to state offices that one of their champions, then Representative Michael S. Dukakis, would lay open to them when he won the governor's chair seven short years later) contemplated Kevin White's regime with excited interest. Then Representative Katherine Kane of Beacon Hill was one early recruit from the remnant vanquished to its fury by John Thompson in the House; she became White's deputy mayor, from which post she evolved (or devolved) into his Hostess of the Revels, running Parkman House on Beacon Hill for the succoring of queens and other dignitaries, and the exasperation of parsimonious, publicity-greedy members of his city council.

What White offered to idealistic Harvard Law grads such as Barney Frank, whose later career would include a stint as Beacon Hill's state representative, a post he left to seek successfully the congressional seat vacated by Congressman Robert F. Drinan, S.J., on orders from the pope, was hands-on experience in government. That prospect had a powerful appeal for a bright young fellow from New Jersey grown bored with studying and seeing his thirtieth birthday looming. People smart enough to spend their first quarter centuries on the earth being nurtured intellectually are smart enough to realize that that is all they've done. Those who have ostensibly severed the umbilicus to campus by accepting the positions of associates in large law firms have not thereby acquired much responsibility. There they find themselves answerable to the senior partners, just as they were at the beck of their mentors in law school and in college before that, just as their contemporaries now on tenure tracks in government departments of the universities still are. They have studied much and at a minimum learned how to curry favor with the elder sages of their professions, but because those activities consumed the time that others in their age group, less favored by fortune, had to spend as combat troops or coming up with wages great enough to support families, they commence to suffer nagging feelings of impotent irrelevance.

The myths of our nation, after all, impinge quite as sharply upon those who go to school for a long time as they do upon those who leave it early to learn manual trades. Not without some basis in reality, those myths specify that school is a device for the cursory occupation of small children who are not yet large enough for serious employment taming wildernesses or wild Indians, making frontiers safe for the defenseless. John Wayne played no stirring roles as a man polishing a seminal research work on the voting trends of second-generation Hispanics who live in mixed rental and owner-occupied neighborhoods of medium-sized mid-twentieth-century cities. Humphrey Bogart's film personae did not include that of informal policy adviser to a promising but unsuccessful candidate for the Newton School Committee. Academic and professional novitiates require much depth of intelligence from those enrolled in them, but little scope for their imposition of their wills on other people. Or, to put it another way: a junior partner in a law firm, an associate professor five years or so away from tenure review: each is free to make just as many decisions as he wishes in the course of an ordinary day or week. The trouble is that he cannot make anyone important pay attention to him, and consequently no one does. This grates upon him.

Government affords him what he calls the Chance to Make Decisions that will Make a Difference. This is a euphemism for power. The perception it expresses is accurate. Long before lawyers in private practice can anticipate with any realism the opportunity to exert power as they see fit, lawyers for the government no older than themselves are exercising it each day. Long before new Ph.D.'s have earned noticeable influence in trivial department deliberations, their contemporaries in the government are setting policy. FDR, that traitor to his class, shanghaied his Whiz Kids from the ranks of lawyers freshly minted by the Harvard and Columbia law schools, drew his planners damp behind the ears from the Yale campus, and impliedly reminded those who studied that our government was formed by relatively young men who would not be given charge of heavy litigation in any of today's big law firms. Private enterprise demands great patience. It promises considerable wealth—an inducement of questionable appeal to activists—and some carefully circumscribed power to him who is very patient for a long time and proves tractable during his probation. That is a lot like school. Government, in contrast, seductively dangles the prospect of excitement before him. It tempts with immediate ego gratification, and the possibility as well that after a brilliant career in public service there will still be flattering opportunities in private enterprise. Government is much more fun than private enterprise or scholarship, and history shows that this indulgence need not exclude the possibility of prosperous private employments later. It may even enhance them.

Thus attracted, eager and energetic young professionals usually prefer an interval in government to an uninterrupted lifetime on the campus or an irkesomely pin-striped eternity drafting land use agreements. They mention "challenge" when they talk about politics, "social justice" and fine stuff like that, and their faces glow with the exhilaration of it all.

What they are talking about is other people's money and how they plan to spend it. Jack Richardson, quondam author and inveterate gambler, drew a distinction between real money (which is the stuff one earns by honest work and disburses for shelter, food, and clothing) and Las Vegas money (which looks like the other stuff but is won and lost at the tables without reference to its currency in the world outside of the casinos). People who have never done much of anything except go to school and work for the government proceed about their duties for the government on the basis of the same sort of distinction. They are capable of great and indignant reaction to the personal expenditure of, say, $30,000 for an automobile, correctly deeming that an extravagance and arrogating to themselves the condemnatory power of disapproval. But they are simultaneously comfortable with the appropriation of several public millions each year until Armageddon for the continued support of an agency and its retiring employees, because that expenditure will demonstrate convincingly that they are serious when they sympathize with the plight of the handicapped or whomever the new agency is supposed to help.

This curious inability to perceive the fungibility of money earned and spent by individuals and money collected and spent by governments is the product of experience limited chiefly to school and government. Those who are very bright and very fortunate escape not only the experience of privation but any real inkling of its possibility, until well into their third decades. Their good fortune—as opposed to the bad luck of the equally bright whom beneficence eludes, so that they do not enjoy the higher levels of education and the luxuries that follow, including that of "unselfish" public service—is either an incident of their good judgment in being born into families of comfortable circumstances, or their later individuation from the herd by someone with the power to dispense scholarships, fellowships, and grants-in-aid. There remains on the campus a perceptible difference in wealth between those whose families have it and those who must depend upon the largesse of tax-exempt funds for their support, but in the academic milieu, as in the real world outside it, it is the majority that sets the style and decrees what is acceptable in taste, and the campus majority is dependent upon stipends from outside sources. Wealthy academics therefore tend to moderate their appetites so as to resemble the majority with whom they rub leather-patched elbows at faculty convocations, thus avoiding envious sniping as much as possible. Penury, more fancied than real, is a sort of badge of membership in the academies, ruefully admitted in what is actually a form of bragging that states the speaker is not in thrall to material possessions.

This smugness neatly finesses the security of the subsistences which is the advantage compensating for their modesty. Rookies entering the Greater Boston academic milieu are welcomed by a teeming community of students and faculty quite prepared to inculcate a *modus vivendi*. It is based upon the proposition that no member in good standing shall ever be obliged to discontinue his education and therefore his style of life because he has run out of money. The first premise of all education is that it is bulletproof against adverse economic news. Public primary and secondary educationalists belabor the taxpayers with that principle every time they open their mouths, but their vehemence is as a soft zephyr of the springtime when compared to the sonorous bombast of those at the university level. For the talented young student who assiduously cultivates his elders in the trade, there is no such thing as poverty that will compel him to curtail his education. He may have to take up grading papers, tutoring the woebegone, or performing other sycophantic chores for some established professor, and his menial duties may absorb his time to the point at which his doctorate is delayed. But if he is bright enough, adept at tugging his forelock to his betters, and defers procreative matrimony until he is finished, he will be allowed to finish.

In the late 1960s, when Kevin White became mayor and Ronald Reagan was a subject for well-bred amusement among cultivated easterners, he who finished his graduate education in or near Boston was assured of a reasonably good job. In those days when students and their teachers had the leisure for expression of their views on foreign policy, Ph.D.'s and new attorneys with law review credentials could be choosy about their first salaried positions. In place of that lurking apprehension of first-generation A.B. graduates then approaching middle age as teachers in the Boston public schools and elsewhere, 1960s campus-fresh professionals had the easy assurance that informs the conduct of a man who *knows* he can always make a decent living. It is not so today, but it was so in those days and it tinted quite agreeably and rosily the vision of those who came of age then.

The combined effects of that sense of personal, albeit limited, security and the persuasion of personal worth and intellectual superiority was for those who were beguiled by government a curious innocence. They approached government as an object for the exercise of their critical powers, the criteria for its assessment being derived from the principles of abstract social justice they had learned in school and the distribution of material rewards that they had observed and received during those years of instruction. They perceived at once that life outside of the academy was not as orderly or kind; it was wanting in that reassuring serenity their universities endeavored to maintain in order that those students who were "promising" would be "freed" for their "important" work. They saw that those who were not very bright, not very fortunate, or both stupid and unlucky, were not exonerated from worries about making livings or from service in the military. Many of them in fact appeared to be leading very messy lives. Nasty. Brutish. Short. They worked in disgusting and depressing surroundings, and they had to perform boring, sometimes dirty, even dangerous tasks. They did not go to those tasks each day with any hope of being entertained by them or finishing their day's work with any satisfaction. Notwithstanding all of these disheartening aspects of their working lives, many of them still did not have enough money, and quite a few could not even secure those appalling jobs.

Very bright and blessed young adults brooded about what they saw. They concluded that it ill comported with the results that they would expect from implementation of the principles of social justice they had learned. They deduced the principles must not have been practiced. Proceeding on the assumption that those learned principles could in fact be practiced, and that they would lead to preferable results if they were enforced, the smart and lucky young adults reasoned that the malfunction in the operation of society must be one of personnel. There were economic, class, and racial dislocations in the city because city government had been in the hands of people who were not as smart, or not as just, or not as fortunate or well informed as they would be in management. Therefore, a term of public service was not only something that held out a shining promise of exciting personal fulfillment for themselves but an obligation that they now saw to be enjoined upon them. It was their duty to go forth and "make the system work," make it "responsive" to "human needs," and see to its transformation into a force for the common good.

This sort of attitude accounts for the dratted, indefatigable nanniness of Massachusetts government on every level. It also lies at the root of a good deal of the damnable meddlesomeness of the federal government, which such people have tampered with at every invitation. By its very definition, modern academic liberalism (which may be a tautology; it's possible that modern American liberalism actually exists nowhere but in the academic enclaves) is an interventionist, activist mind-set. Regardless of their actual genders, Massachusetts liberals are an endlessly bustling, clucking, nagging, and fretful bunch who remind the onlookers of nothing so much as a bunch of old biddies whose lack of offspring and demanding husbands has loosed them upon the general population to chivy and to chide.

Some illustrations: The Commonwealth is beset by such laws as the one that abjures us not to discard empty beverage containers by the highways. This redounds to the consequent enrichment of shopkeepers on the other side of the New Hampshire border where no container deposit is levied; the prosperity of collectors of the empties turned in for the deposits and marked for organized disposal in preference to individual dumping; and the additional expense and inconvenience of Bay State consumers. We have an antigun law that penalizes the unlicensed carriage of a handgun with a mandatory sentence of a year in jail without parole; the existence of this draconian and invariable punishment has succeeded in discouraging the rational policeman from bringing charges against unlicensed citizens caught packing sidearms that they have not used to commit any other offenses. Our campaign practice laws are so strict that our junior senator, Paul Tsongas, was embarrassed when his finance committee was found to have broken the law by contributing to the statewide campaigns of candidates whom he admired; that is no longer permitted. Legislation on our books mandates that our commissioner of corporations and taxation suspend the licenses of doctors and lawyers who have not paid all their taxes, thus raising the unaswered and unanswerable question of just how those delinquents are to secure funds to meet their obligations. And, more harmful, our laws include a statute that forbids racial imbalance in school enrollments and has led to much heartache and distress. The Puritans are all dead now, but the Commonwealth they founded to this day venerates their example by the practice of a secular form of their infuriating code and calls it *liberalism.*

It was this rich vein of limitless potential for annoyance that Mayor Kevin White, bemused by his first victory, began to tap, to the enthusiastic approval of the media and to the silent dismay of many residents of his city. He looked like an enlightened pragmatist positioning himself for a future gaudy with accomplishment. He was setting himself up for trouble.

Public schools 'tis public folly feeds.

—William Cowper
"Tirocinium"

8

KEVIN WHITE'S NEW FRIENDS were fickle, but it would be a while before he realized it. One old stalwart (Anzalone) had been mentioned in bad company on the telephone some years before; the full implications of his indiscretions would not come home to the mayor until 1983. White himself miscalculated gravely during his first term in office; he would run thereafter with a limp for reelections, but he still would win. For the moment as he first took office, winner in a contest that had set a record turnout of 66.2 percent of those registered to vote, he was exhilarated.

It was this exhilaration that caused him to break his word. He had renounced all statewide ambitions, under pressure from the Hicks camp, in the closing days of the first campaign for mayor. Once in place in City Hall, he looked at things differently. He became apprehensive that failure to run for governor in 1970 might very well amount to permanent disavowal of ambitions for the office. Lamely and legalistically he therefore essayed the argument that if he ran for governor in 1970, and won, he would depart from City Hall with but a year remaining on his term as mayor, and that ought to be good enough for those who had elected him to serve a full four years. This did not go down very well with anyone outside his inner circle, nor did it please several who were nestled safely inside, either. He had plighted some sort of a solemn troth with Boston voters when the Hicks camp inspired their suspicions. He had not included in that undertaking any weasel words that he could point to three years later as excusing him from doing what he had said he would do, in the event that some unforeseen events occurred. He had not planned on Lyndon Johnson stepping down from office. He had not anticipated that LBJ's successor would be Richard Nixon. He had not allowed for the possibility that John A. Volpe, who had vanquished Edward J. McCormack, Jr. back in 1966, would decamp from the corner office in the State House to go to Washington. Things had happened faster than Kevin White had planned. He saw no alternative to breaking his word.

He had cognizable reasons for that ugly decision. The state party organization had awarded its convention's gubernatorial nomination to Massachusetts State Senate President Maurice A. Donahue of Holyoke, a charming and intelligent politician of considerable warmth and impeccable integrity. He would begin with the handicap of being little known among the mass of voters concentrated in the eastern half of Massachusetts, and he would confront the curse as well of being a "State House Politician." To counterweight those burdens, he enjoyed that formal Democratic party convention blessing, which in Massachusetts claims the rebuttable allegiance of a comfortable majority of voters, and the opposition of an incumbent who had inherited—not won—the office he held. Francis W. Sargent was officially lieutenant governor of Massachusetts when the time came to elect a governor in 1970. He was acting governor in Volpe's place, Volpe having ceded it to accept Richard Nixon's nomination as secretary of transportation back in 1969. Donahue when nominated early in the summer of the next year (where White vainly tried to engineer conscription of himself) therefore had something of an uphill battle before him, but the incline wasn't all that steep. If he managed to present himself across the Commonwealth as he had in what he preferred to call "the Golden West," he might very well acquire the loyalty of regular party members and then build upon it to attract the independents who deliver landslides in the state.

That notion was anathema to White. If Donahue engineered a Democratic recapture of the governor's office in that 1970 campaign, he would supplant Kevin White as the leader of the party in the Commonwealth. He would be the broker of the Massachusetts backing to be bartered at the 1972 Democratic National Convention. He would be in the position to oppose Senator Edward W. Brooke's Republican campaign for a second term as U.S. senator. The broad influence that White had secured as the strongest of Democrats in the 1966 statewide rout would be wrenched out of his grasp. His prospects for regaining it would be speculative at best. Reasoning that he would not be stronger if he served out his full term in city hall, apprehensive that continuing racial conflict might very well leave him much weaker, White therefore calculated that he had better break his word. He would challenge Donahue in the Democratic primary for the gubernatorial nomination if he didn't get it in the state convention.

He got creamed, although the dimensions of the disaster at the time were not fully apparent. He outpolled Donahue statewide but lost his own city to the comparative unknown by 700 votes. In the final selection in the fall of 1970, Sargent, the ingratiating Republican whose only previous campaign experience had been as the running mate of John A. Volpe, beat Boston's mayor in his own Democratic city by 16,700 votes, noticeably more than the 12,429 margin White had been vouchsafed by that same city when he won election as its mayor three years before. There were angry partisans in that plurality, and they would not be contented with that one rebuke of him. He had broken party discipline when he took on Maurice Donahue, and he would be reminded of that when he made feints later on for the party's anointings.

White would also be haunted by the organizational fall-
out of that desperate move. His armor of righteousness had
been dented irreparably in the estimation of the idealistic
who had been drawn to him as the oracle of principle. His
scheduling secretary, Barney Frank, had decamped to study
Congress in the office of Congressman Michael Harrington of
Massachusetts, oftimes vocal critic of the war in Vietnam.
Frank's public choice for governor in 1970 was Frank
Sargent. And White's fund-raising activities either did or did
not include an expensive breakfast at the Ritz Carlton in
April, at which Theodore Anzalone either did or did not—
Anzalone denies he did—brace some ten or fifteen real estate
developers for campaign contributions amounting to either
$1,000 or $10,000 each. The mayor had created irritating
problems which arose when the time arrived to run again for
city hall just one short year later.

On the surface, the chief obstacle appeared to be the same
one that had made the first campaign so spirited: race, and
what the city ought to do about it. Not much progress appeared in that area, after more than three years of White's
intermittent attentions. Ben Greenspan, fifty-four, made no
effort to conceal his sorrow in commenting to the *Globe* on
the removal of the congregation of Chevra Shas Synagogue
from Ashton Street, in Dorchester, to Newton Centre after
forty-three years in the city: "It used to be a nice neighborhood," he said, "a Jewish neighborhood. It is now a changing
neighborhood, with black people moving in and white people
moving out. The old people remain and are terrorized by
young persons roaming the streets. The victims are black and
white, and they are scared." (*Globe*, 9/1/77, pp. 1–3)
Through the spring and summer White professed an inability
to set the tax rate for the coming year, saying he could not
make his announcement until the Massachusetts Board of
Education made a final ruling on some $21.3 million in state
aid for new school construction, embargoed until the school

committee submitted acceptable plans for the redress of racial imbalances as mandated by state law. Obviously any hopes of swift improvements that White had prompted or permitted to be entertained by his first campaign had been disappointed.

Paradoxically, the fact helped him considerably. In 1967, the *Globe* had been brusque with brave words on the nexus of the racial problem in the city. Endorsing White editorially, it had said:

Everyone is for neighborhood schools—but better neighborhood schools. No one is for busing a child against the will of his parents. That is the law in this state. And that is White's position. Under the imbalance law, busing is offered only for those who wish it. (*Globe*, 11/6/67, p. 16)

Four years later, the *Globe* reacted angrily to Nixon administration retreats from busing as a policy. Noting that parents in Pontiac, Michigan, had burned buses employed in similar desegregation programs while Chinese parents in San Francisco were attacking busing orders in court, the *Globe* spat some of the meal out of its mouth and called for sterner measures. "The furor revolves around busing. Yet few stop to think that 40 percent of all school children in this country are bused every day to regional schools, to parochial school or to private schools. This proves what has been often said, that it's what's at the end of the bus ride that counts." (*Globe*, 9/2/71, p. 22)

It also proved, of course, that taxpayers who agree to furnish public education on a regional basis, parents who elect to send their children to parochial schools, and parents who enroll their children in private schools do not resist having their children transported in deference to their own decisions. This is not the same thing at all as having one's child bused in obedience to a judge's order or conformity to some editor's view of the proper arrangement of society; it was intellectually fraudulent for the *Globe* to suggest that it was or ought to be.

Little Rock, the *Globe* reminded, was peaceful while the buses were being ignited up in Michigan, and so was Birmingham. Smiting Nixon and his spokesmen for their public disapproval of busing—HEW Secretary Elliot L. Richardson, who'd been steadfast against racial imbalances when he was Massachusetts attorney general and lieutenant governor before that, was branded a "turncoat." The *Globe*, unmindful of its placating words of 1967, railed against those who disagreed with its editors.

"The thing that makes the whole performance so shabby is that it comes at a point when school desegregation (almost inevitably involving busing) is beginning to work in those areas where it has been tried out the longest. It comes as cities like Boston at last move forward in this basic area of equal opportunity and equal hope for children who, unlike their parents, do not judge others by the color of their skin." In the *Globe*'s view, desegregation of the schools was the issue of paramount social importance then before it. "And," said the paper, which had assured all who read it only four years before that busing was no part of the controversy, "if it takes busing to get there, so be it." (*Globe*, 9/2/71, p. 22)

This was the *Globe*'s second clarion in aid of the principle of equality in the heat of a Kevin White mayoral campaign. Its executives then grew immediately weary of the allegation that the board of editors who sounded that ultimatum did not include a single parent whose child was enrolled in the Boston public schools. They remain today impatient when the charge is leveled that the people who caused the *Boston Globe* to demand school desegregation at all costs had no personal or parental stake in what they advocated and would not in themselves or in their children have to pay those costs. They argue that what's right is right, what's wrong is wrong, and no personal investment is required to state the difference. The fact remains that the editors who caused the *Globe* to call for busing had no children of their own who were hostage to that principle. Their virtue was unimpeachable, but it was very easy virtue. It was also, perhaps therefore, somewhat hasty. The pronouncement, and the manifest attitude it enunciated, left neither the *Globe* nor those who generally agreed with it much real choice in the 1971 mayoral election. White was opposed once more by Mrs. Hicks, who'd succeeded former Speaker John W. McCormack of South Boston in Congress at his retirement after the 1970 elections. Also running were three city councillors: Thomas Atkins, a black lawyer active in the civil rights movement; John Saltonstall, a Beacon Hill attorney from the famous family; and Joseph F. Timilty, of whom much more would be later heard. Also running was a social worker named John E. Powers, Jr., who at twenty-seven was engaged in ascertaining whether the combined effect of his Socialist Worker party platform and the similarity of his name to a former state senate president's would beguile sufficient voters to win him an election (it did not).

Saltonstall was suspected of being a Republican. Atkins, who was not helped by being black, was a carpetbagger from Indiana, where he'd earned a bachelor's degree and a Phi Beta Kappa key at the university. He had two degrees from Harvard—a master of arts and a law degree—and a firm conviction that the school committee's hapless responses to the segregation problem would never work out because they did not take into account the continuing growth of the city's black population. He was right, of course, but that did not mean he would win, and there was too much at risk for idle flocking to his banner. Given the demonstrated numbers Mrs. Hicks had rallied back in 1967, the persistence of the problem that had inspired their loyalties, and the preeminence of racial justice as a political issue, the contest had to be taken by the liberals as a rerun of the 1967 battle between White and

Mrs. Hicks. From that point of view, Timilty's sole point of relevance was his effect on her.

If her vote were diminished by the appeal of Timilty—he would gather more than 28,000 primary votes to finish third behind White, at close to 47,000, and the lady at some 42,000—that would be all to the good, but White had to have as firm support as possible if justice was to prevail in the city.

This difficulty complicated matters badly in the preprimary campaign. It required many who might have liked to sever their ties to White to stay with him nonetheless. What they had to do was wink at what appeared to be evident corruption. Teddy Anzalone had not been circumspect when he chose acquaintances, and he was still very close to Kevin White.

This suspicion of Anzalone was one of an enormous number generated by the forbidden fruits of FBI inquisitiveness back in 1962. Guessing—wrongly, as it turned out—that the Supreme Court of the United States would approve retroactively electronic surveillances mounted without benefit of the judiciary, agents without warrants bugged the Atwells Avenue offices of Raymond L. S. Patriarca on Federal Hill in Providence, Rhode Island. Patriarca since the end of World War II had been law-abiding society's nominee by acclamation as the leader of the Mafia north of the Connecticut border. His name had been on the lips of every self-respecting fink who had turned up to act contrite and offer public confession of his depredations. Each day from March 2, 1962, to July 12, 1965, FBI men picked up what had been recorded in the Patriarca office during the previous twenty-four hours and shipped it up to Boston for transciption, violating the law just as frequently as they did so.

Early in 1971, Louis "the Fox" Taglianetti, one of Patriarca's subordinates, was convicted in Rhode Island Federal Court of tax evasion. By then the FBI's illicit snooping was a matter of public knowledge, and the Department of Justice, wishing to knock down an issue on appeal, declared that its tax evasion case had not been derived in any part from the FBI surveillance of the Patriarca office. To support this claim, the Justice Department filed with the Rhode Island Federal Court copies of the transcriptions made from the surveillance. The trial court agreed with the Justice Department and impounded the transcripts, so as to prevent their public divulgence and resultant infamy for those whose names were in them.

Louis Fox filed his appeal. In one of those curious developments that occasionally make public stuff that's supposed to be secret, the trial record, with the bugging transcripts, was sent up to Boston and the office of the clerk for the United States Court of Appeals for the First Circuit. There, oddly enough, transcripts that had been secret down in the Providence trial court were open to public access and inspection. And in a further coincidence, Richard Connolly of the *Globe* learned that the documents were open. He obtained permission to sit at a desk in the clerk's office and returned to it carrying a portable typewriter. There he sat for the next eleven days, copying down what he found most intriguing in the transcripts of those illegal wiretaps. That summer the *Globe* published stories he wrote from those transcripts, which by then had been sealed up again.

Those reports were bowdlerized. The *Globe* withheld from publication in August the name of the "mystery man" in Boston politics who had made efforts in the Mob's behalf to cause justice to miscarry in the Boston Municipal Court in Dorchester and who had raised money for political purposes while a public servant. Fortunately for the public's right to know, *Boston After Dark*, a weekly underground newspaper now subsumed into the *Boston Phoenix*, was nothing loath to speculate that it was Anzalone. This enabled mayoral candidates Saltonstall, Atkins, and Timilty to employ their seats in city council to demand investigations of Mayor White's tax assessor and to utter statements pregnant with allusion to the Mafia. (*Globe*, 9/1/71, p. 15) It in turn required *Globe* reporter Connolly to prepare a report on how he had secured the story that had inspired the whole discussion. (*Globe*, 9/2/71, p. 22)

And that, for the time being, looked like the end of it. Louis Fox, *pendente lite*, had had himself and his appeal shotgunned into mootness by a person or persons unknown. Dead men do not appeal. That precluded any possibility of further litigation, which might have left those tantalizing transcripts lying around open again in some hospitable clerk's office. Councillor Saltonstall managed to produce evidence that Anzalone had served as a director early in the operations of Commercial Producers, Inc., a firm taken over two months after it was founded by Gennaro Anguilo, long confidently agreed to be Patriarca's Boston manager (and indicted for racketeering and conspiracy to commit murder in 1983, on the basis of warranted electronic surveillance of his office in Boston's North End), but that did not seem to catch anybody's fancy. White said he doubted "very much of the public thinks I'm intimately involved with the Mafia, or involved at all," and toughed it out with Anzalone by the mild observation that he had done nothing wrong as the assessor. (*Globe*, 9/8/71, p. 10) Public attention, at most temporarily diverted from the racial issue, was speedily invited back to it.

On September 15, primary election day, the city spent about $100,000 to collect the votes of 140,244 citizens, 50.3 percent of those registered to participate in such decision making. White boasted 4,000 or so volunteers, among them John Martilla, his campaign manager, and a good many other comparatively fresh newcomers first drawn to politics by the 1970 antiwar congressional campaign of Robert F. Drinan, S.J. His bag of 46,926, just about one-third of those who voted, was further evidence that he was the preferred candidate of a minority of Boston voters—Hicks and Timilty together garnered half of the vote, and Atkins drew 16,886 who apparently did not fully accept White as the candidate likely to do most for black residents of Boston. And once again, Wards 16 through 20—Hyde Park, Roslindale, Jamaica Plain, and West Roxbury—let him have it: he received 15,728 ballots in those wards, about 31 percent of the total of 50,841 shared by him, Mrs. Hicks, and Timilty.

This made it all the more surprising, six weeks later, when White buried Mrs. Hicks in the general election. Sixty-two percent of the 183,345 who ventured out in the cold rain to vote marked their ballots for him. Wards 6 and 7, South Boston, which, the first time, had sent their favorite daughter out of her home territory with a handsome bulge of 11,335 against 4,489, on second thought provided her with but a 2,492 plurality: 9,013 to 6,521. In Wards 16 through 20 White won 51.5 percent of the 69,793 votes cast. The results as a whole so dispirited the lady that she told her followers that night: "Really and truly it seems to me tonight that all the middle class people have gone to the suburbs. So I think I'll have to go find them there." (*Globe*, 11/3/71, p. 1)

She could have been forgiven that interpretation of the evidence. Running in her eighth contest in eleven years, Mrs. Hicks with 70,226 votes had come up shy almost 20,000 of her 1967 total. White had managed to add but 10,600 to his first mayoral tally of 102,551. In 1967, 278,562 had been registered to vote; 280,779 had qualified by 1971. In the first matchup, 192,673 had appeared to declare their choices; 9,328 fewer came in four years later. Twenty-three-hundred-odd voters had disappeared from Wards 16 through 20; she might have been pardoned for believing them to have been hers.

More likely, though, is the possibility that incumbency was the leading factor in White's improved showing. His campaign directors guessed that at least one-quarter of his 4,000 "volunteers" were on the city payroll. Confronting a single-issue candidate, given a safe-conduct pass from stern attack on the crime issue, occupying the field of available candidates as the most determined moderate on racial issues, he had achieved at the very most a lackluster result. Given the resentment that still lingered after his change of mind on seeking statewide office just one year before, any victory at all was quite acceptable, of course, but this one was scarcely cause for jubilation. What it indicated was that Kevin White could be the mayor for as many terms as he could preserve the uneasy liberal coalition that had been arranged in large part for him by the *Boston Globe*. That meant he would have to make good on his promises to heal the riven city, and that he could not afford to make the liberals feel embarrassment. His continued prosperity depended on that precarious alliance.

As for Doing-good, that is one of the professions which are full. Moreover, I have tried it fairly, and, strange as it may seem, am satisfied that it does not agree with my constitution.

—Henry David Thoreau

9

POLITICS is a variable-sum game, just like the sports from which it draws so many of its metaphors. The winner is the candidate with the most votes; he does not care whether that is 6 of 10, 51 of 100, 501 of 1,000, or 101,000 of 200,000, not if he is shrewd. When he campaigns, it is in his interest to conduct an offense that will galvanize the people who like him better than the other guy to go to the polls and vote. It is also in his interest to avoid inflaming those who dislike him, or merely like the other fellow better, lest they, too, decide to make the effort to mark ballots; that is the defensive aspect of smart politics.

Kevin White excelled in defense. His whole career in politics was bottomed on selection of elective offices that, at the time he sought them, were not strenuously coveted by charismatic politicians. His mountainous pluralities as secretary of state represented the automatic endorsements of habitual Democrats who had visited the polling places for other reasons: to express their preferences for president, U.S. Senate, governor, and attorney general. They voted for White while they were in the building. From those outings he derived nominal recognition, but that accidental recognition of his, when greatly augmented by the effects of incipient racial conflicts and budgetary woes, made his first mayoral candidacy into a greater bolus than his predecessor, John F. Collins, felt confident of swallowing. White's initial motive for eyeing city hall was to get more of the same sort of stuff, and he was unexceptionably candid: he thought he saw in Collins a sitting duck, in a chair from which he might command gratifying attention. By announcing early, White intended to give the incumbent something intimidating to consider in his idle hours as the mayor of the city that had resoundingly rejected his application for promotion to the U.S. Senate, and to freeze at the same time potential contributors disinclined to cast their bounty toward a losing cause. In that purpose he was reasonably successful, and he emerged from the summer of racial unrest into the real primary campaign—which started after Labor Day—needing to beat only an outlander, Edward Logue, in order to square off against the lady bigot in November. Feelings, fears, and baser yearnings played a large part in that contest, without much prompting from him. His task was pretty much to stand there and act reasonable, hoping more voters admired reason than believed in Mrs. Hicks's ability to make things as they were before.

When he ran for reelection in 1971, she was kind enough to take part once again, thus unavoidably creating for the voters a strong sense of *déjà vu* and demanding of them at the same time a considerable leap of faith, that she who had been unable to prevent him from seizing the mayor's office in their first outing somehow now stood a real chance of dislodging him as an incumbent from it. She made perfunctory efforts to suggest that she had changed, retreating from her much scorned proposal to impose a city payroll tax and asserting that the cure for its chronic financial difficulties was to operate it "just like a well-run household." (*Globe*, 9/12/71, p. A5) She said the "Little City Halls," where White had installed a substantial number of those volunteers then canvassing the city for him, cost too much. She was also against

Summerthing, the mayor's program of concerts and other entertainments on the Boston Common. Her platform remained nonetheless based chiefly on her disapproval of the racial imbalance law and the Massachusetts Board of Education interference in the operation of the schools which she perceived, along with taxes, as the cause of Boston's population decline. (*Globe*, 9/12/71, p. 5) She had added some new lyrics, but the melody remained the same. It did not imbue her followers with that same old fighting spirit.

What it did do was revalidate White's occupation of the field of moderates aspring to be mayor and solidify his hold upon the office. Mrs. Hicks exaggerated the drain upon her legions that resulted from the decline in the city's population, doubtlessly, but she did not manufacture it. Those who left Boston for the suburbs did include a disproprotionate number of that middle-class sector of society from which she had recruited many of her followers and on which she had to depend for fresh troops. By winning the first time, White had acquired for himself the same sort of payroll leverage upon hard-core Boston politicians that her school committee job had given her the first time out. The difference of course was that his breadth of influence was far greater than the one she had enjoyed, because it extended into all city departments. When they faced off for the second time, therefore, he had at least as firm a grip on partonage as she had had the first time, and she had relinquished hers to run for Congress. When she lost the second time, he obtained four more years to expand that mercenary army, dealing bread out in that fashion while continuing to stage circuses with Summerthing.

This passive approach to the constituent service aspects of the office proved entirely satisfactory from the politician's point of view, because the racial situation remained utterly intractable. So close to explosion when he ran for mayor the first time, it remained frighteningly volatile all through his second term, to his great benefit. So long as he did not succeed in cooling off that controversy permanently, as of course no human being could have, he remained in a position to declare that he had stopped it from exploding into anarchy. *And no one could argue with him,* because no one could be certain whether in fact his fine hand upon the levers of the city government was not the major reason why the fragile peace had been maintained.

Thus tacitly accepting credit for a negative event, no major racial riots, for which all sane citizens of Boston were profoundly grateful, White was for most other purposes exonerated from all obligations to arrange for desired progress. He was free to select those activities and areas of concentration for his regime that he found most agreeable. He chose downtown rejuvenation as his principal concern, thus availing himself of the results of undertakings by Mayors Hynes and Collins before him and aligning himself simultaneously with those parties of influence who had the most to offer Boston and asked the least from it in return.

Private entrepreneurs with the means to propose and execute vast realty improvements suffer from a painful public disability, which cripples many of their halting efforts to gain social approval. They always have a lot of money, and they know where to get more. Worse, they act like they have lots of money, dressing well and being chauffeured, never risking malnutrition, often showing up with tans when snow is on the ground in Massachusetts. Their faces are not familiar to those gathering for breakfast—two eggs and three pancakes, $1.35—at the truck stop on the corner of A Street and Broadway in South Boston every morning, and their witticisms are not quoted with great fondness in the corridors of City Hall or down at PD headquarters. Many of them do not even live in Boston and most have not used the trolley cars in years. They are not the kind of good guys known to all of the reporters, certified as "all right" down in Cleary Square. They are viewed with deep suspicion. Its true name is envy.

Boston is to envy as Chicago is to wind. They have it in
other cities, but it's meager stuff, somehow. In Boston, which
is large enough to attract and sustain a reasonable number of
highly competitive and driven people but still small enough so
that each of them can know all of the others' business, envy is
robust and vigorous. Her displaced Brahmin families produce
pinched men and parched women who avoid invading principal by making do with mended garments; they demean
swamp Yankees' success over their codfish cakes and beans.
Her Irish churn out florid two-bit lawyers who buy polyester
pants and Korean tweed sports coats from discount merchants who'll accept third-party checks; they ostentatiously
stand rounds of Lite Beer down at Amrhein's in the twilight
and disparage colleagues elevated to the bench. The Italians
in the North End feature ivory-plastic loafers with fake gold-
plated hardware and black suits with shawl lapels; they
hunch over their cannolis and low-rate their gumbahs' burgeoning construction businesses. Jews wrapped in towels take
some steam down at the Boston Harbor Health Club, sneering over cigars at the pledges to plant trees in Israel. Blacks
who parlayed athletic skills into college educations make sure
that their topcoats are correctly draped as they depart from
cutting up their more feckless brothers at the Professional and
Businessmen's Club in the South End. Bostonians of Oriental
ancestry keep their views to themselves and do not share them
interethnically with all the rest of us at the State House, in
City Hall, at Suffolk Superior, and in the federal buildings,
but most likely they are letting the air out of each other's tires
in the same way, carping, caviling, snidely remarking upon
every minor happiness that befalls anybody else. In Boston,
no good fortune is official until somebody has urinated on it.

That is why those who have money and any choice at all
of how to spend it around Boston cherish so their privacy. But
that option of great prudence is denied developers. Like it or
not, they must begin all their projects by first ascertaining

whether there exists some governmental obstacle to doing as they plan. Zoning people, planning boards, those who defend the historic districts, traffic gurus, sewer mavens, folks with other plans: all must be given notice of what rich men have in mind to tear down, build up, or restore in downtown Boston. This means that the rich investor, having it in mind to become richer, must shamelessly expose himself in all his wealth as though he had been courting arrest and brace himself for the sure and certain assault that will follow.

Publicly that counterattack is not presented candidly. The conventions stipulate that some reason other than furious jealousy be offered for challenging what the builder has in mind. This of course is no insurmountable obstacle. His proposed structure will certainly diminish someone's view of Boston Harbor, obscure the consoling sight of the golden dome on the State House, impede someone's access to the Public Garden's flowers, or stir up greater gusts of wind on the financial district sidewalks. If his building will appeal to law firms and corporations seeking office space, as virtually all such buildings are designed to do, rabble-rousers may protest that it will create few jobs for the sullen illiterates whom they purport to represent. Then, too, there's the fact that few such high-rise buildings offer low-cost housing for the elderly and recipients of Aid to Families with Dependent Children; proponents can be abused for that as well. Increased traffic congestion, difficulty in providing fire protection, greater need for police service during evening hours: there's a litany of objections that can be lodged and strenuously advocated, every one of which all by itself would surely justify rejection of the project that's proposed.

To defeat this sort of reaction, the rich person seeking to become still richer by erecting a new building in the city requires a loyal ally in its government, someone who can prevent the potentially rebellious bureaucrat from stymieing his plans. There is no one in the city better suited to such duty than its mayor.

Between 1973 and 1983, Boston acquired fourteen new office buildings. When White first took office, the sixty-story John Hancock Tower in Copley Square was a model on a table in the offices of I. M. Pei and a hole in the ground right across St. James Street from Trinity Episcopal Church. Government Center was in preliminary construction stages, as was the Center Plaza complex just across the street. One Hundred Federal Street, the headquarters of the First National Bank of Boston—now the Bank of Boston—did not exist. Neither did One Federal Street, home of the Shawmut Bank, N.A., 28 State Street, put up by New England Merchants National Bank—now Bank of New England—or 60 State Street right next door. One Boston Place, diagonally across the intersection of State and Washington, was at most a dim dream. One Beacon Street, home of the Employers Union Mutual Insurance Companies, had not become the neighbor of the Parker House Hotel. The block facing the Public Garden on its southerly side, across Boylston Street, was a seedy collection of old two- and three-story buildings which housed Jonny Walker's store for cowboy garb and a Hayes Bickford Cafeteria where the grease was thicker than tradition; when Kevin White prepared to leave the mayor's office, it was an enormous hole being readied for a scaled-down hotel complex finally approved after bitter wrangling over a far more ambitious Park Place project. Nearing completion was the massive State Transportation Building, a brick edifice that was by consensus deemed unneeded by the time it was too late to stop it; it replaced a large chunk of the old "Combat Zone," virtually all that remained of the red-light district after the New England Medical Center complex had displaced the rest of it around the intersection of Tremont and Stuart streets. The deserted Hotel Manger next to the Boston Garden in the West End had been demolished to make way for a new federal building to be named after House Speaker Thomas P. "Tip" O'Neill, but only after the New England head of the General Services Administration had resigned from the post to which Ronald Reagan had appointed him, saying that the new construction wasn't necessary. The Quincy Market–Faneuil Hall project, in its embryonic stages when White took the stage, was alleged to be drawing more visitors each day than Disney World in Florida, and the old stone warehouses and wharf buildings around its perimeter had been gutted and rebuilt to furnish sophisticated urban dwellings for the readily convinced. Next to the expanded Boston Public Library the massive new Westin Hotel dwarfed the nearby and almost as new Hilton Hotel; down on the waterfront loomed the Marriott brick barge hotel constructed by White's good friend developer Mortimer Zuckerman. The site across the street from Durgin Park at the old open-air market had been razed of Giro's Colisseum Restaurant, where the wise guys from the Mob had been accustomed to hang out, and refilled with the Hotel Bostonian. The old Federal Reserve Building in Post Office Square had been partially demolished and made over into the Hotel Meridien, and the Fed was newly ensconced in a striking silver building rising up next to the old South Station, which was next in line for destruction. One survey for the Boston Traffic and Parking Department done in 1983 put the daily number of people coming into Boston between 6:30 and 9:30 A.M. at 459,000, more than half of them by private cars for which parking places were extremely hard to find.

The effect of all this on the city's economy is impossible to calculate with anything resembling precision. Customary guesses put the value of the permanent improvements in the billions. Recurring benefits—wages paid to workers toiling in those structures, taxes levied on them and the real estate, monies paid out to the subsidiary businesses that prosper serving those who are employed in the tall buildings—come to billions more. What can be said with perfect confidence is that Mayor Kevin White presided over a breathtaking reclamation of an urban downtown area unparalleled by any city not first laid waste by modern war. He did not initiate it, as he has at times implied. He did not finance it, as he sometimes seemed to claim. What he did do was expedite it fiercely, midwifing the changes through the Byzantine bureaucracies, more than willing to cajole if that would do the job but quite willing to threaten—and to carry out his threats—when that seemed to become necessary.

The trend fed upon itself. As it became plain that he was really determined to see to the success of projects, more financiers and developers appeared with more new projects. Seeing what was being done, they proposed to do still more. He became exhilarated. He developed a proprietary attitude about the rebirth of what he thought had become, really, his city. Greeting queens—those of The Netherlands and also of England—as the host of this refurbished center, urging casual acquaintances to cast their eyes on what he'd done, he betrayed genuine excitement, the sort of exuberance that reminded the observer of an adolescent youth reveling in the sheer joy of the discovery of what his powers are. When he escorted you through Boston's downtown streets, he had all that he could do to forebear from seizing your lapels to make sure that you saw what he had done and how magnificent it was. He was like that with almost anyone who'd listen.

It was a terrible mistake. The first impulse of the true Bostonian is to suspect that he is being had. The Red Sox are not going to win the World Series, no matter how ferociously a Carl Yastrzemski may invite the contrary assumption. Nothing is ever as good as it's represented. If somebody tells you that he's making all things new, he is giving you the swerve and he is up to something. If this country ever does elect an Irish Catholic to be its president, some son of a bitch will shoot him. If the mayor of Boston claims that downtown is being transformed under his personal supervision, and the consequences will be wonderful, then he's either on the take or he's attempting to distract us from some other wretchedness. If, when God created Eden, He had wanted to ensure man would retain his tenancy, He had only to select the occupants from Boston. The female would have gone out looking for the serpent, found it, and gone screaming back to her mate to complain that it was all a fake, as she'd known all along, because she had found a damned snake in the bushes. And, when he protested that he had not put it there, they would have begun quarreling, never getting to the apple. They would still be at it now, seldom speaking to each other, living apart, mulling divorce, miserable in Paradise.

The reporters and commentators who collect and transmit information to the citizens of Boston harbor the community's envious mistrust of any event or development that at first blush seems to warrant satisfaction, except that theirs is more pronounced. They cultivate it and secure their livings from its continued practice. We—I speak as an admitted practitioner—reserve our professional respect for those among our number who most regularly excel at pranging the presumptuous. For our purposes, the *presumptuous* are those who have attracted our attention by seeking elective office or otherwise behaving so as to suggest that they may think themselves superior to the run of common men. In Boston there is no such thing as pardonable pride. We call it *arrogance* when we encounter it, and that's what we called Kevin White: arrogant.

The accepted—and complacent—rationale for this behavior is that Boston's gaudy history of corrupt mendacity is as much cause for reproach of the newsmen who covered it as for the politicians who committed it. The legendary Curley days, starting with his first election as the mayor in 1914 and continuing until he left the office for the last time thirty-three years later, featured an extremely relaxed journalistic attitude toward political hijinks. *Boston Post* reporters are believed to have participated very actively in the formulation of political debates, colleagues at adjoining desks hiring themselves out as speechwriters to opposing candidates, drafting inflammatory remarks never uttered by their respective clients, swapping the texts back and forth for convenient transformation into wrathful headlines, and spending the remainder of their working hours drinking. Nothing reprehensible was seen in taking pay from an aspirant whom one had been assigned to cover for his nominal employer, and no one was much surprised when the news coverage of a known rogue rather flattered him. For many years, the oral tradition has it, the accepted fee for a reporter's ethics was a new suit of clothes, and the low pay of the trade more than justified the merchandising.

Chary of equation with those buccaneers of old, today's scribblers vie for opportunities to prove by their hard-hitting columns that they are not on the take. So great is their zeal to elude allegations that they have been prostituted in the complete absence of any compromising offers, they upbraid their subjects for extending meaningless civilities. Your prudent politician, running or elected, may without published rebuke furnish coffee and sweet rolls as hospitality for the media representatives invited to his morning press conference. If he proposes to speak later in the day, though, he had better make extremely sure no lobster salad and chilled table wines are offered to the press, because someone in the nourished number will publicly harpoon him for the lavish excess, profligate of public funds or demonstrative of luxurious and therefore suspect campaign funding. What began as a policy of forbidding reporters to accept tempting trips, scarce tickets to the ball games, or gout-inducing spreads, as a measure to preserve their critical independence, has degenerated now unto a point approaching silliness. So great is the scrupulosity of current standards that one is obliged to conclude that reporters are indeed larcenous types, open to subornation of their virtue by the meanest of gratuities.

Kevin White offended against that sensitivity as well. He blundered by welcoming reporters and columnists in Parkman House, the gracious house on Beacon Hill given to the city for whatever use might be devised for it, refurbished and redecorated by the White administration as a charming alternative to receiving dignitaries in the modern-brutal atmosphere of City Hall. French furniture and oriental rugs went to an ambiance indoors that in fine weather opened onto a small garden terrace, and the White administration retained polished caterers to serve the food and wines. It was the work of mere moments to compare such gentility to the rundown accommodations in dangerous surroundings that the city grudgingly afforded to tenants of public housing. It did not take rare wit to perceive that the menus at the Parkman House were somewhat superior to those that were feasible for recipients of public assistance checks. And when White informed the city council that it would be nice to have at his disposal a limousine which the Lincoln-Mercury Division of the Ford Motor Compay would provide cheaply so as to display its flagship carting monarchs around Boston, he was cudgeled for it mercilessly.

The consequence of this kind of behavior was that well before the midpoint of his second term in office, somewhere during 1972, Kevin White had managed to issue a most frustrating challenge to the Boston media. He had, chiefly by the grace of God and the adroit management of such good luck as came his way, achieved the prime objective for which he had been preferred, almost by default, in 1967: there had still not been any lacerating racial riots. He could not be faulted on that score. He had made a prodigious success of downtown urban renewal, and that promised heartening improvements in the city's finances. He had not yet incurred any large debits to his credibility, and he was obviously very pleased with himself. Plainly it was necessary to find something wrong with him and his administration, else its history would turn out to be one long paean to his reign. That could not be tolerated.

The further men are from the ultimate point
of importance the readier they will be [to] con-
cur in a change. . . .

—Alexander Hamilton
Notes taken June 1, 1787, at the
Federal Convention

10

THE PERCEIVED NEED for corrective measures to take Kevin
White down a few pegs had acquired more urgency in 1972.
George McGovern in Miami, learning that infallibility does
not accrue automatically to Democratic nominees for president of the United States, by some osmotic process selected
White to be his running mate. It most likely owed a good deal
to the nationally admiring press that White had been receiving as the necromancer of the spells that were revivifying Boston, inasmuch as McGovern lacked the cozy confidential access to the sages of the region who might have scuttled his
impressions as they formed.

Members of the Massachusetts delegation heard this news
with disbelief that curdled at once into rancid consternation.
Reports naming an arch-enemy of the White-for-Veep proposition are as numerous as were the number of Bay State cog-
noscenti who were in the delegation; a popular version has it
that John Kenneth Galbraith plunged the fatal dagger home,
at the instigation of Senator Edward M. Kennedy. Congressman Robert F. Drinan, S.J., whose blooded ideologues had
gone over in such numbers from his 1970 campaign to
White's 1971 outing, is alleged to have mused on hearing of

McGovern's choice that whoever it was coincidentally appeared to have the same name as the mayor of Boston.

Whoever deserves the principal credit or blame for commissioning the deed, though, he but articulated the consensus of White's putative allies in Massachusetts Democratic politics. Quite regardless of what strengths the man might bring to the McGovern adventure—Irish Catholic, Northeast base, mayor of a big city striving to redress its racial problems and rebuild its inner core—he would be denied the opportunity to deliver them to the national ticket. To the movers and the entrenched shakers in the state Democratic party, he was an outlaw who less than two years before Miami had punctured Maurice Donahue's dream—and therefore their own—of recovering the governor's office. If he was so cavalier about the codes of the state party, he was not to be entrusted with the controls of national power. Furthermore, no follower of Kennedy's was likely to overlook the real possibility that he who secured the nomination for vice president might well find himself elected just in back of a new president whose life expectancy could not be guaranteed; they were not about to install Kevin White in a position where grim fates could achieve that disaster for themselves. Thus was George McGovern freed to select Senator Thomas Eagleton of Missouri, who saw no need to mention his history of mental instability.

Summarily and with jeering horsed and unhorsed from the unofficial ticket in the space of a few hours, White was thus diminished in the eyes of those local observers who had never in their wildest dreams anticipated seeing him nationally exalted. Those in the Boston media were taken aback by the unexpected effect that their daily reports had accomplished, when digested and regurgitated out across the nation by the news magazines and broadcast media. To an extent they participated in the humiliation that White suffered in his meteoric journey through the national consciousness. They, after all, had called uncritical attention to him and conveyed to the whole Republic the impression—now lampooned as idiotic—that he was a politician of unusual merit. If he had been that easy to unfrock, they must have been hornswoggled when they frocked him in the first place.

This had to mean either that the mayor was very crafty and had taken them in badly, not to mention very wickedly, or else that he was a rather ordinary lout and oafish person whom they had quite stupidly mistaken for some sort of political genius. To a degree, the reporter becomes inexorably identified with the candidate whose campaign he covers, as Benjamin Bradlee of *Newsweek* did with John F. Kennedy. As dog owners often seem to develop strong resemblances to the animals they cherish, so the reporter takes on some of the mannerisms, attitudes, and behavioral patterns of the candidate he covers for a long time. Shrewd politicians such as JFK do what they can to foster this, and it is quite a lot. Unlucky politicians such as Kevin White discover that when their lot is ignominy, their admirers in the press start to grow cold.

White in his second term was therefore vulnerable as he had not been in his first. His initiatives, the fifteen "Little City Halls" scattered around the city under the aegis of his Office of Public Service, had lost their novelty as accessible alter egos of the mayor as ombudsman. As government agencies have a way of doing, they were beginning to look very much like handy exemplars of municipal bureaucracies. Summerthing, putting on diversions throughout the city as well as in its center, had undoubtedly accomplished something, the discouragement of civil unrest, but that was a negative; the affirmative was the criticism from the city council that it cost a lot of money. And it was then that the black parents of children in the Boston schools finally ran out of patience with the school committee, the Massachusetts Board of Education, and the apparently inexhaustible willingness of the white power structure to litigate their demands in the state courts of the Commonwealth. They brought suit in U.S. District Court in 1972. The first named of the plantiff parents was Tallulah Morgan. The first named defendant was James Hennigan, the school committee chairman who had succeeded to the position Mrs. Hicks vacated when she ran for Congress.

The case of *Morgan* v. *Hennigan* in the federal court alleged the Boston School Committee had by its official actions and inaction tolerated where it had not brought about, and failed to correct, conditions that in fact segregated the public schools by race, in violation of the Fourteenth Amendment to the Constitution of the United States. That amendment guarantees to every citizen the equal protection of the laws. The factual issues that could be controverted with a straight face were comparatively few. There was no question that the schools were segregated by race. The school committee in the federal court propounded the same defense it had pressed so stubbornly in the sundry state court actions that had gone before, conceding that the individual schools did appear to be racially homogeneous, faithfully reflecting the racial composition of the surrounding neighborhoods, but arguing that this was a development the committee had neither brought about nor had the power to correct conveniently. The parents replied in substance and effect that nobody had said anything about convenience, and they demanded that correction be enforced.

This dispute was drawn by lot to District Judge W. Arthur Garrity, Jr. Under the federal system, which assigns the case to a specific judge when it is filed and leaves it in his hands until its final disposition, that gave him a much more personal role in its administration than had been vouchsafed to any of the state court jurists whose rotating county assignments had taken them in and out of the earlier versions of the litigation. The advantage of the federal system is that the judge initially hearing the matter can and must develop an expertise of the facts and the parties that is simply impossible under the state approach. The disadvantage is that any blind spots, biases, or prejudices he brings to the first day of hearings will remain to influence his final resolution of the controversy. Justice as the federal courts administer it in long and complicated cases is much more personalized, at least in the eyes of the litigating parties, than is the justice meted out in the state courts, and that is by no means always an unmixed blessing.

W. Arthur Garrity, Jr., carried with him to his first day on the Boston School Cases the conditioning of an experienced and able judge who had come to the position in the customary fashion: early in his legal career, he had allied himself with a politician of ambitions and had thus set himself apart from others in his generation who might have possessed equal or superior abilities for the job. He had been fortunate in his choice of politician, allying himself with John F. Kennedy.

In that capacity, the graduate of Holy Cross College and the Harvard Law School had occupied a middle-management position in the midwestern presidential campaign efforts of the senator from Massachusetts. His reward was appointment as United States attorney for the District of Massachusetts. Conformably to the custom of the office as it is observed in the Commonwealth, he immediately ceased active political work. Five years later, his record as the federal prosecutor one of which he could be proud, he was promoted to the bench by President Lyndon Johnson, agreeably to the recommendation of the Democratic senator from Massachusetts, Edward M. Kennedy. He lived in Wellesley, where he and his wife had raised their children out of the public spotlight, and he performed his judicial duties with intelligence, great care, and to general approval. His career until the School Cases could have served quite nicely as a template for the ambitious and talented young lawyer with a genuine desire to be of service to his country in some position that would enable him to use all of his considerable abilities, secure an adequate livelihood, and achieve the esteem and respect of his colleagues at the bar.

His administration of his session faithfully recapitulated his life in the profession. It was orderly and always calm, even when there was a possibility of anger. He was almost always meticulously prepared for the day's work, and he made it plain that he expected equal diligence of lawyers trying cases before him. He brooked no theatrical techniques of trial. If he had any fault, it was that he was capable of taking the most infinite pains to assure himself that insofar as possible he would do justice in each case that came before him. Sentencing bank robbers who had used machine guns to cow their victims, he would interrupt his imposition of punishment to retire into his chambers and reflect a little more on whether he was being too severe. He was by no means always the judge whom the prosecutor would have chosen to preside over a criminal trial, unless the offense charged involved hard drugs, but defense attorneys as well found no edge in having him decide their clients' fates. Nobody worth attention ever said Judge Garrity had not done his level and Herculean best to be absolutely fair. For those who had tried before him, it would have been entirely acceptable if every officer appointing people to the bench had done as well as Lyndon Johnson did.

Presiding over the School Cases, though, he occupied the attention of a much larger audience. Most of those now passionately interested in his actions on the bench were not accustomed to evaluating jurists. His new critics, in the thousands, brought to his assessment only their firmly held convictions that white children should attend schools in their neighborhoods and black children report to the schools located near their homes as well. Arcane disquisitions on equality, patient lectures on the Constitution and the laws, evocations of the names of abolitionists whose eloquence had stirred the city's conscience and the courage of her sons for the Civil War: none of those considerations figured in the estimates Garrity's new critics from the proletariat formed of his *bona fides*. The principles that informed his decisions were of negligible significance; what counted was the substance of his rulings; that substance was precisely what the activist black parents had been seeking, and exactly what the city's white blue-collar families had feared. There is reason to believe he did not understand them, either.

In the two years between the inception of the School Cases in 1972, and the Garrity opinion which set down at length corrective measures in April of 1974, the judge came to occupy in the public's gallery a place adjacent to that which White had perceived himself assigned by the electorate in 1967. Garrity's opinions were approved in the main by the rich, if that term could be said to encompass those who were merely well educated and engaged in financially rewarding occupations. His constituency also appeared to include the minority poor, insofar as those then less opinionated members of society concerned themselves with the formation of opinons on such public issues. His violent opposition was the lower middle class, which, with the energetic assistance of Mrs. Hicks and those who had trooped after her drooping elective banner, had developed an addiction to the cultivation of opinions. Where her campaigns had been strongest, his name had come to be held in greatest odium. His initial order called for busing in two phases, Phase I mandating a good deal of it for academic 1974–75 and Phase II for a substantial increase for academic 1975–76.

Boston had about four months to react to the imposition of Phase I requirements that came with the September 1974 opening of schools. The intensity of that reaction was such that Governor Francis W. Sargent thought it prudent to put 500 Massachusetts National Guardsmen on alert at Camp Curtis Guild outside of Boston. Buses were provided to haul some 17,000 pupils of 94,000 expected to enroll in the public schools across the city. Five hundred policemen stood in readiness to prevent or interrupt violent dissent from the court order, and they were scarcely enough. Rocks were popular means of expression and mobs the preferred mode of public assemblage. Boston made all of the TV networks when 189 public schools opened that September, with some 5,200 teachers more or less in place to aid in preservation of the official fiction that the prime purpose of public education remained the inculcation of book learning. This improvement of the educational delivery system added some $11 million to the school budget.

Phase II, coming a year later, offered to a diminished number of civilian participants a larger number of active supporting roles. Ten thousand students were believed to have escaped a second year of the great experiment. That left an anticipated enrollment of around 84,000 pupils; a full 26,000 of them were instructed to take buses. Teachers had dwindled in number to 4,950, and twenty-six school buildings had been closed either because the declining pupil population meant they were no longer needed or because they were situated in locations that did not lend themselves to the provision of desegregated education. Three times as many cops were on hand to supervise the start of school, a full 60 percent of the 2,500-man force. Assistant U.S. Attorney General J. Stanley Pottinger, chief of the Civil Rights Division of the U.S. Department of Justice, came to Boston to be present for a photo opportunity with Governor Michael S. Dukakis, Massachusetts State Attorney General Francis Bellotti, and the mayor of Boston, Kevin White; Pottinger took the occasion to announce that the Eighty-second Airborne Division down at Fort Bragg, North Carolina, was on standby for a trip to Boston, should its presence become necessary. On Thursday, September 4, about 1,000 gathered in Southie to protest busing. The next day, Judge Garrity ordered Boston police to keep crowds away from all the schools and to establish "peaceful buffer zones" around the installations. Somewhat modifying constitutional guarantees of rights to assemble peacefully for the redress of grievance, Garrity found for the moment that groups exceeding three persons within 100 yards of a school building should be presumed hostile and must be officially dispersed. Twenty-one clerics—nineteen priests, two ministers—and four nuns of the Cardinals' Coordinating Committee urged peace.

In the event, 288 buses were involved in securing the attendance of actual enrollment, which turned out to be 76,127, down 19 percent from the student population that had been expected to show up in the previous September. Seventy-four persons were arrested around K and 4th streets in South Boston, on charges of disturbing the peace. The melee was started by the Committee Against Racism, a Marxist student group. The Boston Police Department SWAT team stationed riflemen on the rooftop of Charlestown High School. Fifty FBI agents were on the alert for civil rights violations.

Kevin White, seeking his third term as mayor of the city, had suspended his campaign as of September 3 in one of those self-righteously statesmanlike announcements that makes the incumbent the sole barrier between the community and chaos, but in the circumstances it was hard to fault him for it. Joe Timilty, his only serious opponent (the other two were Norman Oliver of the Socialist party and Robert Gibbons of the U.S. Labor party), claimed to offer no panaceas; Timilty wished to see the peace preserved if possible and did not upbraid White for his decision. This meant that Arthur Garrity for all intents and purposes was the villain of choice for the white middle-class Bostonian whose kid was being bused in that tumultuous September, a fact that was not lost upon several of the candidates for lesser elective public office. They ran against the judge.

They did so in the shrewd perception that there was a sector of the city that had abdicated its ameliorative position in the community. It had not forfeited its place by conscious choice but had allowed its credentials to lapse. That sector was composed of Irish Catholic Bostonians whose children were enrolled in the parochial schools. Those people, probably to their relief, were excluded from debate over the integration of the public schools because they had managed to exempt their children from what were perceived as the harms of the measures imposed to achieve it. That exclusion, for bad measure, operated to curtail severely the influence the Roman Catholic clergy of the city could bring to bear upon its citizens. Priests and nuns, after all, were the providers of the alternative and parallel system by means of which those barred from discussion had obtained safe passage for their children from the hated rulings of Judge Garrity.

In those southern cities that, to the *Globe's* approval, had by the 1970s learned to live quietly with integrated schools, there had been no such exemption. Birmingham and Selma, Little Rock and Richmond: none of them boasted before integration a competing and established parallel private educational system of the magnitude of Boston's Roman Catholic school structure. The archdiocese today estimates that 44,000 pupils were enrolled in its Boston schools when busing started back in 1974, around 34 percent of the city's total population of school-age children. Cleaving unto Christian principles at what must have been some cost for the financially troubled Catholic school system, Humberto Cardinal Medeiros made it clear that no new students would be taken if their acceptance would hinder integration of competing public schools.

The city as a whole was therefore deprived of the influence of those people whose inclinations toward moderation would most likely have been strongest. Any standing that their relative success in life had earned them in Irish Catholic society, any skills of persuasion that they might have learned, were lost to the peacekeeping effort. Those whom candidates contemptuously inflamed were deaf to the entreaties of the Catholic well-to-do. Some history may be valuable here, as is often the case when Boston Irish behavior is under scrutiny.

The Boston Irish did not secure control of the Boston School Committee until 1913, over sixty years after their ancesters had started to arrive in Massachusetts. The immediate effect of their conquest was the acceleration and completion of the exodus of privileged Protestants from the public schools, both as students in them and administrators of them, pretty much the same effect black arrivals would have on the Irish when their turn came around in the latter half of this century.

When the Irish succeeded to the helm of the Boston Public Schools, their competing parochial system was in place and operating. It had been ever since the first Celtic immigrants had remarked with resentment the ill will of Protestants in public education toward their faith and resolutely bent their wills and energies to the creation of a private system that would accord Rome the fidelity deserved. Boston College, today the largest Roman Catholic university in the United States, with some 13,000 students, was founded by the Society of Jesus in 1863, a mere fifteen years after the Great Hunger had expelled the hordes of the faithful from Ireland. It was built on nickels fiercely saved by unlettered laborers who earned them digging roadbeds for the trolley system and ditches for the water and gas lines. Its flagship existence was demanded for the further education of the students who had graduated from the Catholic elementary and high schools that were going up at the same time. A full century after B.C. was founded, pastors of the churches around Boston were quite capable of declaring that no transcripts of those graduating from their parish high schools would be forwarded to

Harvard, Mount Holyoke, or Smith, because Catholic young people who matriculated in such profane places were in danger of losing their immortal souls.

To those Catholics whose children did not attend sisters' schools, as the parochial institutions were customarily called, that attitude implied a real rejection, and not just a social snub, either. Those whose kids were relegated to the secular system heard regular Sunday sermons, full of brimstone, promising eternal torment for those who did not see to the scripturally enjoined upbringing of their children. They were solemnly instructed that their failure to send their children to religious schools would merit their damnation for ignoring the tykes' spiritual upbringing and would relegate the children of such pagan nurture to the fires of Hell. At children's masses on Sundays, the parochial school kids occupied pews in the center of the churches; public school Catholics sat in pews at the sides. Catholics with children in the public schools grew up with the assurance that they were second-rate in God's eyes and damned for it.

To make this abuse harder still to bear, its subjects had their precise understanding of the cause of it. It was because they did not have enough money. The pastors who strode through the school halls with their cassocks flapping proudly, beaming at the shining faces of the smiling little children, scattering paternal praises on the blushing younger nuns, huddling authoritatively with stern mothers superior, had a virulent habit of outspending the resources of their parishes. There was a congeries of reasons for this pervasive maladministration: the examples of their leaders, William Cardinal O'Connell, who was known as "Dollar Bill" when he was not being mocked for all his traveling as "Gangplank Bill," and Richard Cardinal Cushing, his still more ambitious successor, prompted the belief that the most successful of churchmen were those whose parishes managed to construct the grandest edifices. The archdiocese enforced that belief by rewarding with promotions those whose parishes shone forth and reproving those whose domains failed to manifest constant upgradings of the physical plants that housed them. Then, too, there was the non-Catholic community, which was held ever to be watching Catholics and making scornful fun of parishes that became rundown and decrepit: the Irish were frequently reminded that loyalty to Holy Mother Church was a salvivic reproof to the unbelievers who were avid always in their evil hopes of evidence of slacking in Catholic congregations. And if none of those stimuli achieved the end of consuming Catholic churchmen with greed, there was the sad fact that their finances did not suffice to support easily even quite modest operations. Even when the pastors were resigned to the reality that the means of their congregants were limited, and had no desire to be unkind, and those congregants were truly generous beyond those limitations, there was no blinking the fact that the resultant facilities available were not large enough. There was never enough room in the sisters' schools to accommodate all of the children begat by the faithful, who would never have affronted God by using birth control.

Therefore, whether out of mean vindictiveness toward the tightfisted or helpless inability to admit without regard to cost all the children of the parish into Catholic schools, the priests allocated places to the kids by reference to the contributions their parents made on Sundays. Some denied it, but most did it. In the forties and the fifties, envelopes were supplied for one collection every month. The parishioners were instructed to write their names on the envelopes, along with the amount enclosed. Those donations, plus the ones at Easter and at Christmas, formed the data for the pastor's accounting and the basis upon which he discriminated among applicants competing for scarce seats in the parish school. In time, preprinted envelopes, one for each Sunday, were distributed to every family, sometimes thoughtfully encoded with the amount the pastor thought appropriate from what he had

observed of the family's means; it was still explicitly anticipated that one Sunday every month would bring at least
twice as large a contribution as the other ones. Parishes that
newly arriving pastors found to be in need of capital improvements soon had in addition Grand Annual Collections, for
which less than $100 was deemed shabby stuff indeed. All of
this went into the books of the parish, for convenient inspection when the donor's kids were old enough for school. If
meanness did not provoke selection of the children of the generous, justice likely as not did.

Those whose kids did not get in were therefore of three
general types: fractious Catholics who refused to cooperate in
making records of their donations to the parish, for whatever
reason of rebellion, and could therefore be expected to reject
priestly guidance on other points as well; parents whose behavior in some other respect had won them the disapproval of
the pastor; and parents whose means were not large enough
to permit even minimum donations, that minimum being arbitrarily established by a pastor without consultation with his
victims. Some also were excluded because older siblings had
upon admission proved too stupid or intractable to benefit
from Catholic instruction. In time, as the children matured,
some who were admitted would be thrown out for one reason
or another, relegated to the public schools with the express
statement that they did not measure up to the standards of a
Catholic education.

That underclass of Irish Catholic society expanded every
generation, right along with the parochial alumni who obediently enrolled each new crop of offspring in the sisters'
schools. Its first excluded members sulked every Sunday during mass, well aware of their ineligibility for full status in the
church and the reason for it. The children born to those muti-
neers learned at their parents' knees the debased social standing of the family and imbibed also the resentment that would
come when they, too, in their turn, were excluded. Every

week those kids when they were little were obliged to attend
Sunday school, lest they grow up to be pagans utterly, but
their parents and they also were reminded at the same time
that a brief hour of catechism would at most mollify somewhat the peevish God who was really annoyed that they did
not study their religion every day. When they reached adoles-
cence, they went on to Christian doctrine classes (later collected with Sunday school under the heading "Confraternity
of Christian Doctrine") and were solemnly adjured that they
would not be admitted to the Sacrament of Confirmation if
they did not faithfully attend but instead spent Wednesday
evenings down at the corner playing the pinball machines.
The threatened withholding of Confirmation promised still
another sanction: ineligibility for the Sacrament of
Matrimony—no church weddings for the Catholic canon
outlaw.

Those second-class Catholics were the ones to whom candidates such as School Committeeman John Kerrigan ap-
pealed. They were the ones who voted for him, reviled Judge
Garrity, and threw the rocks. To them, Richard Cardinal
Cushing, dying as Kevin White began his first term in office,
and Humberto Cardinal Medeiros, his successor, were the
chieftains of their own oppression, by their own church. Neither of those clergymen was able to argue with much force to
congregants for generations denied full membership in their
faith that they should cheerfully accord equality toward others in their second-class schools. When the Roman Catholic
clergy of Boston admonished their parishioners not to ob-
struct black enrollments in the public schools to which penu-
rious Irish Catholic white children had been relegated, they
were telling angry laymen that they and their kids were no
better than the blacks. Bigoted or not, those white laymen
resented that and ignored the righteous clerics who had so
long disparaged them. And when those white Catholics un-
lawfully resisted black efforts to desegregate the public

schools they thought were *theirs*, they were as much at log-gerheads with their priests and bishops as they were with Judge Garrity, Governor Dukakis, Mayor White, Assistant Attorney General Pottinger, Attorney General Bellotti, and the Eighty-second Airborne Division down at Fort Bragg, North Carolina. When media commentators marveled at the Boston Irish Catholic refusal to heed the orders of an Irish Catholic judge, backed up by the pastoral letters of a Roman Catholic archbishop, they demonstrated their ignorant assumption that Boston Irish Catholics are fungible, a homogeneous lot that wheels obediently in formation as its ostensible leaders dictate.

Judge Garrity appears also to have proceeded on that blithe assumption. He was not entirely the child of privilege that his circumstances made him seem to be when he first caught the attention of the disaffected Irish Catholic lower middle class of Boston. At his father's insistence, Garrity had combined radio repair studies at the old Boston Technical High School while attending Harvard Law School, just in case things didn't work out as well as they did. Still, Garrity did lack somewhat for street smarts. Frustrated after many months of nudging school officials to develop a workable plan for division of the city into districts for school assignments of their eligible residents, Garrity had seized upon an existing district map that partitioned it by *geocodes*. That map had been devised for the use of the police department. It discriminated among neighborhoods and parts of neighborhoods, according to the frequency of trouble that required police attention. Garrity decreed that children from coded neighborhoods that happened to be black should attend school in coded neighborhoods that happened to be white, and that white children should be bused the other way.

That decision had the merit of speedy facility. The difficulty was that it uprooted intact whole groups of trouble-makers from both white and black neighborhoods and dumped them shoulder to shoulder into unfamiliar schools where they would encounter similarly intact gangs of the other color. Both sides would have every reason to band more closely with their pals and to stand fast against the hostiles. They would fight much better and far longer that way, and the pressure of their peers from their neighborhoods of residence would tend to assure that they would fight well. Plainly, what Judge Garrity ought to have done was devise a new districting plan which would divide the groups of troublemakers insofar as possible and disperse their members widely across Boston. It would have taken more buses, and cost more, but if integration was to be had at all costs, it ought to have been done. Since it wasn't, the potential for trouble was left undiminished.

That potential, adequately realized as Phase II of busing began in September 1975, deferred for about eight years the full impact of Kevin White's personal political problems upon his career. The immediate effect of *Morgan v. Hennigan* was to distract from White's campaign the attention that would cause him to withdraw from a fifth candidacy in 1983.

•   •   •

The long-term effect of *Morgan v. Hennigan,* and the orders Judge Garrity issued in the course of its decade of litigation, was to reduce the student population of the Boston public schools by about 36,000, a full 38 percent of the enrollment expected when school opened in 1972. White enrollment by 1982 had dropped from 56,893 to 18,013. Blacks were not enthused by what they saw, either—31,634 attended in 1972, 28,547 in 1982. Hispanics did increase (5,135 to 9,032), and so did Asians (1,857 to 3,767). The schools, in other words, were more than ever the last resorts of education for those who could afford no better, and more segregated than they had been when Judge Garrity commenced his oversight of them. They were also still engaged in turning out students of extremely questionable accomplishment; average SAT (1978–83) scores showed verbal proficiency averaging 362 out of a possible 800, with math scores 406 out of 800. In February 1982, Larry Johnson, in his capacity as spokesman for the coalition of black parents involved in the controversy before Judge Garrity, asked the judge to end his supervision of the schools. He said the black parents would appreciate it if the federal court would permit them to choose the schools their children would attend. He sounded, in other words, eerily like Louise Day Hicks had sounded, back in 1967.

There are two classes of disputants most frequently to be met with among us. The first is of young students, just entered the threshold of science, with a first view of its outlines, not yet filled up with the details and modifications which a further progress would bring to their knowledge. The other consists of the ill-tempered and rude men in society, who have taken up a passion for politics.

> —Thomas Jefferson
> Letter of November 24, 1808, to his grandson, Thomas Jefferson Randolph

11

THE SOMNOLENT ISSUE was corruption. It was allowed to slumber that year mostly because of busing. But that convulsion and its attendant distempers were not the only major diversion for Boston voters that year. Between Labor Day and November 4, 1975, when the final election votes were counted, the Red Sox furnished the same sort of distraction that they had provided for White's initial mayoral outing in 1967, winning first the Eastern Division of the American League against determined resistance from the Baltimore Orioles and the New York Yankees and then taking the League Championship from the Oakland A's in a series of considerable interest to New Englanders, at least. It was early in the morning of October 22 by the time Carlton Fisk hit the most glorious home run in Boston baseball history, and late afternoon the same day when the seventh game of that World Series with the Cincinnati Reds, regrettably required by major league baseball rules, sent the Reds back to Ohio, victorious in both game and series, 4–3. In the larger scheme of things, so often cited by the stuffy as commanding disregard of sports and games and occasionally invoked by the dull of mind who cannot abide watching that purest of adult contests, baseball, it may not seem proper that the Red Sox should be popularly preferred over politics and that they should thus be a real factor in the outcome of Boston elections. They are, though, especially when it really appears that they might have a chance to seize their first World Championship since 1918, and as many times as they have left us devastated, one game short of triumph, they remain on the whole more emotionally rewarding than the people who aspire to public office.

Their ultimate disposition that year left but twelve days to the voters of the city to collect their wits and contemplate the choices the ballot offered them. That selection lacked for novelty. White's opponent was Joe Timilty, the state senator from Mattapan who had been nudged aside four years before by the mayoral swan song of Louise Day Hicks. Reruns do not usually galvanize the voters of the city. The candidate who falls short, as Hicks had in her first attempt in 1967, usually comes up shorter still the second time around. The presumption seems to be that there must have been some evident deficiency in the candidate which called for the first rejection. If no subsequent disaster occurs to demonstrate that the first dismissal was a bad mistake, another defeat is almost certain.

Busing of course had been a disaster, and it was still one in progress. Timilty, though, could not lay it at the feet of Kevin White, even if there had been some potential gain to be achieved by doing that. The state senator began with the allegiance of those voters who despised White and his ilk as toadies to the blacks. Timilty, a generally decent man, had not inspired or inflamed that attitude, but he did passively receive its benefits as the alternative to White.

Neither could he argue persuasively that those whites willing to accept the blacks, but horrified by violence, ought to vote for him instead of White. The perception was that Garrity was the main architect of busing, egged on by the *Globe* and its adherents, and that White had made a poor best of a bad situation thrust upon him by authorities that he did not control. Scary as the consequences of desegregation had been, they were not as bad as the imagination could devise. The fear was that a vigorous discussion of the racial issue would intensify its heat and obtain literally fatal consequences. Some years after the reduction of that tension to its present level of chronic worrisomeness, it is tempting to remark those who were prominent in the community when the situation was at its very worst but who failed to raise their voices in behalf of sanity. When Humberto Cardinal Medeiros died during the 1983 mayoral campaign between Melvin King, the black, and Raymond Flynn, the white city councillor and former state legislator who whipped King two to one, there was muttering to the effect that the late prelate had failed to exert much leadership in advocacy of racial justice during the times that were truly bad. The fact was that those in his flock who most needed calming down were those who were least likely to accept his counsel with docility and most capable at the same time of responding to it with increased hostility. When Kevin White went to Charlestown on that summer Sunday morning before his afternoon of politicking at the Charles Street Fair in the hot afternoon, Alice McGuff and Patricia Russell of the Powderkeg had powerful claims upon his attention. Those two women represented a tiny minority of resentful lower-middle-class whites who were willing to treat busing as a political issue and not as an excuse for riot. White was therefore disposed to grant them the after-school activities they asked for, and he did it. Timilty, like White, was a responsible citizen, in addition to being a pretty decent one. He was chary of addressing busing at all, quite aware of the fragility of such peace as White had contrived, and unwilling to disrupt it for his own advantage.

Hamstrung therefore on the major controversy, for which he did not claim to have a panacea, Timilty endeavored to make White the issue. His approach began with White's style in the office, dwelling on the Mayor's fondness for elaborate receptions at the Parkman House. It ended with the issue of corruption.

Massachusetts has a national reputation for a colorful tradition of corruption in its politics. Boston as its capital city is deemed at home and therefore abroad as the chancre of that festering tendency to larceny. It is where the naive reps in from the virtuous countryside are plied with booze and women, stripped of their ethics and their scruples, and transformed into the rapacious thieves so beloved of our legends. The engines of their destruction are of course the pillagers who misspent their childhoods and youth in the immoral city and devote their adult years to setting ambuscades for the impressionable.

Over all of these steaming legends hovers the fascinating ghost of James Michael Curley, spellbinding archetype of the felonious Boston politician. Curley ran for everything, it seemed, at one time or another, but from the outset of his four decades of cajoling, haranguing, exhorting, and bamboozling the voters of Massachusetts, he was known as a convict. When he was first elected mayor, in 1914, he took into office with him a criminal record; he had served ninety days in the Charles Street Jail on his conviction for having masqueraded as a friend who worried that his own intelligence would not secure him passage of the civil service exams for appointment as a mailman. With the fine insouciance that was his trademark, Curley ran as a reformer, promising the voters that he'd do away with cronyism and defy the ward bosses who controlled the city politics. Ousted by the one-term limit then in force, in 1918, he returned to the mayor's office in 1922 and used it as a platform for his first attempt at statewide office, losing his bid to become lieutenant governor. Malcolm Nichols occupied the place for four years, after which James Michael reclaimed it for his third term. During that hitch, it was later charged, he accepted $30,000 for ramrodding settlement of litigation that sought damages from the city for harm done to a Beacon Street building during construction of an extension of the subway system through Kenmore Square. A witness with proven experience in perjury gave the main evidence against him, but he was found guilty and ordered to make restitution to the city of nearly $36,000 or else go to jail. He was saved from that ignominy by a fund collected from the public. In 1938 he seized the party's gubernatorial nomination from its convention candidate, Charles F. Hurley, but lost the general election to Leverett Saltonstall, then Speaker of the Massachusetts House of Representatives and later U.S. senator. Undaunted as ever, Curley ran again for mayor in 1941, was beaten, and ran for Congress in 1942; he won. In 1944 he came back to Boston and ran once more for mayor, winning. Serving that fourth term, he was indicted for mail fraud on what was almost certainly a frame-up—the federal charges alleged he had conspired to employ his influence as a congressman to deliver contracts to a company with which he had been briefly involved before Pearl Harbor and from which he was never proven to have received any money. He went to Danbury in June 1947 and was pardoned by President Truman in time for Thanksgiving. Reclaiming his office from the caretaker incumbent, John Hynes, he stood for reelection in 1949 and was beaten by Hynes. He made two more attempts to regain the office, both unsuccessful, and died in 1958.

That career, masterfully employed as the stuff of legend in Edwin O'Connor's 1956 novel, *The Last Hurrah* (Curley told O'Connor his favorite passage in the story of Frank Skeffington's last bow was "the part where I died"), has served as the model for Bay State politicians in the popular mind since the memory of man runneth not to the contrary. Sometimes genially, other times ruefully, now and then furiously, but always knowingly, Massachusetts citizens who deem themselves sophisticated stand ever in readiness to believe that their elected and appointed officials are dishonest. Often enough, special grand juries, empaneled to investigate outrages scented by blue-ribbon crime commissions, have secured evidence that prompted them to hand up indictments leading to convictions. Far too often, trigger-happy reporters and editors, acting on rumors, gossip, and slander circulated by the enemies of those enjoying power, have inspired prosecutions that have relied—as Curley's second and third did— upon uncorroborated testimony from the mouths of infamous persons. Unsupported charges and flimsy indictments have a longer shelf life than the reputations of those named in them, much longer than the time it takes to decide an election. Wooing an electorate long predisposed to take such charges at face value, desperate underdogs have frequently succumbed to the strong temptation to suggest corruption.

Joe Timilty, that second time out, more or less backed into it, nudged toward the corruption ploy by the media.

Boston, in that pennant summer spent anticipating Phase II busing, could look for diversion also to a circulation battle between two weekly papers struggling for domination of what appeared to be a market adequate to support only one of them. Both the *Phoenix*, which prevailed late in 1982 after a very long and bitter struggle, and *The Real Paper* had staff members claiming occupational descent from the city's original underground papers of the sixties: *Avatar*, which suffered from repeated police attempts to shut it down for being obscene; and *Boston After Dark*, which had been gobbled up by the *Phoenix*. *The Real Paper* was published by a sort of commune established in wrathful protest by members of the *BAD* staff who had refused (as they claimed) or had not been asked (as the *Phoenix* claimed) to accompany its masthead into the oblivion of incorporation into the *Phoenix.*

There was real animosity between those two journals and a consequent sharp edge to their weekly efforts to upstage each other. The *Phoenix* was less easily distracted from its principal objective in the struggle, which was to appeal to former radicals who had taken steady jobs, plighted troths and started families, and made some sort of rapprochement with the bourgeoisie. *The Real Paper* either believed that its potential readers had merely camouflaged themselves as burghers and still craved strong rhetoric against the Establishment, or else frequently suffered fits of nostalgic rage and lashed out as it had in the old days of protest. As the summer wore on, *The Real Paper* sought to demonstrate its undiminished integrity by attacking Kevin White—WHITE LIES was one memorable front page screamer—ferociously as the corrupt ringleader of the Establishment and battering the *Phoenix* simultaneously as a sellout rag too scared to attack Kevin White. The *Phoenix* defended itself against these shrill assaults by taking a superior attitude toward the hysterical *Real Paper* and by dutifully attacking Kevin White. The gist of both onslaughts was that Anzalone had acted as White's cat's-paw in attempting to extort $10,000 campaign contributions from developers whom he had invited to have breakfast at the Ritz in April of 1970.

While the two weeklies were slugging it out with each other by competing to see who could hit White the hardest, Jack Kelley, an investigative reporter for Boston's perennially disorganized channel 7, was striving to improve its standing as third-best news station out of three broadcasting in the city by cultivating a reputation as a newsman with sources. One of the questionable characters upon whom Kelley relied was Jimmy Martorano, a second-echelon associate of Howie T.

Winter, notorious as the leader of Somerville's Winter Hill gang (Winter was later sentenced to a long term for interfering in the outcomes of horse races and publicly credited with a good many other evil deeds as well; Martorano disappeared some years ago). Martorano told Kelley that Theodore Berenson, Jr., son of a prominent real estate development family, had been one of the victims of White's 1970 Ritz breakfast shakedown, and he quoted Berenson as telling him that Ted Anzalone had conducted the ceremonies. Kelley broadcast this. Berenson at once called the report "slander" and denied it outright.

Thereupon Francis J. Falzarano, Jr., appeared. He was a contractor and he had done quite a lot of business with the city. He claimed that White in August of 1970 had shaken him down for $10,000. As he told it, he was then engaged in renovating Boston City Hospital under a $600,000 contract. Difficulties were encountered on the job, making it impossible for him to proceed without mayoral approval of a change order. The change order added $73,000 to the contract price. He asserted that the order was not signed until he had promised to kick in the magic ten grand contribution.

Pressed to account for his long silence before telling all this to Steve Nevas, an investigative reporter at channel 4 in competition with Kelley at channel 7, Falzarano explained that after the hospital job and the alleged contribution, he'd been engaged as the largest single contractor for the renovation of the North and South markets in the Quincy Market project for the city, to the tune of $2.6 million in business for his company. Things had not gone well for him, and he had been suspended from that profitable job in December of 1974. Reinstated in February of the election year, he'd been busy until summer finishing the work and had not had time until September, as the primary election loomed, to display his zeal for public probity at Kevin White's expense.

Timilty stopped short of saying Kevin White was crooked.

He contented himself with prim reproofs of White for presiding over a corrupt administration.

White riposted skillfully. He had his police commissioner, Robert J. DiGrazia, denounce those who were denouncing White. DiGrazia, whom Timilty had publicly admired as a top cop immune to the inbred biases and cronyism of the Boston police, announced that the Mob was behind all the charges that suggested White was tied in with the Mob. DiGrazia asserted that the Mob was out to stain Mayor White because eight years of him in office had persuaded the wise guys that they would get nowhere in the city so long as he remained. This of course invited the inference that the Mob was out to elect Joe Timilty and left him unable to reply; neither White nor his commissioner had pronounced that accusation.

That masterful stroke saved White the election. That summer his fire commissioner, James Kelly, had been indicted for conspiring to violate the Campaign Finance Law, shaking down the firemen for contributions to the mayor's election war chest. Not without some reason, Timilty's advisers deduced, as Robert Healy put it in the *Globe*, "that a lot of educated, good government types in the city, whom the mayor locked up six or more months ago, are having second thoughts because of the scandal in the Fire Department and some of, what they consider, the mayor's heavy handed campaign contributions practices." (*Globe*, 9/3/75, p. 21) Until DiGrazia spoke up, "White was losing the concerned liberal voter whom he has to have in order to win the election," Healy wrote just two months later, on election eve. (*Globe*, 11/2/75, p. A7) When the returns had come in, White had beaten Timilty by 7,528 out of 157,846 votes cast, his 81,187 giving him a 52.4 percent majority of those who came out on a sunny day and perceived enough difference between him and Timilty to choose between them—about 10,000 who voted in Boston that day made no choice for mayor. Healy called the victory "a set of blocks, delicately balanced and almost tumbled by the corruption issue." (*Globe*, 11/5/75, p. 19)

Kevin White learned quite a lot from that surprisingly unpleasant summer. He discovered that the friends he had acquired in 1967, when leading citizens feared Louise Day Hicks and gave thanks on a daily basis for the justice of his views, did not know a whole lot about Boston politics.

He had been at the most seriously discomforted by the clumsiness of Jimmy Kelly in strongly suggesting to the fire laddies that they ought to spring for tickets to a $100-per-plate testimonial for the candidate who controlled their numbers and their salaries. Kelly had been extremely stupid, skirting the sactimonious Campaign Financing Law in that oafish manner; any reasonably smart fellow knows that the procedure is to send the dinner tickets to the firemen at their homes. That is how it's done when it is time for the attorneys in the A.G.'s office to appear at spontaneous tributes to their glorious leader, whoever happens to be the chief law enforcement officer of the Commonwealth at any given time. That is how it's done when there's a birthday party for the U.S. senator who awards the appointment of U.S. attorney for the district and approves his choices for assistant U.S. attorneys. Somehow the legal staffs of the district attorneys seem to find out when there is a contributory cocktail party scheduled for the fellow who employs them, and nobody seems to mind. Least of all, it should be added, the attorneys on those staffs who do have some stake in the outcomes of elections that affect their bosses. All that is necessary to observe the letter of the silly law is to eschew distributing the dunning announcements to the beholden during working hours, at the office or the station house. Fire Commissioner James Kelly had been a consummate dunderhead, which fact in and of itself was in the real world the best possible evidence that the mayor had no notice of his actions. What had happened to Kelly, later acquitted of conspiracy charges, was no cause for an adult White supporter of normal intelligence to be scandalized.

So also the rejuvenated reports of the breakfast at the Ritz. That story had been around since 1970 and out in public in time for the mayoral campaign of the following year. By its terms it required the queasy scrupulous to believe that fifteen rich men had submitted quietly to a request from Kevin White that they deliver to his minion $150,000, with the implication that refusal would lead to his determination to torpedo their development projects in Boston. Unexplained was how he proposed to carry out this threat from the vantage point of the office he coveted, that of the governor. Unexplained as well was their remarkable and unanimous disinclination to step forward and corroborate the reports of this arrogance. Striking, too, was the fact that the offices of the district attorney, attorney general, and United States attorney (which was controlled until 1977 by the Republicans) apparently had not acquired any evidence that led their occupants to believe such unlawful exactions had been made. Flogged by the media outlets hungriest for attention—circulation for the weeklies, Nielsen ratings for the television stations—that story about supine real estate magnates looked like a real barn-burner of a prosecution; there is nothing that a Massachusetts prosecutor prefers to a lusty prosecution of political corruption. Yet no one in those ordinarily aggressive law enforcement offices seemed to consider that he had enough to go to a grand jury, just to see if there might be some more. Mayor White could have been forgiven if he was a little disappointed in those liberal friends who wavered in their love for him on that basis alone.

Faced with the inescapable fact that his ideological loyalists were more ideologues than partisans, suffering the sort of personal hurt any human being feels at being publicly excoriated as a crook—even admitted crooks find that experience very hard to bear—he received at the same time some reminders of the true nature of the antagonism he faced in the community. Alice McGuff and Pat Russell, the two Charlestown ladies who conferred with him that apprehensive summer about how to keep the peace when the schools opened in September, came not to bicker with him about how to swerve the federal court or cause the buses carting blacks to tip into the river; they said calmly they were pretty sure that if he could get a good-sized record player to provide entertainment for school dances, devise programs after school to reduce the need for parental supervision, and generally contrive to make the residents of Charlestown believe they were being gently bribed, there probably would not be any major trouble. The ladies didn't ask for very much from him, and he did not promise them miracles; all three involved in the discussion were practicing city politics just as it had always been conducted, and they were quite comfortable. White took from that and many other like experiences the lesson that one way to cool the neighborhoods was to confer some hard benefits on those who were in charge, such benefits as jobs and other patronage.

He emerged from that campaign newly convinced therefore that what he had to do was reduce the animosities he inspired among the middle class of Boston. This meant he would have to sacrifice some of the support he had first enjoyed among the liberals, but that choice was easy for him. If he did not cut it loose, he would lose it anyway. He was going out of fashion.

One great defect of our Governments are
that they do not present objects sufficiently interesting to the human mind.

—Alexander Hamilton
Notes taken June 6, 1787, at the
Federal Convention

12

THE 156,846 who cast mayoral ballots in the 1975 election
represented 82 percent of those who had chosen between
Kevin White and Louise Day Hicks in 1967. In the next four
years, another chunk of the participating electorate would
drop off; the 141,337 who in 1979 trudged to the polls to the
third disappointment of Joe Timilty constituted a meager 73
percent of the 1967 electorate, some 192,673 voters.

During the census decade, 1970–80, bracketed by the sixteen years of Kevin White's tenure as mayor, Boston's population declined by just about 15 percent. Yet as was demonstrated when more than 195,000 came out to give 1983
mayoral victor Raymond Flynn a 66 percent plurality against
Melvin King, those who remained residents of Boston and
those who bucked the trend and became residents retained
the potential to be enthralled by the political process. The
evidence suggests that the record 69 percent participation in
the Flynn-King contest was occasioned by white apprehension that a black man of irregular views might gain control of
city hall. Caucasians rose to the call to deliver formal notice
that Boston remains over 70 percent white and far more resis-
tant to change than myths popular nationally propose, an
inference that tends to controvert the express view of the de-

feated candidate that the relatively genteel campaign had
united the city, but that is another matter. The point is that
the longer Kevin White remained in the office, the greater
became the indifference of the voters.

There are two ways of looking at that phenomenon. The
first, which is by far the most popular, is the view taken with
alarm. It requires the presumption that the objective of the
democratic system is accomplished only when the overwhelming majority of those eligible to vote in it choose to
exercise their franchises. This is Happy Campers Politics. It
makes the candidates into something very much resembling
those indefatigably hearty, inexhaustibly cheerful, usually
bosomy young ladies who cavort mindlessly in scanty cos-
tumes before stadiums packed with spectators presumably attracted by the prospect of observing a football game. Unless
the contestants strive to excite most of the population into
boundlessly enthusiastic partisanship, and the population ex-
citedly responds by going to the polls to show its jolly spirit,
critical observers find the show unsatisfactory. Pejorative
terms are trotted out: *apathy, alienation, cynicism,* and *disil-
lusion* are traditional favorites for description of the uncooperative citizenry. Candidates, and not merely those who've
won such boring, tainted contests but also those bedraggled
poor performers who in losing have failed also to give thrilling accounts of themselves, are held responsible for voter lassitude. Corrective measures are proposed, albeit without professed optimism that they will succeed. Gloom is the overriding mood of those commenting on the situation.

Those dour comments, of course, are delivered by the media, which are themselves implicitly rebuked by sparsely attended polls. When only 25 percent of the city's population
takes the trouble to react officially to about a third of the
news that is presented, as occurred in 1979 when a majority
of some 141,000 Bostonians out of a population of 563,000
returned Kevin White for his last term in office, it raises the

possibility that the importance of the subject has been somewhat exaggerated. Those who are employed by media do not relish that possibility.

The other interpretation is that the purpose of democracy is to afford to citizens of some minimum age and presumed understanding the option to take part in regularly scheduled referenda on the current acceptability of their elected officials, given the available alternatives. This view is incremental. It is based upon the premise that it is seldom wise to fix something that isn't broken. It might be called Known Devil Politics. In this view, the enfranchised citizen need only complete a threshold comparative evaluation of the listed contestants, decide whether it is likely that the defeat of either will inconvenience him more than will a trip to the polls, ascertain whether such an undesirable result is likely to be affected by the casting of his ballot, and then either vote or go about his ordinary business as seems most appropriate.

That attitude, which I think vastly the more common among laymen who derive no cognizable portion of their income from the game of politics or its reportage, probably accounts for the official longevity of incumbents in general, and that of Kevin White specifically. Notwithstanding unrelenting exhortation to the contrary, most Bostonians, like most other Americans, manifest a very measured enthusiasm for their governors, actual or aspiring, and an interest in their doings that is usually at best desultory.

It was not the common people who demanded that no president succeeding FDR would occupy the White House for a third term, not by any means—it was the Republicans. Not yet aware of Dwight D. Eisenhower's comfortable appeal to most Americans, or his willingness to make it as a member of the GOP, they made sure that never again would they be shut out of power by some charismatic fellow from the opposition. They thus foreclosed, quite unwittingly and to their later chagrin, their own charismatic fellow from achieving the same fell purpose. And the two-term amendment they wrought upon the Constitution was not ratified by a plebiscite, after all; it was approved by the state legislatures, teeming, too, with politicians quite as fearful of frustrating careers spent in the shadows of incumbents more resourceful in retaining popularity than they themselves might be in wresting it away. Yeasty years in politics are fermented by unsatisfied ambitions, made memorable—and commensurately newsworthy—by restive people who begin them out of office.

The first four years of Kevin White in charge of city hall had plainly been perceived as adequate by Boston voters when he applied for reelection for the first time in 1971. They were evidently content then with the disciplining they had given him in the 1970 gubernatorial election against Governor Francis W. Sargent, punishing him for his sauciness in going back upon his promise not to make that statewide run. They found Mrs. Hicks no more appealing than they had when she first ran. Five percent of the number of those who had turned out to elect him the first time saw no emergent danger that he would be ejected, and they evinced their qualified approval of the status quo by staying home.

Four years later, when Mrs. Hicks had mastered Christian resignation and Joe Timilty got his first clear shot at the mayor's office, 18 percent of the number who had voted back in 1967 perceived nothing in the contest to give them a sense of urgency sufficient to impel them to the polls. If most citizens of Boston were unhappy about busing, as they most assuredly were, they were still realistic enough to act on the belief that the incumbent devil had handled its inception at least as well as the aspiring devil could. Furthermore, White had the advantage of familiarity with the ongoing situation.

Thus left pretty much without an inflammatory issue on which he could persuasively claim superiority to White, Timilty with a good deal of self-serving assistance from the media resorted to the hoary old corruption issue, and that did not work either. There is a sort of boomerang effect to the corruption charge in Massachusetts. It is so old, and so customary, that the voters have gotten jaded by it. It is something they incline to accept *arguendo:* assuming, as the aspirant asserts, that the incumbent is corrupt, is the alleged crookedness of such a kind and magnitude as to demand his ouster from the office? And if it is, is the evidence of said corruption adequate to prompt a reasonable voter to conclude, not that he is guilty beyond a reasonable doubt, but that indeed he most likely did do what is whispered? Boston has rather elevated standards which must be met to bring affirmative reactions to each of those questions, and both must be answered yes for the incumbent to be fired on the basis of it. The wickedness that Timilty imputed to the White administration, chiefly in the person of Ted Anzalone, was a little dog-eared from its first public inspection back in 1971, when it had been found to be insufficient to kick White out of his office. It had not gained any ballast in the intervening years, and the fresh rebuttal by Police Commissioner Robert DiGrazia had in fact lightened it. All in all, accordingly, the voters did not think it damaging enough to warrant expelling White from office, and another 27,000 residents of Boston decided their votes were not required to influence the outcome of the election.

By the time Kevin White won his fourth term from the people of the city, 51,000 fewer than the 193,000 who had trooped out for his first foray thought the errand of participation in the outcome worth investment of their time and inconvenience. He drew 77,513 nose to nose for the third time with Joseph Timilty, 13,000 fewer votes than Mrs. Hicks had mustered back in 1967, 25,000 fewer than he had drawn that year. Boston's population had declined by about 12 percent; if we assume that those leaving and those newly arrived in that period were as proportionately split between politically active people and politically exhausted people as the stable population of the city, by no means a safe assumption, 166,000 voters should have appeared at the polls in 1979, 25,000 more than actually took part in deciding the mayor's race. If we blithely assume further that those 25,000 nonparticipants in 1979 would have split 53 percent for White and 47 percent for his opponent, as their voting forebears had some 13 years before, White would have tallied 90,573 votes, 88 percent of the 102,551 he garnered in the benchmark 1967 election. Following this convoluted reasoning, from unreliable statistical guesswork, to its logical conclusion, he had lost 12 percent of his support in the city, while the city itself was losing 12 percent of its population.

Since the net loss of white residents during the census decade was 131,000, and the net gain of blacks was just under 22,000, and since the white emigration was most pronounced in those middle-class sectors of the city in which White had had the greatest difficulty in securing support, he was obviously surviving chiefly by means of the advantages of incumbency. As the disgruntled whites departed, and the tractable blacks arrived, his pluralities should have increased quite dramatically. He might not have been acquiring new friends who would throng to the polling places, but he was losing old enemies in vast numbers. True, as he faced down the same old challengers time and time again, his milder partisans could be said to have excused themselves from voting solely on the grounds that he was in no danger, but that left open to nagging question on his part, and intriguing speculation by those who coveted his post, the issue of whether those lapsed White followers would return to his banner when he ran again in 1983, if he should be in trouble.

Political loyalty is usually inspired by some variety of passion—ideology, greed, hope of advancement. Passion does not endure. It is either satisfied or forgotten. When none of one's own money, time, or dignity is at stake, the tendency is to surmise that those loyalists who have gone away will most likely not come back. Old political alliances, however close and personal, tend to resemble old love affairs, more suitable for nostalgic recollection than for revival. Except for the most addicted practitioners, politics is not a game for those crowding fifty, lacking family wealth, unless they have been blessed by their preference in candidates when very young and have been enabled by lucrative professional employments in Washington, state capitals, or major metropolitan centers to go on fooling around with elections because they have no need to worry about earning steady livings in the private sector.

There is no security in a racket that stipulates acceptance of the risk that your employer may be discharged at the polls before you are fairly into the middle years of paying off a medium-sized mortgage. The hours are ghastly, suitable really only for the unmarried or those who are about to be. The work is seasonal, and the most stimulating varieties of it require lots of traveling. Ordinarily the most senior people on a campaign trip are the men and women of the press, who have been covering politics for years. The politicians change, moving up or being thrown out, and the staffs along with the replacement candidates seem to remain forever in their middle thirties. Only the reporters age, wondering from time to time what the hell is keeping them still at it.

That attrition rate diminishes in inverse proportion to the elevation of the office, national political operatives appearing and disappearing far more frequently than primarily state-level aides who never wanted cabinet-rank jobs and may be easily satisfied with judgeships. State loyalists change the guards more often, though, than local henchmen who did not come in contemplating the bench but are delighted to be commissioners of traffic and parking. Still, even on the city level, attrition is a factor in the makeup of all campaigns involving seasoned candidates. It complicates the politician's effort to acquire and keep skilled staffers at top levels, and it confounds in turn the staffers' efforts to maintain foot soldiers in adequate numbers on the precinct level. An observer not tempted to run against Mayor Kevin White at the conclusion of his fourth term would have opined that the mayor would have more than a little difficulty marshaling a staff and legions formidable enough to best a strong opponent, if one rose up to seek to deny him a fifth term.

More interested observers, with a notion to take Kevin on in 1983, could not be so certain, even in reflection on the perfunctory endorsement he had gotten from the voters in November 1979. And they had more need of certitude.

For openers, none of those who seemed potentially serious entrants in the 1983 contest emerged from 1979 with the doubtfully valuable front-running contender's status that had proven insufficient to propel Mrs. Hicks in 1971 or Joe Timilty in 1975 or 1979 into a position of the challenger to beat. Timilty was through, finished and fed up—when the state senate was redistricted on the basis of the 1980 census, he was not entirely surprised but still quite delighted to discover himself the beneficiary of a change that brought suburban Canton into his old bailiwick of Mattapan and Dorchester; he moved out, into the suburban woods.

That left the runners-up. Virtually tied behind Timilty in that year's primary were David Finnegan of the city council, and Mel King, then a state representative, each with 15 percent of the vote. Finnegan had been inspired to run for mayor when he led all city council candidates in the 1975 election but had just finished furnishing still another case study demonstrative of the fact that the willingness of Boston voters to give flattering pluralities to candidates for council and school committee implies no concomitant approval of any larger goals they might choose to entertain. King, who had come in ahead of Finnegan for third place in the primary by 123 votes, in those days alternated jumpsuits and flowered dashikis for his attire in public appearances; with his bristling black beard and shaved head, those uniforms made him rather difficult to take seriously.

Neither did the reserve field of Boston politicians seem to offer anyone with both the obvious capacity to unseat Kevin

White and the consequent ability to vie with him for the heavy financial support that would be needed to meet White on even terms. The 1978 statewide elections had brought one large convulsion to the Massachusetts Democratic party, as Edward J. King dumped Governor Michael S. Dukakis off the ticket in the primary and went on to win the general election against the GOP's Yankee candidate, Frank Hatch, but it appeared to have spawned no restless candidates for mayor of Boston. Dukakis lived in Brookline and proposed to spend his next four years appearing to rusticate at the Kennedy Institute of Politics at Harvard, while rebuilding his shattered political organization into a personal *Wehrmacht.* His lieutenant governor, Thomas P. O'Neill, Jr., the Speaker's son, lived on Beacon Hill and was known to be unhappy with a reelection victory of his own that had left him yoked with King. There were rumors that O'Neill might step down to challenge White, as there had been rumors that he would go after Edward W. Brooke's U.S. Senate seat in 1978, but he would prove much better at indecision than at making any moves.

All of which left Kevin White at the beginning of his fourth term looking very much like the class of any action to be projected for 1983. The only issue that confronted him was the racial conundrum, and while he could not claim to have solved it, he had kept it fairly calm for a good many seasons. He had said in his 1975 campaign literature that he felt his general obligation was to "orchestrate the city," and he could have been forgiven if he believed he had gotten pretty good at it. The only thing that he really had on his mind was the money problem that had been created back in March of the election year, which, when he was elected, really didn't seem that troublesome. Just a small matter, really, of recalibrating state aid for the city, which could be expeditiously handled by the general court when it at last got down to business. He was not wholly satisifed, perhaps, to be merely the devil that was known, but it did seem to be a fairly secure billet for as long as he might want it.

Inequality [is] the poison of all governments. . . .

—Alexander Hamilton
Notes of the Federal Convention
June 7–8, 1787

13

THAT SELF-PERCEPTION of himself as a wary, savvy, ring-wise, and realistic veteran led White during his last term as mayor to do things he never should have done. Concomitantly, it seems to have prompted him to omit actions that he would have in the past been punctilious to see completed. He was off his political feed.

The media consensus of his puzzling behavior was that he had developed terminal arrogance (there was a strident but unpublished minority view that as he had lost part of his stomach to ulcers sprouted during his doomed gubernatorial campaign, so had he parted with some of his reason during the later years). It was expressed regularly in the *Herald-American* by its columnist, Peter Lucas, and its city hall reporter, Howie Carr. It was kept alive in the *Globe* by Mike Barnicle, who likes to strike the mucker's pose in his column every now and then and often employed what he saw as White's airs and graces—dinner parties at the Parkman House, suites at New York's Hotel Pierre, that sort of thing—as the grist for a good spate of sneering.

The alternative interpretation was that he had gotten very stale in the job, had no interest in the day-to-day details of being mayor and therefore sloughed them generally, discontented and frustrated by his inability to fasten upon something else that he could do that would be more exciting.

Either way, he was not in that state a paradigm of the model major-city mayor, as he very much needed to be when things started to come unglued all around him. He had been returned to office more or less wearily resigned to the fact that he would have to manage somehow to improve law enforcement, fire protection, public housing, education, and get Boston's streets repaired and cleaned up, all with much less money that he thought he needed. While accomplishing these prodigies, he would have to satisfy the judges who were overseeing the jails, schools, and duty rosters of the police and fire departments that he was proceeding in all expeditious good faith to reward the long cherished hopes of minority groups who had sued for access to equal employment opportunities, without at the same time infuriating white jobholders with seniority who controlled the unions. For his own peace of mind and the sake of any future plans he might have, he would have to attend to that daunting agenda dependent on the backup efforts of politically influential but managerially distracted city employees whom he had eased into ill-defined but good-paying places on the city payroll by the device of provisional appointment (provisional appointments are permitted by the civil service laws for the unexceptionable purpose of enabling the mayor to secure temporary assistance from skilled noncareer professionals who desire neither the security civil service offers nor the damned annoyance of first taking the exams required to get it. When the city is under scrutiny for its hiring practices, as they affect racial minorities, such appointments also furnish the appointing officer with a convenient means for quiet circumvention of court supervision). In short, he had much to do, cash inadequate to do it, a great deal of irksome interference, and a shortage of good help as he began his fourth term in office. It was *Tregor* that had left him short of cash.

Norman Tregor lived in Newton and owned business properties in Boston. He did not think he was being treated fairly by the city's tax assessors. Long before the voters of the Commonwealth amended the state constitution in 1978 with a referendum permitting tax assessors to apply different standards of evaluation to parcels of real estate according to the uses that were made of them, Boston's assessors and those in most other Bay State communities had been doing just that. They levied on commercial properties by reference to informed guesswork estimates of what such assets would bring if offered for sale in the current market for comparative buildings in similar locations, designed for approximately the same purposes. They calculated taxes due on residential buildings, occupied by their owners, by reference to the value the houses had brought when they changed hands the last time.

That strategy was politically astute, especially for a community like Boston, where the most valuable properties were the tall buildings let out to corporations and other commercial enterprises able to pass on tax-related rent increases to their customers and clients, thus distributing them over a large number of disgruntled but disorganized contributors who would not perceive what was making prices go up and would not be able to do much about it if they did. It had the merit also of offending chiefly people such as Norman Tregor who did not vote there either.

At the same time, that assessing policy reduced the burdens on homeowners generally, people who did vote in the city. Furthermore the degree of mercy increased proportionately to the length of time those homeowners had resided in the city; the net effect was especially nice for those who were most likely to be experienced and active in city politics. For Kevin White and every other city politician who had wits enough to complete nomination papers, this long-standing assessment procedure was a serviceable means of acknowledging the resentful belief of the city's voters that daytime interlopers employed in it ought to share in the expenses of maintaining order, safety, highways, schools, and every other damned thing that the place provided them. Rough justice, perhaps, and from the politically opportunistic viewpoint of such people as Louise Day Hicks and Joseph Timilty not fully satisfactory justice, but still justice in its own way and quite unexceptionable.

Norman Tregor, disagreeing, took his exceptions into court. His claim was that whatever Massachusetts voters might have done to validate this practice in the 1978 referendum, it was not copacetic before that. He argued that the city had deprived him of the equal protection of the laws, guaranteed to him under the state and U.S. constitutions. On March 23, 1979, about nine months before Kevin White secured his fourth term as mayor, the Supreme Judicial Court agreed with Norman Tregor. It ruled that the Boston Assessing Department had wrongfully discriminated against him when it levied and collected taxes on his office buildings greater than those imposed on residential properties of comparable actual worth, and must give him back his money plus the interest that the law presumed it would have earned since he had paid it.

The total, $65,320, was not exactly dancing money but scarcely a staggering due bill for a city that had spent about $863,000,000 in the last fiscal year (1978) before the decision came down ("Boston's Recent Fiscal History: City of Boston Expenditures and Revenue 1960–FY 1982," Boston Redevelopment Authority). The panorama for metropolitan disaster did not open up until the reader of the SJC decision perceived that what the Court had said about Norman Tregor and his dealings with the city applied also and with equal force and effect to every other landlord of commerical real estate in Boston (except those like the developers of the Prudential Center who had cut tax deals with the city as prerequisites for their developments—the Pru's owners pay no realty taxes until 2001). The phone company, then New England Telephone and Telegraph Company, now NYNEX, acquired by the terms of *Tregor* a welcome windfall of around $25 million, and one Fawzi Saleh of Kuwait, investor of oil profits in some seventeen Boston business properties, got a rebate of $2.5 million for what had been done to him. As best the money people in the White administration could judge, Boston had improperly extracted about $143 million from landowners in the Tregor–Saleh–New England Telephone class, and now it would have to pay them back. That was a full 16 percent of the city's total revenues from all sources during 1978. It was 34 percent of what the city had collected in local tax revenues in 1978, $424 million; it exceeded by $4 million what the city had received in aid from the state in that year.

The long and short of the $143 million bill that Norman Tregor had managed to have presented to the city was that Boston couldn't pay it. There was some play in the tax rate because White, in the customary election-year fashion, had exerted all his ingenuity and charm in securing aid funds and juggling accounts to keep it from increasing very much just then. Floundering, he reacted to *Tregor* by pledging new economies in government, while leaning heavily upon the Boston delegation to the General Court to increase substantially the state's share of the cost of running Boston.

That delegation was led by Massachusetts State Senator William Bulger of South Boston, one of Kevin White's pals and among the wittiest of men in a town crowded with them. A classics scholar who reads Greek and Latin for diversion in the evening in his home devoid of television (he and his wife think its fare unsuited to the strictly disciplined Catholic upbringing they provided to their large family), Billy Bulger is short and blond and most mistrustful of the press. Especially the *Globe*. When the 1982 legislative session ended at long last, Bulger encountered a *Globe* reporter at the elevator. "Up or down?" said the reporter, finger poised to punch the button. "None of your trick questions," Bulger said, and made his own selection. He runs the state senate as its president, wielding power and the gavel with monopolistic determination. What he wants done generally gets done, and what he disapproves does not get through. He subscribed wholeheartedly to Kevin White's view that the state must shoulder more of Boston's burdens, and that meant that the senate would cooperate without protesting much.

The house was a different matter. Its Speaker, Thomas McGee of Lynn, was every bit as bent upon complete control of his 159 members as Bulger was demanding of his 39 colleagues, and he was at least as unforgiving of departures from his rule. A Marine who had overcome a crippling addiction to the booze, McGee is a B.U. Law School graduate who never passed the bar exam and claims never to have taken it. He has an extremely foul mouth and actively loathes the media. Mindful of days to come when he would stand in need of favorable action by Bulger's senate fiefdom on pet house bills of his own, McGee was disposed to grant the Boston delegation latitude enough to see whether they could secure house approval of a bailout aid bill but not deeply enough interested to commit his own prestige to the success of such a bill.

This meant that the mayor, through the mouths of Boston's reps and the pulpits of the media, had to convince a majority of some 150 state reps who lived outside of Boston that they ought to divert state funds to its special benefit. Those funds would be substantial, and they would come in addition to amounts of aid that had been pretty large before the Court agreed with Norman Tregor. In effect, he was asking legislation that would concede that the suburbs did in fact owe a large debt to Boston for the use they made of her and should be forced to pay it by additional state taxes.

Massachusetts State Representative Michael J. Barrett, Democrat of nearby Reading, a commuters' bedroom town that straddles Route 128 and derives a good deal of its middle-class white population from the managerial classes of Greater

Boston's white-collar economy, was perplexed by White's appeal. As he recalled in "The Out-of-Towners," published in the Sunday *Globe* magazine on August 7, 1983, his overriding private opinion was that Kevin White had a good case. Accustomed to relying on the educational, medical, cultural, and entertainment resources of Boston, aware of the central city's occupation by transportation and governmental facilities and offices that serve all of the Commonwealth, and cognizant that their payments to the city in lieu of taxes in 1978 totaled just over $20.2 million, 4 percent of the city's total tax revenue, Barrett could see valid reasons to increase the $139 million state aid contribution Boston had received that year. Fifty-one percent of Boston's forty-seven square miles is exempt from taxation, and virtually all of that property is intended to attract, educate, succor, or amuse residents and nonresidents of Boston alike. There is only one city in the United States, Barrett found, that allocates a greater portion of its land to tax-exempt uses, and that is the Federal City, Washington, D.C., established for public purposes and obtaining revenue from the taxation of private real estate holdings chiefly as an afterthought.

Barrett, though, seems not to have reckoned with one troublesome difficulty in constructing an analogy of Washington, and its nationally derived subsidy, with Boston and its appalling financial plight. The far-flung nonresidents of Washington who contribute so much of their money to its daily operation these days cannot recall having been asked at any time whether this is something they would like to do. Or, since they and their forebears have been doing it so long, whether they would like to keep on doing it. The nature of White's Tregor Bailout Bill, as it was commonly called, inescapably posited that threshold question to the state reps who were obliged to debate it and thus to their constituents who lived outside of Boston.

Overlooking that distinction, Barrett was still sufficiently uncertain of his own view to inquire of the voters in his district whether they would like to provide further help to Boston, over and above its proportionate share of state aid, which is based on population, public transit deficits, court administration costs, and that sort of thing, distributed among all Bay State towns and cities. He and a staff member did a telephone sampling of Reading opinion: they learned seven out of ten among his constituents felt no sense whatsoever of financial responsiblity for Boston. Further questions ascertained that this attitude prevailed in 128 homes where no less than 125 separate and significant resorts to Boston's tax-exempt resources—getting educated, finding work, seeking treatment for some serious ailment—had materially improved the lives of the occupants.

Barrett reasoned that this showed his friends and neighbors shared the negative impression of the city. It had led him to hesitate before plunging into legislative debate on the side of the Tregor Bailout Bill. He admitted to his own strong feelings of distaste for Boston, which he said were derived principally from its reputation for political corruption. Granting that to deny state support to the city is a "lapse of responsibility on the part of the rest of Massachusetts, in which Boston has been made a preserve of great institutions and then left to deal with the economic consequences on its own," he predicted that "public support for the city will not appear . . . until one overriding problem is confronted: the corruption of the municipal administration." (*Globe* magazine, 8/7/83, p. 43) In his opinion the suburban citizen, safe outside of city limits, bears the same antagonism toward the city that the sullen Bostonian harbors but can express only by leaving it, and that antagonism is not hatred for intruders of another color: it is for corruption.

The importance of Barrett's inference from his amateur poll is not so much that it was almost certainly wrong, although I am inclined to think it was, but that he, a member of what the eminent historian Samuel Eliot Morison in his *Oxford History of the American People* had declared to be the least efficient and most corrupt of modern American state legislatures, singled out as his major reason for hesitating over the Tregor Bailout Bill the city's reputation for corruption. Barrett's official leader, McGee, was a passionate admirer of the late John Forbes Thompson, the Iron Duke whose career in the same job had ended with his death while under indictment on some fifty charges of corruption. Barrett wrote while the U.S. Court of Appeals for the First Circuit was pondering the appeal of Massachusetts State Senator James Kelley's conviction of accepting bribes while he was the chairman of the Senate Ways and Means Committee. Giving the young Reading representative full marks for recognizing the prime desideratum of integrity in government, one is still constrained to conclude that he blinked the substance of his voters' reaction: they were generally suspicious of governmental plaints that would cost them money to receive with sympathy.

This pervasive attitude, to the astonished dismay of Massachusetts politicians at all governmental levels, was emphatically expressed by Bay State voters twenty months after the Supreme Court nodded in agreement with Norman Tregor and sent Boston's managers into a tailspin. In the 1980 general state elections, voters overwhelmingly approved a referendum question patterned on California's real estate tax cap amendment and proscribed the taxation of any residential real estate, by any town or city, in an annual amount exceeding 2.5 percent of its actual market value. Proposition $2^1/2$, as it was familiarly known, survived intensive mooing and much anguished preelection bleating by the Massachusetts Teachers Association, the American Federation of State, County, Municipal and Federal Employees (AFSCME), and spokesmen for every other union and industry dependent on the public purse for its pocket money. It succeeded because

unorganized and beleaguered middle-class homeowners recognized a rare means to afford themselves a measure of
defense against organized special-interest raiding parties regularly preying on the public bourse.

Until that watershed election, Massachusetts politicians,
local, county, and state, had faithfully recapitulated in their
more modest realms the craven reactions of federal budget
planners supine before all pleaders for new spending able to
muster strident claques behind them. Public debate on such
issues was truncated to exclude consideration of whether the
proposed addition to the panoply of governmental services
was necessary, and if so, whether its cost was one the taxpayers could afford. Selectivity and the necessity to defer gratification, familiar realities to private persons, are strange to
politicians, spending public monies. They can always get
some more. Selectmen wishing to present themselves as decent sorts in the communities where they operated retail businesses, practiced law, provided funeral services, and filled
cavities in teeth, had no ambition to appear hardhearted by
rejecting day-care centers to improve the lot of working
mothers, bilingual educational programs to accelerate the
learning process of recent immigrants, or any of a host of
other beneficial plans. Furthermore, they had no reasonable
expectation of community support, should they choose to demur to such proposals. Parsimony has no lobbyists in place. If
the proponents had identified an actual prospect of arranging
an improvement to the life of the community, the officials'
inclination was to vote to institute it, even though this almost
always carried with it the assurance of an increase in the taxes
upon local real estate. Similarly, county commissioners freely
expanded payrolls and lavished new equipment upon ineffi-
cient highway departments, while state officers fairly vied
with one another to discover new and more ingenious ways to
spend the people's money. Always the taxpayers were told
that that new local program would add at the most a few

coins, perhaps a dollar, to the real estate tax rate. Always the voters heard that the new surcharge on the state income tax, the newly enacted sales tax, the later increase in the sales tax, the hikes in levies upon gasoline, cigarettes, and booze would be earmarked for increases in state aid to the communities, better highways, nicer hospitals, greatly improved schools; the reduction, in other words, of local real estate taxes. And invariably, the next year, those same officials would be standing there before the voters, saying with great melancholy that things hadn't worked out quite as had been planned and more new taxes would be needed to stave off certain ruin. After a few years, and many tax increases, sanctimonious ragtime of that sort becomes a little tiresome, and the listener who is trying to pay off a mortgage by means of his own labor develops the suspicion that he's being had.

I think it was that simmering resentment that Michael Barrett tapped when he polled the Reading voters for their views of whether Boston should be rescued from the clutches of its creditors. Those creditors were people whom the Boston tax collectors had reamed out of monies that they should not have had to pay. By its terms, the Tregor Bill was a state undertaking to impose upon suburban communities, whose own officials had been somewhat profligate, the costs of Boston's greater profligacies; it should not have surprised reps from those other towns and cities that their citizens did not applaud the notion.

Nevertheless, Barrett and those reps did divine by some means or another that the people upon whom they depended for their seats in the state house would not kindly receive news that their state income taxes would be going up, to discharge the bills due for Boston's extravagance. Therefore, lest the house be recorded as invertebrate before the city's demands, the reps made some counterdemands of their own. Boston would have to take the money for its bail as a loan and furnish some collateral to insure its repayment.

The city's first response to this was a proposal to impose a 15 percent excise upon public parking fees. This would generate new revenues, not previously earmarked for some earlier boondoggle, and with new taxes upon restaurant meals and hotel rooms enrich the city's coffers enough to repay the borrowed money. Reps from towns outside of Boston swiftly perceived, or soon had it pointed out to them, that those new taxes would impinge upon the suburban commuter to the city, jacking up the cost of parking his car near his job and clipping him some extra cash when he took time for lunch. There was also the suggestion that a new tax on hotel rooms might not be the best way to encourage the convention trade that Boston had been courting with all of its new hotels. For years those in the suburbs had been smarting under city sneering published in the *Globe*, such as Mayor Collins had indulged himself before the U.S. Senate Subcommittee on Intergovernmental Relations in February of 1967: "They don't make any contribution. Most people who live in the suburbs come into the city to work and then they leave for their nice comfortable homes on an acre or a half-acre lot, sit down and have a couple of martinis, then chuckle over the 'urban problems' that they're twenty-five miles away from." (*Globe*, 2/12/67, p. 72) Now the people in the suburbs had Boston over a barrel, and they were getting some of their own back.

Resourceful as ever, the state politicians holding Boston hostage up on Beacon Hill at last found a way to get it off the hook while doing themselves and their loyalists a little good as well. When the Tregor Bill was at last passed in 1982, it imposed no new parking taxes or other imposts that would fall directly upon the constituents of the state reps and senators who had to vote for it. What it did was transfer ownership of the city's Hynes Auditorium complex, at the Prudential Center, and the Boston Undercommon Parking Garage, from the city to the state, for a price that would with some other minor adjustments set off what the city needed to pay off its tax creditors. At the same time, the bill set up a State Convention Authority and created a new lifetime job as its director, at $75,000 a year; that went to the chief Bulger loyalist on Beacon Hill, Francis Joyce. After, of course, the usual charade of conducting a diligent, intergalactic public search for the best-qualified administrator—it is surprising how frequently national quests for qualified administrators to fill comfortably salaried Massachusetts jobs end with the pleased discovery by the searchers that the best man or woman for the job was right in their midst all along.

During all of eighteen months of horseplay in the General Court, Boston and its mayor verged on desperation. The tax rebates due the landlords under *Tregor* did not in most instances require cash outlays by the city, inasmuch as the creditors still owned the real estate which had been overtaxed and could be made whole by setoffs against their subsequent tax bills. What those refunds did was reduce by the $143 million total the income that the city had to spend. This played the devil with bond and interest payments, which had to be met promptly lest the credit rating drop and future obligations become worthless on the market. That tipped the need to reduce spending, rendered more extreme by Proposition $2^{1}/_{2}$, onto the service departments, at least in Mayor White's view. And it was in the implementation of that view that he achieved new levels of disapproval among his constituents; it was almost as though he had been courting it.

A man that studieth revenge keeps his own
wounds green.

—Francis Bacon
Of Revenge

14

DURING the legislature's year and a half of finagling, the
mayor's initial sense of urgency deteriorated into one of frustrated rage. His sense of perspective deserted him—the dila-
toriness of the General Court, which surely should have come
as no surprise to any Massachusetts politician, overcame his
judgment. He began to do things that made it appear he was
having tantrums.

The trouble was that the tantrums of a mayor have considerably more impact upon a great many more people than
do the spiteful performances of an undisciplined child, an
ungoverned adult, or a senescent elder. White's vindictive determination to hold the feet of Boston's reps to the fire of
approaching insolvency for Boston seemed to him to warrant
the creation of real public consternation. To get the attention
of Representative Billy Galvin of Brighton, a boyish-looking
lad whose oral undertakings are scrutinized carefully in
Massachusetts governmental circles, and Representative Sal
DiMasio, whose district abuts Beacon Hill, Mayor White set
the defenseless citizenry howling. His highway department,
quadrennially energetic to repair road surfaces but otherwise
at best halting in its efforts to refill the potholes and plow the
snow from the streets—it is widely believed that melting is
the preferred mode of snow removal—for all practical pur-

poses vanished. Travelers could have been forgiven if they speculated that the uncollected rubbish littering the city was being conserved for application as landfill. His police and fire departments, restive under hiring policies mandated by the federal courts engaged in overseeing the accomplishment of racial equilibrium on the rolls of their employees, were subjected to Reductions In Force (RIFs) cutting available manpower by as much as 40 percent, and the school department saw its teaching staff similarly depleted; the courts reacted to black complaints of discrimination in a new disguise by ruling that contractual pledges of job security directly proportional to seniority must be abrogated in order to assure that layoffs impinge evenhandedly across racial lines. Long-term white city employees were consequently furloughed while very junior blacks held on to jobs during the Carter recession, thus reversing the inching progress toward assimilation of the races that had gotten under way in the departments.

For those city residents who might not have noticed that there weren't as many cops on patrol as there used to be, had no kids of their own in the public schools, and exercised care in disposing of smoking materials around their homes, Mayor White devised dramatic public demonstrations of his grim resolve in securing passage of the Tregor Bill no matter what the cost to public peace of mind: he started closing district fire and police stations. This left Brighton residents screaming that any needed police assistance would start out from downtown, while East Boston homeowners had no trouble whatsoever conjuring up the consequences when fire apparatus located downtown should be asked to respond to some disaster occuring on the east side of the Callahan Tunnel during the rush hour. White's car was mobbed and immobilized by a demonstration on the Eastie side of the tunnel when he went to visit, and the greetings shouted at him were unfriendly. To all of these anguished complaints, the mayor replied that it was not his fault. He said it was the doing of the reps who were still stalling on the Tregor Bill.

That proposition might have had more chance of provoking sympathy if he had not at the same time made it quite plain that Boston's financial woes did not hamper operations in his Office of Cultural Affairs and his Communications Bureau. Chief Press Secretary George Regan's salary reached $57,000, and his staff expanded to what the mayor said was nine and suspicious onlookers believed was closer to a dozen. There was no dearth of hors d'oeuvres from the gourmet kitchens of Rebecca Karas's restaurant on Charles Street for the nourishment of Parkman House guests who dropped in for a little table wine. Mayoral visits to Our Nation's Capital and to Manhattan called for limousines and first-class hotel accommodations, as the commentators did not fail to note in their reportage to the angry citizens. It was very much as though he had been giving everyone, the entire city and all who cared about it, an almost regal version of the finger.

He picked a rotten time to do it. No matter how exasperated he had become in contemplation of the legislature, and no matter how understandable the vexation that he felt in the intransigent refusal of the populous high-number wards to endorse his candidacies by adoring acclamation, he indulged himself in petulance at precisely the wrong instant in the history of Boston journalism. Quite apart from anything White did, Boston media were in a state of uproar all their own during most of his last term in office. They hungrily eyed vulnerable subjects whose pelts might be taken for prominent display in the game rooms of the media as trophies of competitive superiority. The mayor was a prime speciman, out there in the open and already wounded by those old corruption charges that had slowed him down a little. Now if he was willing to be careless with his previously cherished public pose of "The Loner in Love with His City," the hallmark of his 1979 campaign, he might be nearly ready to bring down.

The attraction of that mission in the first years of the 1980s was a function of an abrupt escalation of competition among Boston reporters. The nasty little contest between the *Phoenix* and *The Real Paper* was in its terminal and most desperate phase for *The Real Paper*, which made bushwhacking Kevin White a mandatory weekly feature for each paper. Channel 7's owner, RKO-General, had plainly lost a battle that had gone on many years, striving to rebut proofs of unfitness to secure FCC renewal of its broadcast license, which had been collected and presented by contending would-be owners—its indigenous news staff under the discredited proprietors was seeking credits that would open hiring doors elsewhere; as those harriers departed they were replaced by equally vulpine successors bent upon embarrassing colleagues at channels 5 and 4. The *Herald-American*, teetering each day upon the edge of corporate euthanasia threatened by Hearst owners in New York fed up with its deficits, struggled to distinguish itself from the comfortable *Globe* in order to annex a little circulation which might goose up advertising and draw an admiring glance or two from some wealthy savior. *Boston magazine*, seeking some restoration of journalistic reputation under its fire-eating editor, John Brady, roamed the fringes of the city's politics, scouting monthly articles that might bust a few blocks and get some respect for the best-fern-bars-and-Bloody-Marys periodical. And suddenly the *New York Times* developed a strong interest in what happened in New England besides commencement at Harvard and the newest information on the double helix to come out of DNA research at MIT, a shift of emphasis the *Globe* did not like at all.

Until mid-1981, when *Times* correspondent Michael Knight left its employment and New England beat, the *Times* had been content to reassure New Yorkers every year that the leaves north of, say, Westerly, Rhode Island, were indeed changing colors once more in the growing autumn chill, following those bulletins seasonably with reports of packed powder north of Brattleboro, adequate supplies of maple sugar in Mud Time, and confidence of a prosperous tourist plucking coming out of Cape Cod around the first of May. At first, when the *Times* replaced Knight with Dudley Clendinen, there appeared to be no major changes in store, but there had in fact already been one. The *Times* had acquired access to satellite technology that would permit it to produce fresh news of New England on a daily basis and deliver it to New England doorsteps in time to be read over the morning coffee. Its management executives paid a thoughtful courtesy visit to *Globe* editor Thomas Winship and informed him that henceforth the *Times* planned to compete aggressively for circulation on the home turf of New England's Largest Daily Newspaper.

Superficially, that notice was ostensibly unthreatening. The *Times* hardly promised to become a competitor for the *Globe*'s daily circulation, hovering around the 500,000 mark in its home territory. Boston's major advertisers evinced no inclination to desert the *Globe*, either. What made the *Times* declaration into one of war was the nature of the surgical strike its operators clearly had in mind: they were after the *Globe*'s influence, which is to say, its power. And that power was what had enabled the *Globe*'s editors and publishers to affect so markedly the way that Boston had been governed since the early 1960s.

Today, robust and rich, the *Globe* is a monopoly in Boston. Other media still exist and publish in the city, but the items on the menu of intense public discussion must be selected and approved by the people who put out the *Boston Globe*. Modestly at first, they will demur to that charge and then with some genteel heat deny it if the accuser persists, but anyone who's written or pronounced for a competing Boston outlet knows they are being disingenuous.

This *Globe* primacy is a product of the same changes that have transformed the city itself since the end of the Korean War, functioning also to winnow and cull its communications media. While the suburbs flourished and drew prospering Bostonians to new homes on its perimeters, the rail system waned under Boston & Maine and New York, New Haven & Hartford mismanagement and folly, leaving the newly minted commuters crowding access roads to Boston every morn and every night. Those choked roads baffled printers of the Boston *Traveler;* they couldn't get their P.M. papers to their old friends who had moved. The new lives sheltered at the wooded ends of those roads were outside their coverage area; they didn't know what new concerns came with the raised ranch out in Reading, and they made no shift to learn. The same sort of indolence, bound up with arrant tendencies to economic mischief, made the *Post* irrelevant and soon bankrupt as well. The Hearst tabloids, morning *Record* and P.M. *American,* obstinately catered to a class of renters who had gotten hold of some cash, purchased small lots of land, and left the city; gradually those tabs contracted into one: the *Record-American.* The *Traveler's* management, perceiving that the A.M. *Herald* was not holding its own with the morning *Globe,* combined the two into the evening *Herald-Traveler* and rested content with the belief that the parent corporation, which owned WHDH-TV, channel 5, would never lose its license from the FCC and could keep the papers afloat on the profits. The FCC revoked that license and transferred it, and in time the *Herald-Traveler* was sold to the Hearst people, who put it together with the merged *Record-American* to create the wallowing hulk that Rupert Murdoch purchased for peanuts late in 1982 and now puts out as the *Boston Herald.*

Through all of this turmoil, the *Globe* grew only sleeker and more dominant of what constitutes the surviving media in Boston. Its readers are the only ones in the Greater Boston area who have been able to nurture their newspaper habits and to tend their loyalties without significant disruption since Japan surrendered and the nuclear age dawned. Except for some minor and unseemly labor troubles which afflicted everyone a good many years ago, the *Globe* adjusted smoothly to change, moving its plant out of downtown Boston to North Dorchester, putting its printing plants in staging areas where the trucks can move out quickly to the stands and the delivery drops, ceding the P.M. suburban market gracefully to such consequently deferential competition as the *Quincy Patriot Ledger* to the south and the *Lawrence Eagle Tribune* to the north, surviving in the shambles as the only major Boston daily paper.

To a generation harassed by television to the point at which surrender to the glowing eye's demands for time not spent at sleep or work begins to seem appealing, that serene longevity in service is the *Globe's* strongest suit. Television doesn't ask much of its consumer, except that he turn it on. Readers have to make a little effort: find the paper where the damned kid threw it this time, spread it out on something so the arms don't go to sleep while reading it, choose among the reports that are offered in proliferation that TV can never match, sometimes even think about what has been printed in them. Proportionately fewer people attempt such exertion now than did in the years before television yammered unattended on and on and accustomed people to the notion that somebody will soon tell them what they need to know. Many of those who persist, and those avatars who have recently acquired the practice of such regular exertions, do so chiefly out of habit. Once broken of that habit, by a newspaper strike that cuts off their source of supply or an uprooting that takes them far away from it, they frequently do not resume it. It is then understandable why the prospect of a strike horrifies newspaper executives everywhere. Continuity is what has made the *Globe* rich and what accounts for the fact that the majority of those who read any newspaper at all in Boston read only the *Boston Globe;* for several years there has been no alternative. That the paper is also pretty good is quite irrelevant.

The expansion of New England coverage promised by the *Times* did not put that numerical dominance in hazard. Reports had it that the *Times* had no realistic expectation of acquiring more than 40,000 daily circulation in the *Globe's* area (it came in with 41,000 on Sundays). The likelihood was that the *Globe* would keep most of the households that decided to accept the *Times,* at least for the foreseeable future. Even if the New York paper's Boston coverage proved regularly intriguing, it would not come wrapped in movie listings, local sports, or reports about sewer bonds held up by Boston area selectmen. At the most, the *Times* would come to occupy a new place of its own in those homes and offices where the *Globe* had been routinely taken, an additional source of information for the intelligent and cultivated professional whose interest in affairs outside of his personal world is great enough to move him to subscribe to another paper every day and take the time to read it.

That was what bothered the *Globe.* To the readership of which it was proudest, the power elite of the city, it stood to lose the exclusivity of its authority to determine the agenda of discussion and eventual action. It had always acted upon the occasionally grudging presumption that national and international priorities were for American newspapers the primary responsibility of the *Times,* the *Washington Post,* and from time to time the *Wall Street Journal.* Carved out of that hegemony, and jealously guarded in its isolation, was the *Globe's* monopoly of definition of Bostonian issues. Its endorsement of Kevin White over Louise Day Hicks in 1967 was in its view a decision taken with deserved solemnity, in recognition of the fact that it deemed the situation grave enough to warrant imposition of sanctions stayed for these seven decades during which the *Globe* had endorsed nobody. Plainly, the editors acted with a sense that they were doing something momentous.

The outcome of that effort emboldened them. In 1971, 1975, and again in 1979, albeit with perceptibly diminishing enthusiasm, they endorsed Kevin White for reelection. They did so with the expectation that attention would be paid, and since the election returns conformed to their explicit wishes on each of those occasions, they could have been pardoned for overlooking the possibility that the fallacy of *post hoc, propter hoc,* infected their reasoning. Then, too, because the candidate whom they had endorsed each time had won by respectable margins, four precedent decisions had been recorded to instruct future candidates on the power of the *Globe.* Those later contestants might also question privately whether *Globe* approval was a prerequisite for victory, but to be on the safe side they would exercise special pains not to affront the *Globe.* Power, whatever its corrupting effects, begets greater power.

If the *Times,* by regularly impressing Boston's movers and shakers, gained a foothold of credibility on local matters even remotely similar to the authority it has long possessed on the issue of national affairs, that *Globe* power would be challenged. The crippled *Herald* might inveigh against a *Globe* selection as it wished, without anyone paying it much heed, but if the *Times,* even stopping far short of an editorial pronouncement, drove home the opinion that the *Globe's* choice in a given race might be open to some doubt, then that choice would be doubted. To a lesser but still worrisome degree, the *Times,* by appearing to endorse the same candidate favored by the *Globe,* could dilute the *Globe's* power slightly, implying that not one but two imprimaturs made the standard approval.

The *Times* notice of competition in the local market therefore prompted the *Globe* to air out its drawers of long

undisturbed linens. Some cosmetic improvements were instituted, among them a weekly Sci-Tech section aimed at preservation of the devotion of Route 128 and university scientific
and technical types who spend all of their time fooling
around with microchips and much of the money they spend
advertising the devices they build from those chips in the *Boston Globe*. Completely recovered from the disappointment
suffered in discovery of the difference between the cost of
maintaining a Tokyo bureau during the Vietnam War and the
number of world-beating stories that came back from it, the
Globe began to look eastward for new bureau sites. It sent
a man to London in 1983, there to compete with The
Associated Press, Reuters, the *Washington Post–L.A. Times*
News Service, and God only knows how many shoestring operations covering an entire continent.

While all of that was going on, the *Globe* kept a close eye
on its local turf. What it observed the *Times* doing there did
not make it feel cheerful. Clendinen had no sooner set up
shop at Knight's old desk than he was reinforced, perhaps not
to his unalloyed joy, by Fox Butterfield. Butterfield had just
completed a book wrapping up what he had learned as
the *Times*'s first Peking, China, correspondent since the
Communist Revolution. To natives inquisitive about his evident redundancy as second man in what had always been a
one-man bureau, Butterfield cited his roots in Cambridge, his
wife's family ties in North Andover, and their ten years' residence outside the United States in the service of the *Times* as
the makeweights of his request to its management that he be
allowed to roost awhile in Boston. He said his intentions were
to explore new breakthroughs in deep thinking around
Cambridge. Nobody gave much credence to this, especially
when Butterfield began asking questions about Kevin White.

Inspirited by that activity, the *Globe* moved to retaliate by
beefing up its city hall coverage and applying that new mus-
cle to its principal tenant. This meant that the *Herald*'s one-

man band, Peter Sleeper, had not one but two prosperous dailies on the scene, each with forces at least double his own, and the television folks as well to goad him to greater efforts. Dan Rea and Andy Hiller out of channel 4; Kirby Perkins of channel 5; Howie Carr, ex-*Herald* staffer then at channel 7; Tom Sheehan and Michael Rezendes of the *Phoenix;* Clendinen in chivalrous tacit competition with his colleague, Butterfield: all were there to remind Walter Robinson and Charles Kenney of the *Globe* that the supremacy of their journal in the coverage of Boston was still very much a disputed question.

The standard of performance, against which all of the participants were measured at least weekly, was which of them had managed to convey most strikingly the unmistakable hypothesis that Kevin White was crooked. He was not without a strong supporting role in the production, although he had by his own choice comparatively few dramatic lines.

That play of conflict ran almost a year, from the spring of 1982 until White delivered his own mayoral eulogy on May 26, 1983. A highlight of the first stages came on July 14, 1982, when the *Globe* dumped him.

During the course of this administration and in order to disturb it, the artillery of the press has been levelled against us, charged with whatsoever its licentiousness could devise or dare. These abuses of an institution so important to freedom and science, are deeply to be regretted, inasmuch as they tend to lessen its usefulness, and to sap its safety; they might, indeed, have been corrected by wholesome punishments reserved and provided by the laws of the several States against falsehood and defamation; but public duties more urgent press upon the time of public servants, and the offenders have therefore been left to find their punishment in the public indignation.

—Thomas Jefferson
Second Inaugural Address
March 4, 1805

15

IT SOUNDED so good starting out, the *Globe's* revocation of its sponsorship of Kevin Hagan White. It began with a bow of affectionate nostalgia: "Ten years ago this week, at the Democratic National Convention, he was the most important person in American politics—for about four hours. Kevin H. White, the mayor of Boston, was the first choice of Sen. George McGovern for the Democratic vice presidential nomination.

"After weighing the pluses and minuses of other candidates," the *Globe* recollected fondly, "Gary Hart, the McGovern campaign manager, focused on White as the consensus choice. He was a young, articulate Catholic from the Northeast, a fervent opponent of the war in Vietnam, fresh and politically 'clean,' free from any taint of corruption or scandal."

That was an interesting statement. Taken on its terms, it meant that the *Globe* exonerated White of any odor of wrongdoing that had been imputed to him in the miasmic allegations dredged out of the Patriarca tapes. It also meant the *Globe* rejected any notion that real estate developers had been shaken down in the Ritz for large contributions to his 1970 gubernatorial campaign. After all, both those sets of charges had been aired out pretty thoroughly during the 1971 mayoral campaign; if White had been pristine a year later, the *Globe* clearly believed that there was nothing to them.

Calling to mind the destruction that John Kenneth Galbraith and affiliated Bay State liberal Democrats had wreaked upon their putative soul mate in Boston city hall— "Their objection to White," the *Globe* observed wryly, "was that he was a politician"—the *Globe* characterized local reaction to the short national celebration of the mayor as "at first incredulous, then more thoughtful, agreeing with White that McGovern's active consideration was 'a heck of a tribute to the city.' "

The *Globe* said that the Kevin White of the McGovern nomination vintage "was known for his innovation, his openness to new ideas, his presence in the neighborhoods, his insistence on choosing intelligent, dedicated and honest people." This was where the note of regret began to get insistent, always a good place for the subject of an encomium in progress to pull his head down and make plans to cover up. The first rocket usually arrives right after such wistfulness for bygone days of glory is read into the record, and this occasion was no exception to that general rule.

"In 1982, as he enters the third decade of his political career," the *Globe* began to scold, "Kevin White is no longer known for these traits." Note that the *Globe* did not accuse him of exhausting his supply of innovation, his hospitality to untarnished thoughts, his willingness to persist in visitation to the neighborhoods where the neighbors had become a trifle testy watching fire and police stations close down, or his determination to hire smart, devoted, and scrupulous people, although all of those allegations could have been leveled with some justice. The *Globe's* complaint was that the *image* was no longer one of a man with those admirable qualities. "For this reason, the *Boston Globe* urges him not to run next year for a fifth term."

It amounted to a declaration that White shouldn't run again because the editors of the *Globe* didn't love him anymore and wanted a divorce. They wanted him to know that it was nothing personal, of course. "The mayor is an intelligent, often introspective, man with a sense of history. He can best spend the remainder of his term in office affirming his historic mark upon this city. He can best spend the next 18 months trying to unite the city, leading it through fiscal, political and racial troubles ahead."

That, of course, was what he thought he had spent the last 174 months doing, three times taking time out to renew his forty-eight-month leases on the office, each time with an endorsement on his application from the *Boston Globe*. If, as the *Globe* now seemed to be suggesting, he had either failed to cure the division of the city he had inherited, or worse yet, had exacerbated it, there was very little possibility that a year and a half more of his attentions would improve the situation, even if he spent the interval undistracted by concern for reelection.

Curiously, the *Globe*, having stated that it would not welcome more than eighteen additional months of White's management of Boston, appeared at the same time to be reasonably satisfied with the results of his service to date in his office. Saying that the city's growth is "a healthy, ongoing process to which Kevin White has contributed greatly," it expressed the confidence that his successor would "inherit a strong legacy." Presumably this would include the fiscal, political, and racial problems that White had but eighteen months to correct, given his inability to resolve them before July 14, 1982—some legacy, that bag of cats.

The heir to this mixed collection, in the *Globe*'s published estimation, could be almost anyone, and surely ought to be. Noting that "[o]f the half dozen candidates preparing to run next year, three received their start in politics working for Kevin White," a fact the *Globe* found pleasingly demonstrative of his influence upon the city still so badly divided as to be in dire need of somebody other than the influential Kevin White to lead it through its problems, the *Globe* said impatiently: "Any of them would be preferable to Kevin White in 1983."

That was not a reasoned appeal to the body politic. It did not put forth a set of facts demanding a conclusion, offering an argument for serious consideration by the thoughtful Boston voter. It was an emotional outburst, the same sort of garbled *cri de coeur* that the *Globe* had uttered in White's benediction on November 6, 1967. Then, scared to death of Mrs. Hicks, its editors had fabulized a Kevin White personifying principle, some sort of gray-flanneled paladin who would bring peace to a city of irrationally frightened citizens wrongfully believing that school busing might be forced upon them. Four years later, without so much as a sheepish concession that its calming words of "no forced busing" might have been the slightest bit misleading, the *Globe* brusquely called for precisely that corrective. And now, as the fifteenth anniversary of its first anointing of Kevin White approached, the *Globe* snatched its skirts away from his now muddied progress.

The outburst made a total of three gross excesses performed by the *Globe* on its own editorial page in the excitement that it felt to run the city: one to put itself into the business of providing moral advice to its eager readers, two more to recant the advice it had given that first time, so as to position itself to deliver new maxims. As its autopsy of its mayoral hero showed, getting out of an endorsement without giving the real reason—or a good one—is an awkward piece of work.

"White has survived less because of political and more because of theatrical skills," it said. "He has become the Marlon Brando of politics. His brush with Potomac fever a decade ago was his *On the Waterfront*. The performance was as poignant as Brando telling Rod Steiger, 'I coulda been a contendah. I coulda been somebody.' " *Coulda* been somebody? Kevin White *had* been somebody, the *Globe's* designated defender of the "principle of equal treatment for all people" for God's sake, back in 1967—wasn't the Hub's twentieth-century version of Abe Lincoln "somebody" in *Globe* terms by 1982?

Well, actually, no—it wasn't fun anymore. "As Brando gradually began to play himself in character roles, so did White—the aloof Godfather, the 'loner in love with his city.' But the critics aren't cheering and the audience is dwindling." The mayor's ratings were declining, in other words, so it was time to cancel his show for the coming season.

"In 1972, some of Kevin White's people worked for him diligently and left the city payroll for distinguished public careers. Now, a new set of Kevin White's people includes two who have left the city payroll to go to jail. One of them, a ward coordinator, had a criminal record when White hired him as an 'administrative assistant' on the city payroll.

"In 1981, facing reduced revenues, White did not dismantle his political machine. He did not lay off his political ward coordinators and precinct captains, whose sole allegiance is to him and not to the city. Instead, he trifled with the security of the city, treating police officers and firefighters as yo-yos, laying them off and rehiring them as a political 'symbol' of Boston's fiscal distress. This was not a gesture of 'love with his city.'

"This 'symbol' created anxiety for hundreds of thousands of Bostonians and reduced Kevin White's own credibility to the vanishing point. A new mayor can restore the city's credibility on Beacon Hill and in Washington merely by being inaugurated.

"No political leader wants to become a lame duck sooner than necessary. Kevin White is a man of occasionally gifted vision and of singular political talent. He can still lead the city and will be treated more fondly by it if he realizes it's time to leave gracefully." (*Globe*, 7/14/82, p. 12)

The impact of that editorial, while personally devastating White, severely damaged his vote-getting potential among Boston's trendier liberal set, where such pronouncements are taken very seriously. To the full-time politicians, organizers, and the more disgruntled of rich favor-seekers, it was a peremptory suggestion to be incorporated into preparations for negotiation with the incumbent mayor of Boston. To his friends and to his implacable enemies, Kevin White's formidable aspect as an active foe owed much to his perceived sponsorship by the *Boston Globe*. These were men of the world, quite able to discount sniping at him in the stories printed in the *Globe* as necessary demonstrations of the paper's evenhandedness toward all candidates, perhaps even means of keeping him in line. Until that editorial disowned him, the received wisdom was that if White ever did find himself in a tight spot, this side of indictment, the *Globe* after some hemming and some hawing would protect his interest.

That sort of unmentioned leverage is extremely precious to a politician; it gives him at the outset of any acrimonious exchange the unspoken option to nullify his disputant's capacity to bring public embarrassment upon him. Developers who play hardball when their building plans are bottled up; union bargaining agents; community activists with ambitions to annex for themselves important authority over city decisions: people like that in the end can harm an uncooperative elected official only by threatening his public ignominy. When they begin with the belief that that avenue is closed to them, as most did when approaching Kevin White during his long romance with the *Globe*, they are much easier to deal with. On the afternoon of July 14, 1982, therefore, Kevin White's effective operating power had been diminished by the *Globe's* dismissal of him as a candidate for reelection; the extent of that diminution would take a while to determine, but it was significant.

At the same time, a scuffle began for early foot in the race among other hopefuls to replace White in the *Globe's* affections. The obvious path to that bower of delights lay to the left of the centrist and rightist ideological plateaus where the numerical majority of Boston voters were believed to live. The left fork looked like an easy route for Mel King, the black activist candidate who had gathered in enough votes for third place in the 1979 primary, given his oft-stated belief that the first function of the government is to finance all programs of potential benefit to those in poverty. Ray Flynn, concentrating by then on his city council duties after quitting as state representative from South Boston to make time available to run for mayor, believed he could nudge his ideas far enough in that direction to make a *Globe* endorsement feasible. David Finnegan, narrowly trailing King in the 1979 race, had since become host of an evening talk show on WBZ radio, which made him the darling of the geriatric set while giving him much practice in developing a rap style. Finnegan had intended to present himself as a clone of Kevin White but without all the bad companions and the nasty gossip clinging to the mayor. That approach seemed to him a likely suit to press before the *Globe*. Lawrence DiCara, the ebullient Italo bachelor of Dorchester with the Harvard degree and the ob-

session to be mayor, had renounced the city council to prepare himself for the fight, and he brought Kennedy Institute
credentials to increase his stature when he called at the *Globe*
as Boston's latter-day Fiorello LaGuardia. Robert Kiley,
ex-CIA manager of international student fronts, had been
very effective as White's overseer of busing and head of
the hideously balled-up Massachusetts Bay Transportation
Authority and had put down his transplanted upper-midwest
roots on Beacon Hill, gaining much fealty there. He thought
he stood a decent chance of winning the *Globe*'s heart. Fred
Langone said he was going to run, too, calling on his fellow
sexagenarians to turn out in acknowledgment of his dutiful
service on the city council—the *Globe* was in favor of the
elderly, Fred knew, and wasn't he one of the six the *Globe*
said would be better? There was hope for everyone.

More ominous than all of those discouragements for Kevin
White in that welter of confusion all around his office was the
sharp signal that the *Globe*'s action had sent to the rest of
media and to prosecutors. The corruption issue had achieved
third billing in the *Globe*'s list of particulars for advocating
Kevin White's retirement. It trailed in importance the vindictiveness he'd shown while Tregor was still chewing on his consciousness; it was a very poor third to its central argument,
which was chiefly that the *Globe* was sick of looking at his
face. In fact, the whole question of whether he was crooked
had been pretty well fudged by the editorial. All he was directly blamed for was hiring an ex-con (an act the *Globe* has
generally applauded in stories about rehabilitating ex-
offenders), who with another hireling had come to a bad end.
Scrupulous not to judge him guilty even by association, the
Globe had seemed to cite those two exemplars as proofs that
his recruiting policies were going slack along with the rest of
his public act, an arguable premise but hardly an inflammatory one. Nevertheless, deposing him from his favorite's position, at least in its disappointed eyes, the *Globe* prepared

itself to treat him just like everybody else—everybody else in this instance being a class limited to those persons whose every act was under scrutiny by the federal grand jury and whose associates and confidants were frequent though unwilling callers to its secret sessions. Every one else, in short, who invited a Godfather innuendo. That position was new for Kevin White, and one he was not likely to enjoy.

The effect of the *Globe*'s repudiation of the mayor it had done so much to promote thus posited a question that for almost sixteen years had been entirely speculative: Given the manifest fact that there was a public White *imago*, quite separate from the actual person who is Kevin White, how much of the elected figure was the manufactured candidate devised by the living person and the media who formed him, and how much was really Kevin Hagan White? This question lurks behind the celebrity of every well-known politician, every celebrity, in fact. Those who are egregiously celebrated—Ted Kennedy, for instance, and his brothers before him—by the sheer proliferation of media products inspecting, extolling, upbraiding, or excoriating them become in time the subjects of still further media attention directed to ascertaining how much of the first gouts of media product were in fact balderdash and pap. White did not reach that peak of media redundancy, for which protracted and insatiable national attention—at the very minimum; international notoriety is better, or worse if you are the topic—is prerequisite. What made him stand out was that the question arose on the purely local level, and he didn't seem to know the answer either. In high summer of 1982, after all those years in politics, he appeared destined to discover just which Kevin White, the real one or the one that transacted public affairs, was the fellow who had acquired so much fame.

> The men with the muck-rakes are often indis-
> pensable to the well-being of society; but only if
> they know when to stop raking the muck.
>
> —Theodore Roosevelt

16

THAT CYNOSURE appears to have been the Kevin White coop-
eratively designed and produced by him and the media. This
was good news for the Kevin White who lived with Kathryn
on Mount Vernon Street, once he relaxed a little and enjoyed
it. If the Kevin White that everybody maligned was the illusion, then the real one would not be accused of committing
felonies, always a disagreeable experience. It seems to have
been bad news for almost no one, unless the entire electorate
of Boston is deemed as a class to merit sympathy.

The surmise that the White *imago* and not White himself
was the agent provocateur of all the uproar rests largely upon
the attitude of the prosecutors, and the media, of course, to
what remained of the official critter after the announcement
that it would not be presented as a candidate for reelection.
As far as could be ascertained, his announcement of retirement took most of the fun out of it for both kinds of participants in the hunt.

The relationship of prosecutors and the media needs some
explanation here. In Massachusetts, by tradition, the prosecutors and the media maintain the same sort of relationship developed by the prosecutors and the national media when the
quarry was Richard Nixon and the year was 1973. It is sym-
biotic and it is iterative. Each party, in its own bailiwick,

develops scents and clues useful to the other in its realm of operations.

The press, by allying itself with the prosecution, obtains at one remove the ability to impose the ultimate sanctions of infamy and imprisonment that our society permits for the degradation of individuals but in theory reserves for application by the government acting conformably to the due process of the law. The media, by publication of names, innuendo, rumor and conjecture is afforded informal nominating powers to say who will be subjected to subpoena, summoned before the grand jury at times and places known in advance (which materially facilitates the taking of pictures), and, if all goes well, disgraced by indictment.

The prosecutors, by seeing to it that the media are not inconvenienced by overmuch scrupulosity about rules of grand jury secrecy, can assure that the reporters and cameramen not waste their time barking up unpromising trees, which invariably makes them angry. The prosecutors also obtain at second hand the benefit of confidences made to newsmen by informers who would not be caught dead chatting with the government, and the fruits of the media's liberty to proceed about investigations unfettered by the tedious rules of due process that apply to prosecutors.

When the joint enterprise succeeds, i.e., brings down some well-known figure and puts him in the dock, the prosecutors and the media divide a common jackpot: the media gets a bodacious story, which makes the reporters who have covered it look good, and it is about the prosecutors, which makes the lawyers who have moved it forward relatively famous in their communities. All lawyers, especially trial lawyers, have constantly in mind the abundance of fellow tradesmen competing for advantage in private practice and believe that name recognition gained as prosecutors survives the transition into private litigation later on. Everyone involved has a good time, in other words, except of course the fellow who must go to jail in order to provide the satisfying denouement of the investigation.

The prosecutors who held jurisdiction over Boston and any wickedness done in it during Kevin White's regime as its mayor occupied the office of district attorney of Suffolk County, attorney general of Massachusetts, United States attorney for the District of Massachusetts, and the chief of the New England field office (Strike Force) of the Organized Crime and Racketeering Section (OCRS) of the Criminal Division, United States Department of Justice. The United States attorney had at all times putative control over the field office, but that hegemony seldom required invocation.

The district attorney during most of Kevin White's administrations was Garrett Byrne, by whom White had been briefly employed as an assistant D.A. when he was a rookie lawyer. That did not mean much. Byrne's roster of assistants has included many promising young politicians, including Edward M. Kennedy, whose operational mark upon the criminal justice system in that office was minuscule. Byrne was generally believed to harbor no ill will toward Mayor White and reputedly regarded him with some paternal affection. Byrne was succeeded, very much against his will, by Newman Flanagan, who was reliably believed to have been stayed in the effort to achieve his own mayoral ambitions only by his friendship with Mayor Kevin White. In all of the flap and commotion about whether Kevin White was on the take, nobody seriously looked to the D.A.'s office for thrilling new disclosures of importance to the chase.

The attorneys general during White's reign included Elliot L. Richardson, who took that office at the same time White became mayor and left it a year later to join the Nixon administration; Robert H. Quinn, Speaker of the House of Representatives voted in by that body to serve out the two-plus years remaining of Richardson's term; and Francis X. Bellotti. Richardson was in office when the Patriarca tapes

were circulated among New England law enforcement officers. The material in those tapes was examined carefully by
the lawyers in his newly established Organized Crime Section
of the Department's Criminal Division, who worked closely
with the lawyers assigned by the U.S. Department of Justice
to its New England Strike Force. I was one of the lawyers in
Richardson's OCS, a circumstance that obliges me now to
tread a fine line between coyness and violation of the obligation of confidentiality imposed by official access to those records. It is safe to say, I think, that the transcripts (AIRTELS)
of the FBI surveillance of Patriarca's office on Atwells Avenue, in Providence, were studied closely in the attorney general's office and were obviously examined in detail in the
Strike Force offices. Those who evaluated the contents of
those tapes did so mindful of the fact that they had been
made in violation of the Fourth Amendment to the
Constitution of the United States, so that no information contained in them could be introduced as evidence at a trial in a
court of law in the United States. Further, leads developed
from that information could not be employed to secure evidence not itself set down in them because such information
would be "fruit of the poisonous tree" and also excluded from
admission at trial. Finally, the events and transactions mentioned on the tapes commenced no earlier than March of 1962
and were concluded by the end of July 1965; the Massachusetts Statute of Limitations for all offenses except murder and
treason is six years from the date of the offense; the federal
statute tolls five years from that date. In the event, inspection
of the Patriarca tapes did not lead to any prosecutions by the
Commonwealth of persons named in them for acts that had
been mentioned in them.

Neither did it instigate federal prosecutions under the direction of Chief Attorney Edward F. Harrington, then head
of the Strike Force, or U.S. Attorney Paul Markham, W.
Arthur Garrity's successor as federal prosecutor for the Dis-

trict of Massachusetts. Harrington had not then developed his later, unreasoning obsession about politics and politicians. Markham's administration of his office was impeccable.

By the time that Kevin White mounted his ill-starred gubernatorial bid in 1970, and the major real estate developers either were or were not called to a high-ticket breakfast at the Ritz to solicit their substantial support, the changes in tenancies of national political offices had completed their ripple effects in Massachusetts. Herbert F. Travers, Jr., former chief of the Criminal Division of the attorney general's office under Edward W. Brooke and then under Richardson, had been successfully sponsored by then U.S. Senator Brooke to be the new U.S. attorney for Massachusetts. Travers brought over to the U.S. attorney's office a fair number of the lawyers who had worked under his supervision in the A.G.'s office. I was one of them. Former assistant U.S. attorneys under Markham genuflected to what was then considered the rule that subordinates left office when the more partisan U.S. attorneys bowed out in deference to a changing of the party guard in Washington; several found managerial positions in the attorney general's office under the Democratic sway of Robert Quinn. Harrington resigned as head of the Strike Force to open a partnership with Markham and was succeeded by Gerald F. McDowell.

The offices of prosecutors take their tone from the chief and their daily trends from the work of the lawyers who actually go to court. All chief prosecutors promise as they take their offices that they will be seen regularly in the trenches of the courtrooms, questioning witnesses, arguing with judges, combating the sly efforts of the defense bar to thwart the accomplishment of justice. Those appearances in actuality number fewer than the visits made by Santa to the hearthsides of the children who've been good. If the office is well staffed, the person running it will have trouble staying abreast of the assistants' requests for authority to secure indictments, obtain search warrants, sustain informers, and extend surveillances; the time needed to prepare a major case for trial does not exist in his schedule.

The cadre of prosecutors that shuttled between the attorney general's office, the U.S. attorney's office, and the Strike Force—McDowell's successors included Jeremiah F. O'Sullivan, who had been an assistant attorney general under Robert Quinn—was extremely energetic. We were also, I venture to say, regularly insufferable by outsiders. This was the dawn of the era of the professional prosecutor, incarnated to replace the part-time prosecutor (PTP) whose pursuit of evildoers was a mere sideline to his private practice. Evolving wisdom had it that the PTP lacked the dedication and the time to become as expert in jailing people as the full-time defense lawyers who opposed him were at keeping them out. Search-and-seizure law, all by itself, was becoming an intricate discipline for monkish mandarins. Furthermore, there was the lingering suspicion that PTPs informed their judgments about whether to go after someone, or how hard to go after someone who clearly had to be nailed, by referring to the probable long-term effect of such decisions on their presumably thriving private practices. PTPs, the theory went, pussyfooted around powerful politicians and rich pillars of their communities because they were protective of their future professional careers. Full-time prosecutors (FTPs), their integrity untroubled by such coarse temptations, would investigate fiercely and indict fearlessly, bringing equal justice unto all whether they liked it or not. Collectively we were a bunch of bloody bores.

Nevertheless, sanctimonious, self-righteous, and censorious as we were, there was among us no dearth whatsoever of shrewd, calculating ambition. With but very few exceptions we had no intention of retiring from our prosecutors' slots with the grateful thanks of Commonwealth or country, after forty years or so of meting out justice (the exceptions were the

Strike Force lawyers, who really were career justice employees). What we had in common were middle-class family backgrounds which did not include illustrious forebears in the legal profession. We were, most of us, the first of our families to graduate from law school. We had no footholds in the profession, and our grades in law school had not been good enough to make us catnip for the hiring partners of major Boston law firms. We had gone into government for precisely the same reasons that the political science hotshots acted upon when they escaped from the campuses to join up with Kevin White. In government we could be sure of rapid advancement as trial lawyers, regular court appearances, and the responsibility for conducting major trials against the lions of private litigation, before we were thirty. We believed that the way to impress a major law firm was to take on the best of its trial lawyers and thrash him soundly, or failing that to take on the best of the celebrated privateers—e.g., F. Lee Bailey— and give him a run for his money out in front of God and all the people, thus becoming well known while still young as "a bear in a man's suit" in the courtroom. We did not take dives for Kevin White or anybody else; we were so unbearably self-righteous that nobody even tried to give us directions to the pool.

That prickly attitude endured in the prosecutors' offices. It was still in full currency when the *Globe* punctured the official Kevin White balloon on July 14, 1982, and let out all the stale, hot, liberal air. Harrington had proceeded from the Strike Force quarters on the sixteenth floor of the federal building in Post Office Square, via his private offices with Markham, to the best office in the U.S. attorney's digs on the eleventh floor, with the election of Jimmy Carter in 1976. There Harrington put in four years of increasingly public and astonishingly strident public posturings in which he declared his complete disapproval of political corruption. He also saw to the initiation of investigations and prosecutions which if nothing else demonstrated that he wasn't fooling when he started hollering.

The biggest of those cases, and certainly the most troublesome, was the prosecution of Massachusetts State Senator James Kelley (D), Oxford, on charges that he used his position as chairman of the Ways and Means Committee to extort bribes from firms doing business with the Commonwealth. It had nothing to do with White but displayed Harrington's zeal. It was initially tried to a jury before my close friend and former boss, Judge Joseph L. Tauro, who had succeeded Herb Travers as U.S. attorney before going to the bench (James N. Gabriel, now a bankruptcy referee, served as interim U.S. attorney between Travers's departure and Tauro's arrival, becoming U.S. attorney himself when Tauro was named to the court). Tauro dismissed the jury as hopelessly deadlocked after two days of deliberation (11–1 for conviction), a decision that infuriated Harrington and prompted him to engage in a public denunciation of Tauro. Retried, Kelley was convicted before another judge.

His appetite for splashy—and therefore political— prosecutions barely whetted, Harrington was put out of office by the 1980 defeat of Jimmy Carter. That departure, though, resulted only in a change of public demeanor in the U.S. attorney's office. Harrington's Republican successor, William Weld, did not carry on as Harrington had, to the amusement of the press, but he was quite as eager to prosecute politicians and their hangers-on. Weld had been the GOP candidate for attorney general, swamped by Frank Bellotti in 1978. Still in his thirties and with his political ambitions surviving if somewhat dampened by that first run statewide, he was quite as agreeable to hooking White as Harrington had been, albeit much more circumspect in his public utterances to that effect.

He started off with a bang, two bangs if you were counting. In the fall of 1981 he bagged John Williams and George Collatos.

Williams, a ward heeler appointed by White to oversee commercial real estate rejuvenation projects in Dorchester, was in due course convicted of shaking down one prospective venturer. Williams was the ex-con to whom the *Globe* alluded in its Dear Kevin editorial of July 14, 1982. He was portrayed in court as the ham-and-egger that he was—the victim he selected to shake down for $50,000 was an FBI stool pigeon transplanted to Boston from the Southwest under the government's relocation and fresh-start program for organized-crime case witnesses who have discharged their ends of the bargains. There was lavish speculation and much diligent exertion aimed at elucidating a close link between the crooked appointee and the mayor who'd appointed him to the post he had misused so clumsily, but it was never proved.

More significant, perhaps, was the prosecution of George N. Collatos, a former assistant with the Boston Redevelopment Authority. Collatos, too, had been caught shaking down a contractor, his target being the Lawrence Ready Mix Concrete Company. Company officials invited the FBI to overhear the conversations between them and Collatos, and he was given three years for extortion.

Soon after Collatos was carted off to Danbury to do his penance for abusing Lawrence Ready Mix, Weld had him back up before the grand jury. Collatos was asked whether he had solicited and collected funds for White's 1979 campaign; he lied and said he hadn't. He was asked whether he had organized two fund-raisers for the mayor; he lied and said he hadn't. He was asked whether he had gone to someone on the governor's council to intercede in a court case involving Lawrence Ready Mix; he lied and said he hadn't. Weld could prove he had solicited and accepted campaign funds, had organized the two fund-raisers, and had put the influential arm on the governor's council; he could prove Collatos denied doing those things while he was under oath. Weld secured an indictment charging Collatos with four counts of perjury.

Collatos, being of at least occasionally sound mind, pleaded guilty. Judge W. Arthur Garrity, Jr., sentenced him to two more years in the cooler, on the understanding that the sentence would be reviewed if he became vociferous before the federal grand jury. Collatos, then sixty-two and too old to be doing time, was considered likely to ponder that option carefully. By early May of 1983 there were reports that he had not been seen in and about Danbury since the middle of April, having been moved to the Plymouth County House of Correction, about thirty-five miles from Boston, in order to be more accessible to federal marshals delivering witnesses before Weld's grand jury.

All of this was lovingly recorded in much detail by the media. At the end of September 1982 Butterfield of the *Times* printed the Collatos story; except for the assertion that an unnamed source in Weld's United States attorney's office had identified White as the real target of the Collatos effort, it was for Boston readers a rehash. For those outside of Boston, though, relying on the *Times* to designate what is news in the country, it was fresh meat and very appetizing. Among outlets whose appetites were whetted were *Newsweek* and *Time*, the television networks, and even *The Economist* across the Atlantic. Tardily, the nation that had been briefly titillated by White's 1972 flirtation with the Democratic nomination for vice president of the United States was now officially advised that the shining lad of a mere decade ago was being stalked by the federal prosecutors. The *Globe* shuffled its city hall lineup as soon as the state elections were over in November, transferring Walter Robinson from his single-handed demolition of the gubernatorial hopes of Republican John Lakian (he caught Lakian puffing up his academic credentials with Harvard studies that he'd never pursued) and Charles Kenney off the Hill, against the grain of *Globe* tradition which regards the state house beat as by far the more important of the two. The objective merits of the story had not increased noticeably, but the journalistic antes were being raised dramatically, and since the significance of any given news item is in the first instance the importance attached to it by the outlets that cover it, the story of Kevin White by the end of 1982 was a much bigger one that it had been at the beginning. This mutation was not overlooked by the other media who were putting newsmen on it and deciding how to play it at their shops.

In January 1983, Butterfield retreaded an old wheezer of a tale about a formerly abandoned residential building at 23 Unity Court in the North End, now fabled in local legend as "$250,000 townhouse." Back in the early seventies, Joanne Prevost, White's director of the Office of Consumer Affairs and Licensing, purchased for $1.00 and other consideration title to a small, rundown house at that address. The property had changed hands just before that to a contractor who had development rights for other property on Boston's waterfront and a vague intention of rehabilitating it as a residence for himself and his wife. Under some pressure to conform to White's administration rule that all of his department heads live in the city, Prevost, who had an apartment in Waltham, asked her boyfriend to look around for something that she might buy cheap in Boston. He contacted Robert Cucchiella, who was friendly with the contractor, and in due course the property was sold to Cucchiella's sister, Claire, for $5,500, which Prevost provided, paying the state and federal excise taxes on the transaction. Prevost then took a deed from Claire Cucchiella, which would complicate any efforts a third party might make later to trace the transfer of the property from a contractor doing business with the city to an employee of the city, but did not make it illegal.

This was cozy and it was devious, but it was not worth punishing. The district attorney's office, which might be suspected of having given White the benefits of nonexisting doubts, had long since so concluded, and the prosecutors' offices with concurrent jurisdiction and full awareness of the matter (obtainable from Tom Sheehan's story in the *Phoenix* in January of 1982) had not acted either. Had they acted on the facts known of the transaction, the most they could have charged was that Prevost, a city official, had with the assistance of her boyfriend euchred a beholden city contractor out of some real estate he hadn't planned to sell and had tried to conceal her part in the transaction. That might have given Prevost some anxious moments, along with the boyfriend who had since married Prevost and moved into the rehabilitated house, but in a court of law it's very hard to perceive how such accusations could have been expanded to put Kevin White in jeopardy.

In the media, of course, it was a vastly different matter. Joie Prevost's townhouse had been news in 1982 and become news resurrected as the election year came 'round because Joie Prevost's helpful boyfriend was Ted Anzalone. Prosecutors mindful of the need to limit accusations to what can be proved to have been done against the law lack the latitude of media to allege that when two colleagues of a suspect combine to pull something cute, he is to be held responsible. The *Times* used to disapprove of that sort of tactic, when Senator Joseph McCarthy (D-Wis.) was engaging in it. The *Times* changed.

Much the same ought to be said for the "Paintgate" or "Couchprobe" revelations first exposed to public view by Butterfield's *Times* stablemate, Clendinen. Looking over the campaign fund-raising reports that White's committee had filed on January 12, 1983, he came up with figures showing it had spent about $10,000 fixing up the basement of White's home on Mount Vernon Street. The big ticket was a bill accounting for nearly $8,500 of that sum, paid to Roche-Bobois, a chauncy furniture store whose Boston outlet is located on the now fashionable waterfront. That was for, among other things, a nifty leather couch, and since the store offered great visual opportunities for TV camera crews, it made a frolic for the media. Once again, though, the facts bleated out over the whole Republic did not in their most sinister possible interpretation warrant imposition of criminal sanctions upon Kevin Hagan White. The acquisition of the couch and other gear, after all, had been disclosed by White's own committee, scarcely the act of someone scheming to conceal what he had done. He said that he had planned to use the space in his home for conducting campaign business, and since at that time he was still at least mulling a campaign, there was nothing unlawful about that. The most that could be said of the refurbishment story was that Kevin White had lavish tastes and was not too proud to indulge them at the expense of his campaign coffers, a charge that went to contradict only his already ruined reputation as an ordinary Joe with common, everyday tastes and otherwise impugned him not at all.

With one exception, the other instances of improprieties flung at White's head publicly also failed to strike him solidly. The Massachusetts State Ethics Commission, in 1981, found that a "birthday party" planned for his wife, Kathryn, at the Museum of Fine Arts was actually a ploy to extract $100-per-person "gifts" from city employees, which was prohibited by law. Caught out fairly and squarely, White canceled the party and ordered the contributions in hand to be returned to their donors. These came to about $122,000 and the task of giving them back was greatly complicated by the fact that a great many of them appeared to have been made in cash, in amounts totaling around $1,000 each. When the ostensible donors were identified by the media, they had trouble recollecting how they had come up with so much currency, given what appeared to be their modest circumstances. There was some suspicion that gratuities of prohibited size had been disguised in those bloc purchases of tickets by unprepossessing and forgetful city workers. But once again there was a distinct shortage of evidence to prove Kevin White had committed a criminal offense. It was all very well for allegations of laundering ill-gotten gains to be bruited about the media, with vague attributions to federal grand jury witness lists, but no indictments were ever handed up.

In all, fourteen city employees in addition to Collatos and Williams left the payroll under duress during White's sixteen-year tenure as the mayor of Boston. Deputy Real Estate Commissioner Francis Tracey was convicted of evading taxes on $6,000 in contributions to White's campaign funds which he put in his own pocket—he got eighteen months in the slammer, but he had nothing mean to say about the man whose money he had taken. Budget Director William McNeill got two years for ten counts of mail fraud bottomed upon ten letters that he received in the course of collecting a city disability pension he had lied to get; Maurizio Paul Rendini, a city budget analyst, was convicted of the same sort of finagling—both of them obviously acted on their own. Robert Toomey, demoted by White from a $42,000-a-year city job to a $35,000-a-year job, was also accused of mail fraud in collection of a disability pension. He had taken out the last of nine private disability policies the day before the "accident" he cited in applying for a $32,000 city pension. White was not charged. Richard Rizzo, a city health inspector, drew suspended sentences for seeking bribes from a noodle factory under his inspection in Chinatown; White was not involved. Parks Commissioner Anthony Forgione got six months suspended for conflicts of interest arising from a North End building project—White was not involved. And eight people hired to collect the money from the city's parking meters were accused of omitting to turn in $700,000 in quarters which they used to purchase homes and other comforts for themselves; no one said White's campaign funds had a big surplus of coins.

That was all the mud the media and the prosecutors had come up with on Kevin White before he took himself out of the 1983 campaign on May 26, 1983. After he did that, the circuits that transmitted all the tales of his corruption for all practical purposes went dead. If the prosecutors were still cajoling the convicted perjuror, George Collatos, to produce some testimony that they might corroborate sufficiently by other evidence to make a solid case, no easy undertaking when your principal prospective witness is a man who has already confessed that he'll lie under oath when it is necessary, the media appeared to be no longer interested. Kevin White was left to spend the summer in the sun, all but totally unbadgered, while the media pursued the ten worthies who were jostling to succeed him, each vying with the others to convince the voters that he would cure all the city's ills, stop its inhabitants from fleeing to the suburbs, and revive the industrial base that had started to decline right after World War I. You could see why the mayor seemed to be a little sad and perplexed.

> If a man found himself so rich-natured that he could enter into strict relations with the best persons and make life serene around him by the dignity and sweetness of his behavior, could he afford to circumvent the favor of the caucus and the press, and cover relations so hollow and pompous as those of a politician? Surely nobody would be a charlatan who could afford to be sincere.
>
> —Ralph Waldo Emerson
> "Politics"

17

POLITICIANS and reporters are adrenaline junkies, each depending on the others to provide his needed dose. Their mutual moralities of dealing with each other are grounded in the fiction that what they say is important to the multitude.

For politicians whose intentions and capacities are not basically evil, this is a harmless fantasy. It can be argued that a man like Kevin White, whose sincerity nobody questioned when he proposed to remake the tired city, accomplished substantial good for many who would otherwise lead lesser lives without him. White did not reverse the processes that had commenced to change the city before he was born, nor did he conjure up the trends that left it brighter, more opulent, and newer than he'd found it. What he did do was contrive to keep its fragile peace, a prodigious and profound accomplishment, and urge its downtown rebirth onto the levels that it might never have reached under a lesser mayor. He did not manage what he had promised, but then nobody could, and in the attempt to deliver he achieved more than he might actually have dared to guarantee.

For newsmen who imputed to him undertakings he had not himself chosen and made that their message to the multitude, the adventures of those sixteen years were heady stuff and, like most intoxications, seem afterward to have been a bad idea. Reporters and editors ought not to fall in love with politicians whose careers they are engaged in covering, nor should they fall into hate when those careers disappoint them. By investing Kevin White in 1967 with almost knightly powers which he had not claimed or shown, the *Globe* and the rest of the Boston media whom it easily leads bought for themselves an emotional investment in the candidate that was almost bound to depreciate. And depreciate it did, quite catastrophically.

The result of that infatuation was that Boston got a mayor who was nowhere near as good as its voters and the man himself had been led to believe by the media. Thus installed in what may well be an impossible job for any human being, he at once began to display the imperfections of his character that the media had themselves chosen to insist did not exist. His practical determination to employ his patronage powers to assemble a machine to support him were evident in his first campaign pledges to open "Little City Halls"—did the media imagine that he'd staff those offices with enemies lustful for his destruction? His impatience with the stalling and the tricky foolishness taken for granted in the state house had in the first instance moved him to extricate himself from his safe office as the secretary of state for the Commonwealth, to secure in exchange direct levers of power which he could work to annex greater power for himself. It should not have startled anyone when he blew up as the general court dawdled over Tregor, or that he did rash things that he should not have done in order to accomplish what he wanted. It did startle people, though; it was the last straw.

The first and weightiest straws came from the corruption issue. It caused him the greatest personal hurt, in my estimation, unjustly so. In the real world of American politics, the candidate is supposed to enjoy the option to invent his own integrity. If he is dead honest, that is fine. If he is cute enough to make sure city employees are braced off city property by mutual friends of theirs, he is and should be golden. And if he is a crook, but a devilishly smart one, he is, in the contemplation of the law, as good as if he were dead honest.

The laws that are supposed to govern baser inclinations toward larceny, bribe taking, and the like, as silly and as convoluted as so many of them are, were not drafted to punish anyone who is not caught breaking them. Suspicions, however strong, should not be deemed sufficient to invoke sanctions, unless they are supported by probative evidence adequate to warrant both indictment and conviction. Such support was not to be found for the suspicions against Kevin White, in the opinion of several prosecutors who would not have minded in the slightest seeing to his accusation and conviction in the courts they served. It was in the media that those suspicions were articulated, and in which he was subjected to the penalty of disgrace. The punishment was far less than the courts might have imposed, to be sure, but it was decreed and carried out by institutions that were not constitutionally empowered to inflict it.

Such violation of the right to due process of the laws, when threatened against members of minority groups or found to have been perpetrated against them by the operation of population shifts, was regularly deplored by the institutions which on an *ad hoc* basis punished Kevin White. The April 1983 issue of *Boston* magazine featured as its cover story "Stalking Kevin," by E. J. Kahn, Jr., illustrating the summary of the frenzy among newsmen with a grainy photograph of the mayor overprinted with a yellow bull's-eye. The question Kahn raised and put to his fellow reporters but never really answered for *Boston*'s readers was, "Will the media get the mayor?" Not whether the media ought to be in the business of getting anybody, but whether the effort would prove successful. The article itself was a contribution to that effort.

The answer to Kahn's question turned out to be Yes. The media got Kevin, just as the media had made Kevin, for what seemed at the time to be the best of reasons. If good intentions really were the paving stones for the road to Hell, there would not be a pothole today in the streets of Boston.

AFTERWORD

For those wishing background information of facts arguably influential of the views I have expressed, this note is provided.

I lived in or near Boston during Kevin White's entire service as its mayor. One of my periods of city residence included the 1975 election. I voted for him in both the primary and the general elections. My personal contacts with him totaled less than half a dozen; all occurred during my efforts to prepare articles I had been commissioned to write for periodicals, but for two receptions at the Parkman House to which I was invited with a slew of other people. The food was good and the wines were satisfactory.

I was a columnist at one time or another during White's administration for *Boston* magazine, the *Phoenix*, the *Boston Herald-American*, and, most recently, the *Boston Globe*. I have never been an employee of any of those journals; my oral agreements with their editors called for me to write regular columns for which the editors would see that I got paid set rates if they were published. My columnist's relationship with *Boston* proved to be co-terminous with the tenure of the editor who hired me. I left the *Phoenix* stable of contributors because I had a strong hope, which proved to be justified, that I could write more frequently, for more money, for the

Herald-American. When an incoming editor of the *Herald-American* proposed to revamp his gallery of columnists by reducing my contributions from five columns per week to three, I repaired to the *Globe.* My contact with each of those journals was limited to those visits that were necessary to deliver my copy and collect my mail—none at *Boston* magazine, none at the *Phoenix,* brief forays into the *Herald-American* building, and weekly calls to the *Globe.* In each relationship I have understood my function to be the statement of my views on subjects of potential interest to the readers of the paper. I have never been asked to reflect the views of any of the journals that have purchased my work, nor have I sought to do so.

Details of my association with the Office of the Attorney General and later, the Office of the United States Attorney, are incorporated in the text because I believe them to be germane to the reader's evaluation of what I have had to say about the activities of those offices during Kevin White's administration. I did not take with me from either of those offices any files or other materials that I might have used to refresh my recollection of matters discussed in this book, nor have I had access to any, directly or indirectly.

The research for this analysis was deliberately limited to printed materials published contemporaneously with the events they describe and to statistical abstracts prepared by the Boston Redevelopment Authority. I reviewed the *Globe's* coverage in the newspaper microfiche room of the Boston Public Library; I neither requested nor had access to the *Globe's* library at any time for the purpose of developing this analysis.

Since the focus of this inquiry was what people said and did during Kevin White's career as mayor of Boston, and not what they may wish today they'd said or done, I did not solicit the current views of any of the participants in the events I have covered. It seems to me that the implications and effects of words and deeds spread out over sixteen years are best to be gauged by looking at what has resulted from them, not from taking down what the speakers and the actors now believe to have been their intentions at the time. Personal memory, as I have learned from research forcing me to alter and amend many of the recollections I formed, or thought I formed, at the time of events over that time span, is quite as unreliable as my training and experience in cross-examination of witnesses had made me suspect. The memory plays tricks with the sequence of events, the authorship of remarks, even the content of them, and it seems to me that the risk that someone was misquoted long ago is nowhere near as great as the probability that he will misquote himself today when asked to comment on the event. We are all very wise in Boston, and we know a lot of things; many of them are not so.

Most of our troubles are directly attributable
to our refusal to sit quietly in our rooms.

—René Descartes

INDEX